Building a Successful Professional Practice with Advertising

IRWIN BRAUN

Building a Successful Professional Practice with Advertising

ama
com

A DIVISION OF AMERICAN MANAGEMENT ASSOCIATIONS

Library of Congress Cataloging in Publication Data

Braun, Irwin.
  Building a successful professional practice with advertising.

  Includes index.
  1. Advertising—Professions. I. Title.
HF6161.P89B7   659.1′023′73   81-66214
ISBN 0-8144-5598-0   AACR2

First Printing

To Marilyn and Karen

> **Stuart and Lincoln,** Attorneys and counsellors at law. Will practice jointly in the courts of this judicial circuit. Office no. 4. Hoffman's Row. Upstairs. Springfield.

Advertisement run by two young lawyers, John T. Stuart and Abraham Lincoln. Sangamo Journal, *Springfield, Illinois, August 1838.*

Acknowledgments

When the American Management Associations first proposed that I write a book on professional advertising, I thought the idea was far-fetched. But about a year later, after seeing a barrage of low-image professional advertising and a host of articles on the subject, I decided the proposal was plausible after all. The need for a book on how to create tasteful, practice-building advertising had become evident.

As with any effort that explores a new field, I recognized that I would need the cooperation of professionals, advertising people, entrepreneurs, and others with experience in professional advertising. From these pioneers, there was a great deal to learn. And learn I did from the many professionals who were kind enough to meet with me personally, allowing me to tape their views. All in all, they gave me a tremendous amount of pertinent information, and insight into the marketing of professional services.

To these people, who so generously gave me their time and advice, I owe a debt of gratitude. A special thanks goes to Dr. Frederick Seltzer, Arnold Siegel, Robert Hodges, Gail Koff, Julius Phoenix, Jr., Dr. Allen Gutstein, Ira Neiger, Aline Bricks, Aaron J. Broder, Carolyn Patten, Dr. L. Lee Bosley, Sandra Nelson, Robert J. Feurzeig, Robert Purcell, Ed McMullen, Howard Kamin, Robert Froehlich, Gil Liberman, Charles Kinsolving, Alfred Koffler, William Harrison, Jr., and Anthony Formichelli.

I am also grateful to the firms and associations that supplied a good deal of material and information for this book: American Dental Plan; Creative Surgery Center; Sieck & Zelinka; Jacoby & Meyers; F. Lee Bailey & Aaron J. Broder; Universal Dental Centers; PMI/Strang Clinic; Deloitte Haskins & Sells; Siegel, Sugarman & Seput; Laventhol & Horwath; Froehlich & Richter; Horlick Levin & Hodges; Metropolitan Lawyer Referral Service; Minnesota Dental Association; Razidlo Advertising; Popofsky Advertising; TDI/Winston; New York Subways Advertising; Newspaper Advertising Bureau; Magazine Publishers Association; TV Bureau of Advertising; Radio Advertising Bureau; American Association of Advertising Agencies; Institute of Outdoor Advertising; Transit Advertising Bureau; National Yellow Pages Association; and WCBS Radio.

Irwin Braun

Contents

The Ripple That Caused a Tidal Wave

ON JUNE 27, 1977, the United States Supreme Court ruled that state laws and bar association rules prohibiting lawyer advertising violated the free speech guarantees of the First Amendment. In this landmark decision (*Bates* v. *State Bar of Arizona*), the Court held that lawyers could advertise the prices of their services in newspapers and couldn't be prevented from doing so by bar associations or state law.

Justice Harry E. Blackmun, writing for the majority, pointed out that the bias against lawyer advertising originated in England as a rule of etiquette rather than ethics at a time when trade was regarded as unseemly and the law was more a form of public service than a means of earning a living. "Since the belief that lawyers are somehow above trade has become an anachronism, the historical foundation for the advertising restraint has crumbled," wrote Justice Blackmun.

The argument that advertising reduces professionalism found no sympathy with Justice Blackmun. He wrote, "The assertion that advertising will diminish the attorney's reputation in the community is open to question. Bankers and engineers advertise, and yet these professions are not regarded as undignified. In fact, it has been suggested that the failure of lawyers to advertise creates public disillusionment with the profession."

Justice Blackmun predicted that advertising would reduce the cost of legal services to the consumer without encouraging shoddy work. He was right. As more and more professionals advertise to build their practices, it is apparent that high professional standards and ethics are being maintained.

CHAPTER 1

Beyond the Supreme Court Decision

"IT'S A DISGRACE." ... "It's not for me." ... "It won't last." ... "It demeans the profession." ... These are some of the comments I have heard from professionals regarding advertising by their colleagues. It doesn't surprise me. Recent surveys of lawyers, dentists, and physicians indicate that the majority are against advertising at this time.

So why am I writing this book? Because I can confidently predict that in the not too distant future the vast majority of professionals will be engaged in some form of communication. It could be on radio or TV; in the Yellow Pages, newspapers, or magazines; by direct mail; or outdoors. This prediction is based on current trends in professional advertising, the new concepts in the marketing of professional services, and the changing demographics of the tradition-bound professions.

Advertising by professionals has intensified since the Supreme Court ruled in 1977 that lawyers could advertise their fees. Most professions have seen their local and state associations draft new codes of conduct regarding advertising. Some have simply prohibited the use of false or misleading claims. Others have adopted strict codes prohibiting the use of guarantees, discounts, endorsements, or free consultations. Professionals are also prohibited from engaging in sensational, comparative, or flamboyant advertising.

Despite all the restrictions, *The New York Times* reported (February 12, 1979) that there had been widespread violations and abuses by professional advertisers in New York State. One lawyer ran an ad which contended that he never lost an uncontested divorce case. These violations prompted the New York City Consumer Affairs Commissioner to conclude that professional advertising is "a mess."

But who are these advertising professionals? According to a study conducted by the American Bar Association, they are mostly attorneys whose income is low. The American Bar Association found a definite relationship between advertising and income. When a lawyer's income is low, the likelihood of advertising is high. As income rises, the incidence of advertising decreases.

In most cases, these advertising professionals are recent graduates of professional schools who do not want to wait ten years to build a practice. This is a generation that was raised on mass communications and knows its impact. And these young people recognize that advertising could be a medium not only for attracting patients and clients but for educating them as well.

One young lawyer who opened a practice in a suburban shopping center said, "Advertising helped get my name known." He opened his practice without a client. A dentist in Tucson said, "Why should we exclude advertising from the other tools we employ in our practice? Properly handled, it helps us to reach out and treat people who might otherwise never receive proper dental care."

On the other hand, some professionals who advertise are established practitioners who are trying to reposition their practices. Noted criminal lawyer F. Lee Bailey and his associate, Aaron J. Broder, used small classified ads in Chicago and Los Angeles and on the front page of *The New York Times* to advertise their specialty in aircraft disasters. This prompted *Advertising Age* (January 15, 1979), the leading publication in the advertising business, to state, "With F. Lee Bailey, who is probably the nation's best-known lawyer, opting to advertise and doing it on the front page of the country's most influential newspaper, it is rather clear that legal advertising is here to stay."

MARKETING PROFESSIONAL SERVICES

The influence of these advertising professionals is already beginning to be felt. The prices of certain routine services have dropped considerably where there has been intense fee advertising. One physician who set up a cosmetic surgery center said, "Advertising promotes healthy competition, and competition promotes lower fees."

The 1980s will be a decade when professionals will experience a new kind of competition. The number of professionals is increasing each year, and the government is forecasting surpluses even for physicians in a few years. There is already an oversupply of lawyers, and the competition continues to grow. Furthermore, the increased scrutiny of professionals by the media, government, and consumer groups has also heightened competition. Finally, we can anticipate that competition in the marketplace will grow as more and more professionals devise new concepts for marketing medical, dental, and legal services. These mavericks would like to do to their professions what H&R Block did for tax preparation: standardize the service and deliver it to the greatest number of consumers.

One such innovator was a dentist who was rapidly setting up dental centers in a retail chain throughout the country. "Dentistry," he said, "is still being practiced as it was 75 years ago, with dentists barely tapping the market of this $10 billion industry." A young lawyer who was busily setting up legal clinics all over the United States predicted, "You will see a real revolution in the way professional services are delivered in this country." This revolution is the marketing of professional services for the first time to the American public. What is marketing? Simply stated, marketing is analyzing the marketplace and taking advantage of the results of the analysis. It is the way most businesses sell a product or service. More than any other business function, it seeks to expand volume and profits by determining the needs of consumers and satisfying them.

To market your services, you need to identify what your clients/patients want and then fill the need. And you have to determine how much they are willing to pay for these services, so that you can still make a profit.

Marketing can give you a certain image, which may appeal to either a broad or limited segment of the population, depending upon what you want to accomplish. A practitioner can't be all things to all people. Define what makes you unique, and communicate this to your specific audience.

Communication has always been a vital ingredient in the marketing mix. Without it, selling any product or service in this communications-oriented society would be practically impossible. No matter how good a product or service is, you still have to sell it to the ultimate consumer. The old adage "Build a better mouse trap and the world will beat a path to your door" will not work in this age of communications.

Some of the largest companies in this country, like Procter & Gamble, are known for their marketing expertise. They use research to develop new products that fulfill a particular consumer demand and need. They then use all the components of the marketing mix—advertising, public relations, sales, and promotion—to deliver a product or service to a target audience at a competitive price.

Some of the recent trends in marketing professional services are discussed below.

Clinics

Clinics are springing up all over in malls, shopping centers, storefronts, and department/discount stores—as daring professionals devise new techniques for delivering dental, legal, and medical services. These clinics recognize that the middle class has always been shortchanged when it comes to professional services. The middle class is being squeezed as the price of these services soars beyond the inflation rate. As a result, nearly half of all Americans do not seek regular dental care, according to a survey made by the American Dental Association in 1978. Similar findings for legal services have been well documented in major research studies. Close to 70 percent of the U.S. population do not have adequate access to attorneys. Furthermore, lawyers are consulted for slightly less than a third of all problems that could be called legal problems, reported the American Bar Association Commission on the Need for Legal Services in 1978.

Recognizing a need, lawyers have been opening clinics at an unprecedented rate. "There may be a legal clinic in every neighborhood in five to ten years. It is inevitable that this kind of operation will succeed," said Gary C. Huckaby, chairman of the American Bar Association's Committee on Delivery of Legal Services.* Before 1977, just a handful of clinics existed; by 1979, the number had soared to over 700.

What are these clinics? They are simply high-volume, high-efficiency firms. They range from local operations to multistate chains, from sparsely furnished offices to plush facilities employing the latest technology. The key to the clinic concept is to reduce the work load in the office by using preprinted forms, standardized procedures, and work sheets that can be handled by paraprofessionals and staff personnel. Equally important is the use of ancillary personnel to perform routine procedures that were previously done by professionals. Traditionally, lawyers have billed their time on an hourly basis: $75, $100, or $200 per hour. Clinics work on the principle of being more efficient and getting more done within the hour so they can then pass on the savings to the consumer.

Equally important, clinics concentrate on recurrent problems of the average citizen so that they can keep costs low. Legal clinics handle a wide variety of problems, including criminal cases, uncontested divorces, domestic relations, landlord–tenant cases, bankruptcies, real estate closings, and name changes. Complex litigation is handled by outside consultants who are hired on an "of counsel" basis and share the fee charged by the clinic. The administrative work is done by the clinic.

Clinics also save money by buying supplies in volume and using in-house services (like dental laboratories). Computers are used to store and retrieve information, as well as to assess the management of each office.

Clinics depend on a large number of clients walking in and have

---

*"Legal Clinics: The Bargain Bar," *National Law Journal,* February 12, 1979.

learned that the road to success is paved with advertising. Stephen Meyers of The Legal Clinic of Jacoby & Meyers said, "Advertising is what makes it possible to generate a clientele large enough for us to deliver services efficiently."

Professional Service Centers In Chain Stores

More and more mass merchandisers, such as Montgomery Ward (#1), are setting up professional service centers where store customers can find legal, dental, optical, health-testing, and other services. The stores lease the space to the professionals or have other financial arrangements. Because of the large volume of clients, the fees charged by these professionals are generally lower than those charged by solo practitioners.

The professional center is a response to the one-stop shopping trend that is sweeping the country. Now that close to one out of two women work, people want the convenience of going to one place for all their shopping needs. They want to save time and money. And because of the high costs of operating a car, people are confining their shopping to one or two familiar stores that they trust.

Convenience is an important benefit offered by these in-store professionals. In addition to being centrally located, the service centers have day and evening hours, are open seven days a week, take credit cards, and have ample parking facilities.

The professionals recognize the importance of store traffic. One practitioner who opened a chain of dental centers said that "close to one out of three new patients is produced through store traffic." The loudspeakers in these stores announce the availability of professional services. Store circulars, flyers, and signs also point the consumer toward the professional center.

In addition, centers advertise continuously in newspapers and on radio. They also use transit and outdoor advertising. These centers enjoy another advantage: What they pay for advertising media is a fraction of what others pay. Because the chains in which they are located purchase large amounts of newspaper, radio, and other advertising, they pay the lowest possible rates. The professionals benefit from the volume discounts earned by the store and, consequently, they run extensive ad campaigns.

Group and Association Advertising

Groups of professionals are banding together to advertise under an umbrella name. This is happening among lawyers, dentists, oral sur-

geons, chiropractors, and accountants. These groups have anywhere from ten to several hundred members who pool their financial resources to hire advertising agencies to create programs that attract new patients and clients. One such group of lawyers uses radio exclusively and promises to put consumers in touch with specialists for their particular problems. Another group of dentists advertises in newspapers only, under the caption "Personal dental care at low fees," and lists the fees in the ad. In many cases, these advertising groups are associations, such as the American Dental Association, the American College of Surgeons, the American Medical Association, and regional and state bar associations. Some are trying to create favorable images for their members, while others are actually acting as referral services.

A lot of professionals like this approach because their names are never mentioned in the advertising. The only time an individual name is revealed is when the consumer calls a central telephone number for additional information.

Prepaid Legal, Medical, and Dental Plans

Another trend that we can expect to see more of in the future is the rise of prepaid legal, medical, and dental plans. This is occurring throughout the United States as companies, unions, and credit unions offer employees/members extra benefits. They can buy these services in volume at a greatly reduced cost. These organizations can also see that quality control is maintained and that their employees get the best services at a reasonable cost.

Health maintenance organizations (HMOs) are typical of these types of prepaid professional plans. HMOs emphasize preventive medicine in order to eliminate the need for serious treatment later on. Payment is generally administered by a third party—an employer, a union, or a professional organization. The employee does not have to contend with bills, claim forms, or deductible payments.

The growth of HMOs is unprecedented as companies and unions question the effectiveness of their present third-party health programs. They want to see more innovation and greater efficiency in medical care. They also want lower premiums to reflect these changes.

Various national studies indicate the effectiveness of the HMO. Compared with conventional insurance plans, HMOs have an average of 200 fewer hospitalization days per thousand members and 25 percent fewer surgical procedures. Employees subscribing to HMOs have a 17 percent lower absenteeism rate compared with employees covered by standard insurance plans.* Other professional plans are also growing in size. The National Resource Center for Consumers of Legal Services reports that by 1985 an estimated 20 million Americans will be covered by prepaid legal plans, as compared with about 12 million in 1979.

Franchises

There are significant indications that many professionals may go the franchise route. Government statistics reveal that 90 percent of all franchised businesses succeed over·a two-year period compared with 20–30 percent of all independent businesses. The franchisers hope to do for the professionals what Century 21 did for real estate: establish an image of professionalism with a saturation advertising program.

The management of these franchises will consist of entrepreneurs and professionals, each having control over different aspects of the operation. Many professionals recognize the value of working with marketing, management, and advertising experts who can guide them in building a successful practice. The businessmen will be involved in developing marketing programs, including advertising and promotion. They will use television and other mass media to build an image for a particular franchiser. They will also be concerned with setting up management systems to help the practitioner become more efficient. The professionals will be responsible for establishing quality assurances and defining the parameters for acceptability from practitioner to practitioner. Quality control will be a major concern for these franchises.

In some cases, franchisers will seek independent practitioners; in other cases, they will set up offices in chain stores and then franchise them to individual practitioners to operate. The cost of buying a franchise could be several thousand dollars. In most cases, there will be a monthly percentage-of-gross charge to help cover advertising and management expenses. The financial arrangements will vary from franchise to franchise.

Packaged Professional Services

In the future, you can also expect to see major American packaged goods companies getting into health care, legal, and other services. For example, a dentifrice manufacturer might set up dental care centers where dentistry is practiced and toothpaste, brushes, fluoride mouth rin-

---

*National Association of Health Maintenance Organizations, *National Report*, 1980.

ses, cavity-proof plastic sealants, and other related products are sold. Such companies have the marketing expertise and financial strength to deliver services to the vast majority of Americans. They recognize that by using the latest technology, they can deliver a variety of professional services and products at a reasonable cost.

THE GROWING NUMBER OF PROFESSIONALS

Another reason I can predict that the majority of the professionals will be engaged in some form of advertising in the future is the number of new practitioners entering the ranks each year, with a resulting increase in competition. Professional schools are turning out practitioners at an unprecedented rate, and the numbers keep increasing. Just look at the figures:

Profession	Total Number Employed (1979)	Number Entering per Year
Lawyers	420,000	35,000
Physicians	350,000	14,000
Accountants (CPAs)	190,000	15,000
Dentists	110,000	6,000

As surpluses build up, the reluctance to advertise will lessen. Also, it appears that the acceptance of advertising is greatest among the younger lawyers, dentists, accountants, and physicians. Recent studies of students in professional schools indicate that a good percentage of these future practitioners are in favor of advertising to build their practices. One dental school conducted a survey of its freshmen and found that 32 percent planned to advertise upon graduation. *Medical Economics* (August 6, 1979) surveyed medical student leaders and discovered that these leaders "see nothing wrong with advertising and are likely to use it in their practices."

THE GOVERNMENT'S ROLE

There is another important factor that I would like to mention: the role of the government. The Federal Trade Commission has assumed an aggressive posture to see that all attempts at curtailing competition in the professions are eliminated. The government recognizes that the cost of dental, medical, and legal services has gone up way beyond the current rate of inflation. Medical costs, for example, soared 240 percent between 1968 and 1980, faster than the cost of any other basic living need, including food. One out of every 11 dollars spent by consumers is on health services. The government is inclined to keep these costs in line. It recognizes that open competition will bring the fees down on dental, medical, and legal services, and it will be pressing national, state, and local organizations to drop restrictions on professional advertising.

ADVERTISING CAN PRODUCE RESULTS

Has advertising by professionals worked? Yes, whenever the practitioner used knowledgeable advertising people. In many cases, however, professional advertising has been poor indeed. The ads, full of bold black type, tend to sell too hard and to make other professionals resentful and uncertain as to where it will all end. You see these low-image ads everywhere: "Dentures $50." "Divorces—Uncontested $150." "Dental Examination Free." On radio and television, you hear boasts of "surprisingly low cost" or "just tight budget" professionalism. From what I have observed so far, most professional advertisements tend to be amateurish and one-shot deals with no understanding of the need for continuity. In fact, an American Bar Association commission study concluded that most advertising by lawyers has been poorly planned and ineffective, both in spreading the message about legal services and in attracting new clients for specific practitioners.

Advertising has become a very sophisticated business over the last decade. It is no longer a hit-or-miss proposition. Advertisers want to know what they are getting for every dollar spent. They want accountability, and they use highly developed techniques to determine advertising effectiveness.

The average professional doesn't have the expertise or time to create innovative, effective communications programs. But with a little knowledge of advertising and what to expect from it, practitioners working with communications experts can create practice-building programs that project their individual strengths to specific audiences.

CHAPTER 2

The Value of a Communications Program

WE LIVE TODAY in a world of mass communication. It's all around us. Messages are stuffed in our mailboxes, thrown at our front doors, blared over the airwaves, flashed on TV screens, displayed on newsstands—and even confront us on highways, trains, and buses. Every day, the average American is exposed to 1,800 commercial messages—from 8,600 radio stations, 725 TV stations, 9,500 newspapers, and 9,800 magazines and professional and business publications. They are all competing for our attention to communicate something.

What is communication? The definition as found in *The Random House Dictionary* is "the imparting of thoughts, opinions, and information by speech, writing, or signs." However, Peter Drucker, the management guru, defines communication as a feeling, sensation, or perception that is received. It is conditioned by the receiver's cultural and emotional background rather than by his intelligence. Drucker advises, "To improve communications, work not on the utterer, but the recipient."* Successful communication is a transmitted message that evokes a response in the recipient.

Communication should cause something to happen. Whether it takes the form of a personal message, an advertisement, or a news story, it should convince the recipient about some product, service, or idea. And when it does—in the manner set forth—you are communicating.

The average practitioner might ask, "Do I really have to get involved in mass communication? I've lived without it all these years; do I need it now?"

The answer is an unequivocal yes! Everyone needs a communications

---

*Quoted in John J. Tarrant, *The Man Who Invented the Corporate Society*, New York: Warner Communications, 1976.

13

program today—especially the professional who deals with people. How you use communications will determine your future success with the public. If you establish a reputation as a professional who knows his specialty and treats his clients/patients (C/Ps) with courtesy and respect, the referrals will flow in. And referrals are the heart of any successful practice, and the key to its growth because every year a professional can expect to lose a number of C/Ps through normal attrition. So enthusiastic C/Ps and word-of-mouth recommendations are extremely important. This is also the best type of communication: it's the least expensive way to reach potential C/Ps and certainly the most believable.

You are in a people business

The philosopher Maimonides recognized this over 800 years ago when he wrote, "The physicians should not treat the disorder, but the patient who is suffering from it." A well-known dentist recently noted in a leading dental journal, "We have to recognize that we are treating people, not teeth."* And a physician writing in the *American Medical Association Journal* (March 1979) said, "There are no illnesses, just patients."

Unfortunately, most professionals are not familiar with the humanistic approach to treating people. Professional schools teach students how to write a brief, perform surgery, fill a tooth, audit a company—not how to deal with people.

When you are involved with people, you must communicate with them. In this era of consumerism and increased C/P rights, the professional who places himself above the public is in for trouble. People want to know, and it is up to the practitioner to educate and encourage C/P involvement.

You must establish a lasting rapport and a warm and personal relationship with your C/Ps so that they believe in and trust you. If they understand what you're telling them about their problems, they will benefit and so will you.

THE FORGETFUL CONSUMER

Communicating is not easy, particularly if your time is limited. Though you may carefully explain facts to a patient, most of the information will be forgotten within a few days. In fact, a University of Minnesota study indicated that, immediately after listening to someone talk, the average

---

*Interview with Dr. Arthur Labelle ("Maybe the ADA Should Sell Toothpaste"), *Dental Economics*, August 1979.

person remembers only half of what was said. The results seem to be consistent, no matter how carefully the person listens.

In addition, recent studies indicate that consumers do not listen to professional advice. For whatever reason, only one out of three people follow instructions carefully, while two out of three either totally ignore the advice or follow it occasionally. More important, the researchers found that consumers "are often subtly discouraged from asking questions." Some felt intimidated and rushed by the practitioner, who never bothered to ask if they had any questions.*

It's no wonder that some of the largest companies in America are now running advertising campaigns to promote listening. They claim that Americans listen on the average at a 25 percent efficiency level. Some of these companies are sponsoring training programs to encourage their employees to listen carefully. "We're convinced that effective listening adds a special dimension to what we can do for our customers," stated Sperry in a recent advertisement.

EDUCATING THE CONSUMER

It is truly amazing how little American consumers know about health care, their legal rights, and tax laws. This may be due to the constant changes taking place and to the professional's reluctance to tell too much, as well as to the poor listening habits of consumers. It takes time and effort to educate consumers—and time is the professional's perishable commodity.

"Your [the patient's] lack of knowledge," remarked one dentist, "for the most part is not your fault; it's the fault of your doctor, who never told you anything. If a patient doesn't ask, the doctor will never volunteer any information. Most dentists feel the less the patients know, the better off they are."

Consumer education has played an important role in building acceptance and awareness of innovative professionals who are marketing their services. These professionals have located their practices in high-traffic areas—namely, chain stores, shopping malls, and storefronts—and their advertising and publicity stresses convenience, low cost, and professionalism. "We're taking the mystery out of professional services. We're educating the public; the more they know, the more they'll trust us," remarked one professional engaged in a mass communications program.

---

*Bob Levoy, "Are Your Patients Failing to Follow Your Instructions?" *Dental Economics,* August 1979.

METHODS OF COMMUNICATING

The number of communications devices that have been created is truly mind-boggling. Audiotapes, telephone facsimile transmissions, video cassettes, direct-to-home TV satellites, video discs, and video data services are just a few recent developments. There are three basic methods of communicating, however, that all professionals should consider—personal, group, and mass communication.

Personal Communication

To some degree, most professionals are already involved in a communications program with the public. Call it "personal communication," if you like. It is probably the most widely used method of communicating at the present time. This interpersonal exchange can take place in a conference, on the telephone, or through the mail. It might be a lawyer meeting with a client to discuss a will or a dentist showing a youngster a flip chart on how to brush teeth properly. Your relationship with your C/P is not only for your client's benefit but for your future success.

Group Communication

Many professionals recognize group communication as a way to build a successful practice. Group communication might involve an accountant lecturing on tax-saving investments, a dentist speaking to a group of third graders about a visit to the dentist, or a cardiologist speaking to a church group about heart attacks. In any case, it is a professional speaking to a group about a subject of common interest. This is the bond that brings them all together, and the talk might take place in a room, theater, or lecture hall.

Mass Communication

Mass communication involves sending out messages to large numbers of people through such mass media as newspapers, radio, and television. It includes advertising and public relations. By controlling the message and choosing the appropriate media, the professional exposes the selected audience to appeals that affect its desires, attitudes, and decisions. Both the message and the media are extremely important in getting the public to react.

The ultimate purpose of mass communication is to exact a response from the target audience. The target audience is the group of people you are trying to reach. The group shares similar characteristics, such as age, income, gender, education, occupation, or life-style. The response desired from a target audience could be in terms of feelings, thoughts, or actions that will help you to achieve your objectives.

ADVERTISING AS MASS COMMUNICATION

American business spent an estimated $54.7 billion on advertising in 1980, according to *Advertising Age* (February 16, 1981). That is an expenditure of over $230 for each person living in this country. Businesspeople recognize that advertising works—it sells products and services—or they wouldn't make the investment. They know that advertising is the tool for reaching the greatest number of people who might be interested in buying a product or service.

But what is advertising? One professional described it as the dissemination of information to consumers by a sponsor through selected paid-for media, with the intent to influence the recipients to react in a desired manner.

The types of mass media used in advertising include:

Print advertising: Newspapers, magazines, supplements.
Mail advertising: Newsletters, personal letters, direct-response mailings, postcard reminders.
Printed matter: Brochures, folders, booklets, stuffers.
Signs and transit advertising: Indoor signs, outdoor signs, billboards, transportation posters, spectaculars.
Broadcast advertising: Radio—AM and FM; TV—VHF and UHF; public broadcasting stations; cable TV.

Anything that uses mass communication with a controlled message to try to sell a service is advertising—whether it is a tax newsletter, space purchased in a local newspaper for a weekly column on dental health, a full-color brochure inserted in a Sunday newspaper by a group of lawyers, a sign in a train station promoting a firm that handles uncontested divorces, or an illuminated sign outside a physician's office.

All these advertising techniques have two things in common: They are trying to communicate something using different types of media, and they are trying to convince someone to do something.

For the practitioner, advertising can be a golden opportunity to inform existing and potential clients about specialties, fees, and the availability of professional services. Advertising could be the vehicle that educates the vast majority of Americans who have rarely used professional services.

There is also a clear need for consumer education regarding fees for professional services. A study by the American Bar Association in 1977 indicated that nearly 80 percent of the survey respondents agreed with the statement that people do not go to lawyers because they have no way of knowing which lawyer is competent to handle their particular problem. The consumer is at a disadvantage because of lack of information.

More important, the study showed that consumers overestimated the cost of lawyer fees by 91 percent for drawing up a will, by 123 percent for 30 minutes of consultation, and by 340 percent for reading and giving advice on a two-page installment contract. Obviously, informing the public about the cost of legal services is a primary need if people are going to use professional services.

Advertising Can Work for You

Many professionals may question the effectiveness of advertising. Studies by research firms and advertising agencies show that advertising can accomplish the following:

- Attract C/Ps to practitioners in large numbers.
- Educate the public regarding the need for and range of professional services.
- Influence consumer attitudes.
- Allow specialists to address specific markets with related information.
- Cut overhead expenses by better utilization of a professional's total available time.
- Reach prospective C/Ps at a lower cost than many other marketing techniques.
- Raise the consciousness of the public toward the profession.
- Inform C/Ps of fees for professional services.
- Create awareness of your firm among university students seeking professional careers.
- Be a positive force in motivating your own staff.
- Demonstrate to your present C/Ps that you are concerned about educating the public about your profession.
- Reassure C/Ps who already use your services that they made a wise decision. These individuals are most important in recommending you to other people.

To Advertise or Not to Advertise

Making the decision to advertise has been easy for some practitioners. "Our decision to advertise," stated an official of the accounting firm

Deloitte Haskins & Sells, "does not indicate any lessening of our commitment to excellence, but rather it indicates our intention to make that commitment more widely known." A young dentist wrote in *Dental Management* (October 10, 1979), "You can sit and wait for your practice to build. But why wait? Why should you deny the public your talents? Why should you deny the public the education about the good preventive dentistry that it deserves and that you can perform?"

Many professionals remain skeptical about the need for and results of advertising. They cite many of the abuses that can occur, such as misleading information and fees, and anything that demeans the profession. They ask, "How can you place a fee on services that are not routine?" And, "Who is going to judge what a routine service is?" But one Federal Trade Commission regional director decried this thinking when he wrote, "Professionals fail to consider the sophistication of the public about advertising, the flexibility of advertising as a means of conveying needed information, and the intolerance of our present law enforcement system for misleading advertising in areas affecting the health of the public."* From this it would appear that the government is committed to the public's right to know.

What Consumers Think of Professional Advertising

A number of surveys have been conducted to find out what Americans think of professional advertising. In each case, consumers overwhelmingly supported advertising by professionals. For example, *Advertising Age* (December 24, 1979) reported these findings:

Lawyers. 69 percent of all adults (over age 16) said lawyers should be permitted to advertise; 13 percent said they should be forbidden; 18 percent had no opinion.

Physicians. 65 percent of all adults (over age 16) said doctors should be permitted to advertise; 17 percent said they should be forbidden; 18 percent had no opinion.

Eight out of ten consumers felt that professional advertising served a useful purpose. The vast majority of respondents indicated that they would like to be able to compare prices in ads before they make a decision on an uncontested divorce, a closing on a home, or an appendectomy.

---

*Harrison J. Sheppard, "Should Dentists Advertise?" *Dental Economics.* September 1977.

Two-thirds of the consumers who favored advertising by physicians and lawyers said that they believed that these professionals should be actively encouraged to advertise.

Consumers favor advertising by professionals or other reasons, too:

o Advertising helps them find out about the qualifications and specialties of professionals.

o Advertising helps them compare fees.

o Advertising encourages competition and stimulates free enterprise.

Advertising as an Investment

As long as you make a decision to start an advertising program, don't look at it as an expense. It's really an investment in yourself and your practice. The best investment you can make is in building an identity and an image.

Many studies on advertising effectiveness have been conducted by companies, advertising agencies, and research firms. These studies show that money invested in advertising should be regarded as any other investment that a practitioner makes in equipment, people, or salaries.

In order to get the most mileage out of your communications program, however, you must plan and spend every dollar wisely. It will require research and constant monitoring to determine the effectiveness of your campaign.

A communications program also has a definite cumulative effect. The public will start to identify with the image you project, provided you do it on a continuous basis. Advertising increases consumer awareness of your practice.

If you think of your advertising as an investment, you'll recognize that it also has a definite monetary value—if you develop a thriving practice, it will become more valuable. When the day comes for you to sell it, you'll get a higher price than a practitioner who has never achieved any recognition.

"I have noticed that when purchasing a practice," wrote Arnold Siegel of Siegel, Sugarman & Seput in the *California CPA Quarterly* (March 1979), "the price one can expect to pay could be as much as 150 percent of the acquired firm's gross annual billings. Thus, if a firm had $100,000 to invest, it could expect to acquire gross annual billings of approximately $67,000 if it purchased a practice. However, if this same $100,000 were invested in advertising, they might expect to acquire gross annual billings of $200,000." This was based on his firm's experience in advertising its services.

CONSIDER PUBLICITY FOR MASS COMMUNICATION

In addition to advertising, every professional should consider using publicity for mass communication. Advertising, as discussed in the previous section, involves buying broadcast time or space in newspapers to promote your ideas. Publicity, on the other hand, involves sending out information that has news value to gain public attention, understanding, and support for a person or service. The space and time given to the stories are free, since they appear as regular news articles and features.

The key to all publicity is news. Stories that you submit to the press or broadcast media must have new information of interest to the public. When you submit a story, there is no assurance that the media will decide to use it. More important, if they do decide to publish your story, there is no assurance of what they will print. In advertising you have complete control over the message and the timing; but in publicity the message can be changed and distorted by a journalist, and you never know how much space or time the media will give your story.

Publicity, however, has greater believability than advertising. The message of the story, therefore, has a great deal more impact. Many professionals have used publicity successfully to build a practice. Writing articles, lecturing at colleges, being interviewed on radio and TV programs, and speaking before community groups are all techniques that have been used by practitioners to obtain publicity.

Publicity is only part of a total public relations program. Public relations is the developing and maintaining of a favorable public image between practitioners and their public, suppliers, and staff. This is most important in building a successful professional practice.

CHAPTER 3

Taking a
Situation Analysis

SHOULD YOU LAUNCH an advertising program? It's not an easy decision, and you're the only one who can make it. So before you start an advertising campaign, take a situation analysis—ask yourself the 14 pertinent questions discussed in this chapter. The answers will help you determine your current situation and whether it can be improved with mass communication. They will also help you set realistic goals.

1. *Who am I?* Be honest with yourself and your practice. Make a list of your strong points and weaknesses. Try to find out what your clients/patients (C/Ps) think of your practice. Research techniques discussed later will help answer this and other questions. If you find some procedural deficiencies in your practice, try to correct them. Or you might want to contact a professional practice consultant, who advises professionals on every aspect of achieving a successful practice, including communications.

2. *What is my specialty?* If you are an attorney who practices all phases of law, or a dentist who is in general practice, then your methods of attracting new C/Ps will be different from those of the specialist who obtains his C/Ps through referrals.

Many specialists, however, can't wait for referrals and decide to promote their practices by advertising. One such specialist was a young ophthalmologist who located his practice in a large Eastern city. He was trying to build his practice quickly because of the large debts he had incurred going to medical school and setting up a practice. He couldn't sit back and wait for referrals. It would just take too long. He decided to do something about it—namely, advertise—and started with one-minute commercials on a local station and ads in a neighborhood newspaper. His ads were mainly educational, and he found that the campaign clearly produced results. On the basis of his experience, he predicted "A lot of doctors will be changing their minds about advertising for patients in the future."

If you are a general practitioner, you might want to consider developing some technique or concept that sets you apart from all other practitioners in your community. You might be a dentist who practices preventive dentistry or a physician who is strongly committed to holistic medicine. Whatever it is, try to find your own niche that makes you different.

3. *Is my practice set up to handle additional C/Ps?* "Advertising used properly does work," claims the American Bar Association booklet on lawyer advertising. You can expect an increase in new C/Ps over the duration of your campaign, and you will require additional time to give your new C/Ps the proper attention. Be prepared to handle these people and resolve the following details before starting an advertising program:

- o Can you handle all the new C/Ps, or will you have to get additional professional help?
- o Can you expand your practice with your present facilities?
- o Is your office efficient enough to handle increased paperwork and billing?
- o Do you have a printed fee schedule for routine services?
- o Do you have interview and disclosure forms to assist you in handling new C/Ps quickly?
- o Will you accept credit cards? Third-party payment plans? What about financing?
- o What kind of C/P cases will you take, and what kind will you reject?

4. *Is my office tastefully decorated and up to date?* Make no mistake about it, the first impression a client gets about you is from your reception room and office. Is it tastefully furnished? What kind of lighting and decor is there? Does it reflect your unique personality and specialty? When was the last time you redecorated your office? Is your equipment relatively new or is it outdated?

Where you practice is so important that one professional group—the American Dental Plan—sends out licensed hygienists to visit the offices of dentists applying for membership. They conduct an unbiased survey of the dentist's practice, evaluating the appearance and cleanliness of the office, as well as dental procedures. If a dentist does not meet the standards set up by the organization, it will not include the dentist's name on its recommended list.

Universal Dental Centers, one of the largest dental chains in the United States, also recognizes the importance of layout and decor (#2). Located in discount and department stores, the firm not only hired an interior de-

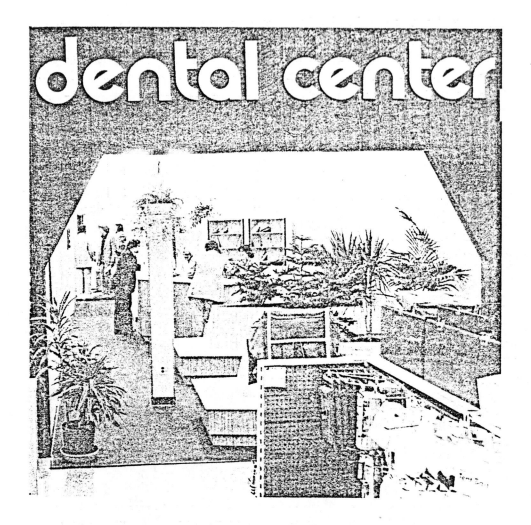

signer to lay out the facility but also engaged a psychologist to make recommendations.

The centers are designed so that the reception area and information desk are open to public view. In fact, the aisles in the store lead directly into the center. As people walk past the appliance area, they suddenly find themselves in the dental reception area.

The psychologist strongly urged that the reception area be open and visible to the public to offset people's fear of dentistry and their reluctance to visit a dentist. If shoppers see people sitting in an attractive area, they will be more inclined to come over and inquire about the service— and that's half the battle in attracting new patients. If you can get them into the office—and answer their questions by selling your service—then you can convert them to patients. Once the person elects to have work done on his teeth, he is taken into an enclosed area that is the equal of any modern dental practice anywhere.

In addition to the layout, the psychologist also recommended specific colors for the dental center. She picked bright colors—yellows and greens—to create a cheerful and tranquil environment that would not create any additional anxiety. The psychologist also suggested the apparel and fingernail polish the hygienists wear. (Neutrals instead of red, because people identify red with blood.)

5. *Who are my current C/Ps?* It is truly amazing how little professionals know about their C/Ps. What is the average family income? Are they professionals, business people, or blue-collar workers? What ages are represented? What is the education level? This information will be extremely important if you decide to initiate an advertising program.

6. *Do I need C/Ps?* No one has to tell you whether you need C/Ps or not. If you're just starting a practice, the answer has got to be yes. Very few practitioners start out with a clientele, so they have to devise ways to get C/Ps—and the fastest way to do this is to advertise.

If you're an established practitioner, just look at your appointment book. If you have appointments booked weeks and weeks in advance, you obviously don't need more C/Ps. But if you have a thin booking of appointments, you might want to consider a program to increase your C/P load.

The most obvious reason for any advertising or public relations program is to increase the number of new C/Ps. Every organization and person I interviewed cited this as the major reason for advertising, although other reasons were also mentioned.

One young dentist who opened a new office without patients in an established neighborhood said, "I was thinking I've got to do something to make people realize who I am. If I wait, eventually I'll get referrals. But I had a big nut to crack—a lot of overhead—and I decided to help things along. Something had to make it go quicker. I felt that advertising and public relations would be the catalyst to push things along." Within a year and a half, he had built a successful practice that was the envy of established practitioners in his area.

7. *What kind of C/Ps do I want?* Think about it. Many different types of consumers use professional services. There is the type who wants the best possible services and will pay any fee to get them. There are people who shop price first before considering what kind of professional help they will get. There are other people who need a specialist to help them with a particular problem. And there are people who don't use professional services because they think the fees are too high or they are just frightened to use them.

An ophthalmologist who had been practicing many years had a patient problem. His inner-city practice was undergoing a population shift from white middle class to predominantly black. The physician did not want to relocate his practice, so he decided to appeal to the black consumer, who was now in the majority in his neighborhood. He instituted a communications program, contacting local black newspapers and national magazines. The result: He was able to turn his practice around by attracting black consumers in his area.

8. *What kind of practice do I want?* Only you can make this decision. It has to be based on your philosophy of practice. You may decide to engage in a low-volume, high-fee practice that is based on a personalized approach, giving each C/P sufficient time and attention. Or you might want to offer low fees and service as large a clientele as possible. In this case, you'll probably have to be open ten hours a day, seven days a week.

The disadvantages of engaging in a low-fee, high-volume practice are obvious. As the time spent with each C/P declines according to the volume of your practice, a dehumanizing effect occurs. You and your C/P are deprived of the rapport and communication so necessary for a personalized practice. You end up treating a problem, not a person, and you're no longer able to render an individual service.

9. *Who is my competition?* Yes, competition—you don't practice in a vacuum. Today more and more methods are being devised for delivering

professional services. Legal clinics, high-volume dental centers, and health maintenance organizations are a few examples. They stress low fees, convenient hours, easy-to-get-to locations, and quality care. You'll have to think twice about opening a practice in a highly competitive area.

Even the largest accounting firms recognize the new reality in competition among professionals. Deloitte Haskins & Sells stated in its house organ,

> Every year audit committees want to know what we are doing for the clients and how we do it. Increased visibility has inevitably led to greater competition among the firms. Competition has always been there, but now it is more intense. All firms have responded to these changed conditions and become more aggressive. Operating in a new environment of open competition is now a fact of professional life.

If you locate in an area that is oversaturated with professionals in your specialty, you can expect difficulty in building a practice. You should know the strengths and weaknesses of your competition. There are always shortcomings among your competitors that you can take advantage of. These might be fees, financing, or third-party payment policies. Or your competitors might have such strengths as up-to-date techniques and C/P education programs.

By studying the competition, you can also determine where *your* weak and strong points lie. You can establish a new image that will set you apart from your competition.

You can obtain information on local practitioners from your county or city professional association. You can also obtain information from the local chamber of commerce or by just talking to people. You might also want to look in your local Yellow Pages or check your local library for various professional directories.

Your research should show that you have benefits to offer C/Ps. If not, you will have to create a unique position for yourself in the professional marketplace.

10. *In what kind of geographic area is my practice located?* One of the important factors in any practice is the geographic area where it is located. Here are some important points to consider:

○ The demographic breakdown of the population and how it relates to your specialty. If it's a low-income area, then it certainly is not the place to be practicing corporate law.

○ The geographic limits of your area and the people you want to reach in that community. Concentrating on a small community will make it easier to reach potential C/Ps at a lower cost. If you want to reach a wider area, then obviously you will need a larger advertising budget to attract potential C/Ps. The accepted rule is that the larger the area and population you want to influence, the larger the budget you will need.

o The ethnic and socioeconomic factors of your area. In many cities, neighborhoods can turn in a few years from middle-class populations to people living on welfare, and vice versa. And in most cases, the ethnic and racial mix will change with the income levels. The economic health of the community is also important. A depressed area will not be able to sustain a large number of professionals, and you might consider relocating somewhere else.

One professional who decided to relocate was a dermatologist who had a successful practice in New York City. He saw his neighborhood changing and considered moving his practice. He opened a new office in a stable upper-middle-class neighborhood. He had a problem, however. It is hard to build a practice quickly, particularly when you consider that dermatologists in a new area find it difficult to get referrals from physicians. How was he going to get his name known to the new community? The answer: Advertising and public relations.

o Accessibility to transportation and parking. If you are located in an area that is easy to get to by mass transportation, it will be to your advantage. If an automobile must be used to reach your office, you should have adequate parking facilities.

11. *Do other local professionals advertise?* If you are located in an area that has professional advertising, you are less likely to be criticized by your colleagues if you launch your own advertising and public relations program. A young lawyer located in El Paso, Texas, started a newspaper advertising campaign—much to his regret. "I was the only one advertising here," he said, "and I caught hell. I was castigated for stepping out of line. The response I got couldn't have been more negative." A young dentist who opened a practice in an established neighborhood on Long Island also received criticism from older practitioners in the community for his educational advertising in a local newspaper. But, as he wrote in his weekly column, his philosophy was: "It's the responsibility of a doctor to inform, not just perform . . . and this is my medium."

12. *Are my partners or associates committed to an advertising program?* You should have the support of everyone in your firm. One of the worst things is to commence a campaign and discontinue it because the initial support was lukewarm. Many programs are discontinued before achieving their objectives because one of the partners was ambivalent about instituting a communications program in the first place. When the accounting firm of Deloitte Haskins & Sells considered advertising, it appointed a study group of partners and a communications task force. After considerable thought and discussion, the decision to advertise was made unanimously by the firm's policy committee.

13. *Do I have the resources to sustain an advertising program?* You have just opened a new office and outfitted it beautifully with the latest equipment and furniture. Should you now appropriate a budget for a continuous advertising program? Only you can make this decision based on your financial resources and other commitments. One of the reasons cited for the failure of a large legal clinic in Boston was undercapitalization. The clinic started an advertising program and had to cancel it because it ran out of money. Don't start a campaign unless you are totally committed to it—in philosophy and with the money to back it. You don't want to start a program and have to discontinue it because of lack of funds.

14. *What are the current state and county regulations regarding advertising?* If you decide that your practice can benefit from advertising, it would be wise to check with your state associations and societies. Many states restrict the advertising message as well as the media that can be used. Under existing guidelines, many professionals are limited to the use of print, radio, and TV. The use of other media, such as direct mail, billboards, and bus cards, is prohibited by some state associations.

In addition, what you can say and show in the ads may be limited. Some societies prohibit endorsements, guarantees, comparisons, self-lauditory statements, or anything that can be construed as misleading.

The American Bar Association* also suggests that you consider:

o What limitations does the jurisdiction in which you are licensed to practice and/or intend to advertise place upon the type and content of advertisements?

o Do any of the bar associations of which you are a member maintain

---

*Individual Lawyer Advertising: A How-To Manual. Chicago: American Bar Association, Commission on Advertising, 1979.

codes of ethics and professional responsibility that differ from those of the agency having licensing jurisdiction over attorneys in your locality?

○ Will your advertisements cross state lines and attract persons in jurisdictions other than the one in which your practice predominates? How will or should this affect the content of your messages and the media you use to convey them?

○ Does your state have criminal or civil statutes—"little FTC acts"— that may impose liability on you on the basis of your advertising efforts? Will your credit practices fall within any existing statutory or regulatory prohibitions once you start to advertise?

○ If your firm is a professional corporation, does the statute under which you are incorporated require any special activity if you advertise?

○ Are there any local or state assumed-name registration laws of which you need to be aware if you intend to use another name when advertising?

○ What is the status of specialty designations in your jurisdiction? Will you have to make any applications or filings, or obtain any certifications, before you advertise your willingness to accept business in any given area of law?

Whatever the restrictions, it would be wise to obtain them in writing from your local society or association. It can save you a lot of headaches later on.

CHAPTER 4

Doing Your Own Research

One of advertising's greatest copywriters, John Caples, when asked about research, wrote, "It is one of our most important tools." In my opinion, he created more memorable advertising than anyone and knew the value of research.*

Do you need research? Yes, if you intend to create an advertising campaign that is unique. Many of the questions raised in the previous chapter can be answered if you use the techniques discussed in this chapter. Research will identify potential problems as well as existing ones. Professionals who have started to advertise have recognized the importance of research. Creating a communications program by guessing not only wastes your time and money but could hurt your business as well.

What is research? It is the systematic and objective search for information and the analysis and use of it to solve your professional problems. When properly organized and conducted, research is a highly methodical activity designed to increase knowledge and understanding of a problem as a basis for making an informed decision.

The reason for most advertising research is to identify a market opportunity. The opportunity may be the need for a service that does not exist at present. The consumer may not even recognize such a need, but your research will probably indicate otherwise and you should act on it.

THE GROWING NEED FOR RESEARCH

The need for research is growing as economic and demographic changes occur. The mainstay of the new life-style is a population that is committed to self-fulfillment and enjoyment of life to its fullest dimensions. Recent trends that will affect professionals are described below.

A low birth rate. The American woman is bearing fewer children today

---

*Willard Pleuthner, ed., *460 Secrets of Advertising Experts*. New York: Thomas Nelson & Sons, 1961.

31

because the decision to build a career outside the home and the need for a second income is receiving priority over raising a family. The continuance of low birth rates has enabled physicians and other professionals to care for the needs of senior citizens.

An aging population. Because of the lower birth rate, the population is growing older. The median age is expected to advance from 29.5 in 1980 to 32.7 by 1990.

A mobile society. People are on the move. According to the 1980 U.S. Census, by region, 27 percent of the population in the West move at least once a year. In the South, 22 percent move each year. In the North Central region, 18 percent move; and in the Northeast, 14 percent move each year. The average mover is between 21 and 34 years old, married, with 1.7 children.

The growth of one-family households. Changing life-styles are bringing a surge in one-person households; as the divorce rate soars, marriages are delayed, and women seek careers instead of families.

RESEARCH BY BUSINESSES

The biggest companies in America use research for all phases of their businesses. They use it in product development, package design, product naming, advertising, and promotion. Consumer acceptance or rejection of each element is carefully considered in the final analysis, and changes are made before the product is put on the market and advertised.

There are many case histories where research indicated that a change of name or packaging could increase sales. When changes were made, the acceptance of the product or service was shown by a surge in sales. This was demonstrated when Allegheny Airlines changed its name to U.S. Air. Research had indicated that consumers viewed Allegheny as a small, regional airline. By changing its name to U.S. Air, Allegheny took on an identity as a national airline—which is precisely what it is. Airline bookings rose dramatically with the launching of a saturation advertising campaign announcing the name change.

RESEARCH BY PROFESSIONALS

Most practitioners, whether they know it or not, are conducting research. For instance, when you ask a new client/patient (C/P) who recommended you, you are conducting research. The research might be informal and unstructured, but it is research.

Practically all professionals involved in a communications program are involved in research in one way or another. They may have started advertising by guessing who the market was, but after a short period of time—using in-office questionnaires—they have been able to pinpoint the market. In addition, they have also been able to determine what message and which media produce the greatest number of new C/Ps. Examples of professional research include:

○ Deloitte Haskins & Sells, prior to deciding to advertise, sponsored a national opinion study to determine how the public accounting profession is perceived by various groups with which the larger certified public accounting firms have professional working relationships. The study involved six groups: corporate financial officers, attorneys, members of the investment community, members of accounting faculties at colleges and universities, audit committees, and members of the American Institute of Certified Public Accountants not involved in public accounting. The opinion poll found that none of the CPA firms ranked higher with its clients (those who know a firm best) than did Deloitte Haskins & Sells. But they also found it was important to become better known to the business world. Advertising, the firm believed, was an effective way to tell its story.

○ The American Dental Plan is a group of solo practitioners in the New York metropolitan area. They offer lower fees to consumers who sign up for the plan. Before launching an advertising campaign, the American Dental Plan researched and tested copy appeals to gauge consumer reaction. It found that many people could not believe that the group could offer lower fees for personalized, private-practice dental care. It solved the problem by asking in its ads: "What's the catch?" The answer: Through the American Dental Plan, the dentist gets a continuous flow of patients and therefore can offer reduced fees. The American Dental Plan addressed this problem in its follow-up direct mailings to people who responded to the advertising.

○ The Metropolitan Lawyer Referral Service (MLRS) is a nonprofit organization that puts people with legal problems in touch with a lawyer who specializes in the caller's particular problem. A client questionnaire was prepared to pinpoint demographic information about the client and how they heard of the MLRS. The market was defined as black and Chicano ethnic groups, blue-collar workers (often transient and thus unfamiliar with the area's legal resources), and the low-to-middle-income first-time legal user, aged 28–48. The education levels were high school graduates with some college education.

○ When Jacoby & Meyers legal clinics first started to advertise, they had not done any market research to define the target audience. Nor did they know the size of the market. They did not even know whether people would be attracted or repelled by advertising. But they did know from bar association studies that the middle class in this country needed legal services at a reasonable cost. They set up a "sourcing" research system, where each caller who responded to a TV commercial was recorded with the time of day, name, address, and type of case. These data, plus other demographic information, were collected a second time when the caller showed up for an appointment.

o A dentist who advertised continuously in a suburban community conducted research after the patients received treatment. They were provided with a questionnaire that asked them how they chose him and what they thought of his office procedures and personnel. From this information, the dentist was able to determine where his practice stood at that moment—and how to make changes to improve it.

DEFINING THE PROBLEM

Before you start any research, define the problem that needs studying. No matter how small or how involved, the problem should be defined carefully, and it must be agreed upon by everyone in your firm, especially your partners. Seek out the advice and counsel of your associates, employees, and practice consultants. Their opinions might be helpful in narrowing the range of questions to be asked.

Also seek out the advice of C/Ps who are friends. Every practitioner has C/Ps who are close and whose opinions and judgments he or she can rely on. Go to them and explain what you are trying to accomplish with your research. Ask them to be objective, and solicit their opinions.

IDENTIFYING YOUR PROSPECTS

One of the major purposes of all research is to identify the key prospects—your target audience. What you are doing is identifying the segments of the total population that are most likely to use your services. You must know the people you want to reach and their life-styles—*who* they are; *what* they are doing; *why* they are doing it; and *where* they are doing it. With this C/P audience profile, you can create a message and develop a media program that will communicate with them.

As a practitioner who wants to build your practice, you should know the following about your prospects:

1. How did the C/P hear of you? Was it through advertising, referral, recommendation, news article, or some other means of communication?
2. Where does the C/P live?
3. What are the demographics of your C/Ps (income, age, education, sex, occupation)?

All these factors, and many more, will determine whether you will advertise, what your message will be, and which media you select.

Much of this information is readily available. Other facts will have to come from your own research. Be sure that the data are correct and up to date. You don't want to base decisions on outdated information and slipshod research.

In addition to determining the best prospects for your practice, you should be able to recognize those aspects of your practice that make it truly unique. After you determine these benefits, you still have to communicate them to your target audience.

USING SECONDARY SOURCES

No professional should undertake a research project without first seeing if the information is available from other (secondary) sources. Check your library to find out if research related to your problem has been previously done. There are many organizations—the government, marketing research firms, advertising agencies, professional associations, trade magazines, banks, chambers of commerce—that conduct research that you can draw from on a variety of subjects.

Some advantages of using the information obtained from secondary sources are:

1. If you have to do your own primary research, the information can be used in planning your study.
2. Using secondary research is not only less expensive but also much quicker than conducting primary research.
3. It will give you background information that will help you determine the total picture before you focus in on a specific problem.
4. Statistical information is published regularly that can give you information on recent professional trends and how you compare to the rest of the profession.
5. You might be lucky enough to find that the research you want has been done by someone else. You'll have to determine how complete

it is and whether it serves your specific needs. You'll also have to see how current it is, who collected the data, and whether the research is carefully done, the facts are accurate, and the study is objective.

Sources of Secondary Research

External data sources provide information free or at a reasonable cost. Many of the references are available at your local library, the libraries of nearby colleges or universities, or local and national associations. Some sources of information are discussed below.

Federal government. If you are looking for basic statistics on health care, dental care, law, or economic conditions, the federal government should be your first source. There are a number of ways to get information from the federal government:

1. Go to your local *library's reference section* and explain your problem. Libraries have reference sections and document rooms that maintain files of recent government publications. There are also approximately 500 depository libraries in the United States; these contain documents that are made available to anyone. A list of depository libraries is available from the sources listed here.

2. Write to the *Superintendent of Documents*, U.S. Government Printing Office, Washington, D.C. 20402.

3. Contact your *congressman's office.* His staff should be able to obtain information for you or tell you where to get it.

4. Use the *Federal Information Centers.* They are operated by the General Services Administration and are designed to answer your questions about government programs, activities, or agencies. A list of the addresses and telephone numbers of these centers appears in Appendix 1.

5. Write to the *Department of Commerce.* This is probably the best source for statistics and information in the business field. This department provides information on the population and its social and economic makeup. It also has information on housing. Data on income, trends, market potentials, and economic forecasting are also available on a national and state level. For more information write to the Chamber of Commerce of the United States.

6. Contact *other government agencies.* Many other federal agencies offer a variety of studies on the health, employment, economic, housing, and social changes of the American population. These reports include infor-

mation on dental care, specific diseases, national and state statistics, employment, income, housing, and so on. A partial list of government agencies appears in Appendix 2.

Local, state, and regional sources. The information available on local and state levels varies from area to area. The stage agencies that monitor the activities of professionals are different in each state. These agencies have established a number of restrictions regarding advertising by professionals, and it would be wise for the practitioner to check these agencies before engaging in a campaign. In addition, these agencies compile information on the economy of the state and on health and dental care, as well as statistical abstracts of current data and other information.

County chambers of commerce and regional planning boards collect and maintain data on the business climate in the region. The larger banks also collect and publish data on economic conditions. Newspapers and radio and TV stations conduct research on the demographic breakdown of the local population and on the strengths and weaknesses of local business. Public utilities maintain records on local population trends, housing, and business conditions.

For additional information on state or local activities, refer to the State Industrial Directory Corporation, 2 Penn Plaza, New York, N.Y. 10001.

Professional Journals. There are hundreds of professional journals and management magazines published by associations and business organizations. The publications that deal with practice management (e.g., *American Bar Association Journal, Dental Management, Medical Economics*) are excellent sources of information on recent trends, since they periodically conduct surveys of subscribers and studies of consumer attitudes toward the professions. In addition to research surveys, many of these publications have articles on all phases of running an efficient practice.

There are many indexes published that list subject matter, titles, authors, dates, and page numbers of recent articles. Also, all magazines publish indexes of articles that appeared the previous year. Once you identify the article you want, write to the publisher for a back issue if your local library doesn't have a copy.

If you want specific information and can't find it, you might want to call the publisher and speak to one of the editors. They can be very helpful in providing information or giving you ideas on where to get it.

Associations and societies. Every profession has an association. In many cases, these associations overlap. The best source for information on professional associations is *The Encyclopedia of Associations* by Nancy Vakes and Denise Akey.* The book is published in regional editions, with an executive index, and is probably available in your public library. You can also write to the publisher.

The quality of associations and societies varies from profession to profession. Many act as public relations agencies for their members, while others collect data on trends affecting the profession. See Appendix 3 for the names and addresses of key associations you can request information from.

DOING PRIMARY RESEARCH

Since not all information can be obtained from secondary sources, you might have to do your own surveys. One form of primary research is to gather information from your present or potential C/Ps.

Internal records are an excellent source of information on your C/Ps— where they live, who recommended them to you, and other demographic information.

Surveys are a versatile, flexible, and inexpensive method for collecting data about a specific problem. They might include the solicitation of suggestions, ideas, and comments from a sampling of C/Ps. This will permit you to predict how best to communicate to your overall audience of C/Ps.

There are eight basic steps to conducting a survey:

Set objective of survey.
Determine information needed.
Select type of survey.
Prepare a questionnaire.
Set a deadline.
Determine sample size.
Collect data.
Evaluate data.

Setting Research Objectives

Clearly define the specific objectives of your research. Determine the most important facts about what you want to know. Consider how this information can be used in helping you make decisions.

---

*Published by Gale Research Company, Book Tower, Detroit, Mich. 48226.

To do effective advertising, you should know a good deal of the information listed below. Surveying C/Ps can be one of the most successful methods of obtaining this information. Some typical research objectives include determining:

Your target audience.
What type of C/Ps you want to communicate with.
Desirable benefits of your practice.
Customer needs for professional services.
Attitudes of C/Ps.
Competitive conditions—services, costs, and so on.
Range of services to be offered.
How your strengths and weaknesses affect your practice.
How C/Ps learned of your service.
Why C/Ps decided to use your service.

Obtaining Demographic Information

One of the best places to obtain demographic data is from your personal information forms for new C/Ps. An amazing amount and variety of information can be collected from these forms. The Preventive Medicine Institute/Strang Clinic, was able to pinpoint its target audience by determining the educational level, age, area of residence, occupation, race, and marital status from personal records.

Selecting the Type of Survey

Select the type of survey that will provide you with the data in the most efficient manner. The three different survey methods are: the in-office questionnaire and interview, the telephone survey, and the mail survey. Each has advantages and disadvantages that should be considered.

In-office questionnaire. With the in-office method, information is sought either in a personal interview or through a questionnaire filled out while the C/P is waiting in the reception room.

The advantages are:

○ You are reaching the right audience.
○ The interviewer can make additional observations about the respondent (ethnic group, sex, etc.).
○ You have better control than with other techniques.
○ Respondents can ask questions if they are uncertain of what is expected of them.

o You can usually get a higher percentage of completed questionnaires compared with other techniques.
o It is relatively inexpensive to conduct and can be done by your existing staff.

The disadvantages are:

o Since respondents are identified, they might be inclined to equivo-
   cate—whether they intend to or not—about certain facts (e.g., income, occupation).
o It's time consuming for your office to conduct such a survey.
o The interviewer might prejudice the response.

Telephone survey. Usually the telephone survey deals with well-defined
concepts or subjects. The information to be obtained is limited in amount
and of a nonconfidential nature. If you are going to conduct a telephone
survey, it is wise to have questions prepared and places to put the answers. It is generally used to supplement other research techniques.

The advantages are:

o It gets answers quickly. You don't have to wait for someone to come
   into the office or mail a response.
o It's relatively inexpensive to conduct if you are calling in a local area
   or using a WATS line.
o It's easy to call respondents back if they are busy.
o It can be used in a wide or narrow geographic area—the nation,
   state, county, or town.
o It may produce an unrehearsed reaction that is extremely informative.
o Because the respondents are not seen by the interviewer, they can
   be induced to speak more freely. Here's a flattering approach you
   might use when introducing yourself: "You are one of a select number of clients whom we are calling to find out how you feel about
   our legal service. Can you tell us _____ ?"

The disadvantages are:

o The amount of information to be obtained must be limited to one or
   two questions. Don't try to get a lot of information, because the respondent will only hang up on you.
o People are annoyed with nuisance telephone calls. Since many people try to sell things over the telephone, consumers are reluctant to
   cooperate with telephone interviews.
o It should not be used to obtain personal data.
o You might have to hire an independent telephone survey company
   to conduct the survey.

Mail survey. In a mail survey, a questionnaire is sent out to people famil-iar with a specific service or problem. If the group is small, the question-naire can be sent to everyone. If the audience is large, a representative sample must be selected to survey. A mail questionnaire package usually consists of a cover letter that explains the purpose of the survey, the ques-tionnaire, and a postage-paid envelope to mail the questionnaire back in. Sometimes an incentive might be offered (a book, half-dollar, etc.) to en-courage the recipient to answer the questions.

The advantages are:
○ Wide distribution is possible at a relatively low cost.
○ Because respondents are anonymous, they are much more likely to reveal their innermost feelings.
○ There is no interviewer who might bias the outcome.
○ Respondents have more time to answer the questionnaire.

The disadvantages are:
○ You *must* have an up-to-date and accurate mailing list.
○ The attitudes of the people who respond to your survey may be completely different from those of the people who do not respond. This is because people who answer such surveys generally feel strongly about the subject. Unless the percentage of return is high enough, the sample may not be representative.
○ The type of questions and length of the survey have limitations. Questions may be misunderstood, particularly if you are surveying a technical subject.
○ The percentage of response will be lower than in other types of sur-veys because questionnaires are time consuming to fill out.

Writing a Questionnaire

Writing a questionnaire isn't easy. Show it to others for their opinions and advice. It may require several drafts before you get a final version that you are satisfied with. Here are six guidelines to writing a workable questionnaire:

1. *List the information you would like to obtain.* Then narrow down your list of questions. Be unmerciful in cutting down the list. Get others to help you, since it is important to get additional opinions. The process of re-ducing the number of questions you will ask is vital to the success of any questionnaire.

2. *Don't ask the respondent to do too much.* Make it simple. If you ask peo-ple for information that requires them to work, they'll throw the ques-

tionnaire away. For example, if you ask "How much did you spend on dentistry last year?", I'm sure that the information can be obtained, but the respondents are not apt to do it, because they have better things to do with their time than to figure out the amount they spent. Instead, ask "When was the last time you had a dental examination?" They will probably be able to answer this offhand. The thing to remember is to keep your questions easy to answer.

3. *Make it clear.* It is important that you test proposed questionnaires with enough people to make sure that the questions are not ambiguous. If there is any possibility of a misunderstanding, it will occur. Respondents have different educational levels and cultural backgrounds, so that the phrasing of a question may evoke different responses. Women sometimes react differently than men. And people of different ethnic backgrounds may have difficulty understanding the questions you pose.

4. *Pay attention to appearance.* Looks count! The appearance of the questionnaire—the paper it's printed on, the form and flow of the questions—will affect the responses that you get. Do not print a questionnaire on inexpensive paper. Leave wide margins and plenty of room for writing answers. The questionnaire should look important and substantial and be fun to do. To be successful, it must evoke the interest of the C/P.

5. *Keep it short.* A questionnaire should be long enough to cover the subject matter and not a bit longer. If a questionnaire has all the ingredients for success, it can run several pages without cutting the response rate.

6. *Make it obvious to the C/Ps that it is for their benefit.* There are a few crucial seconds when a respondent picks up the questionnaire and considers whether to answer it or not. If people think it's not in their interest to answer it, they'll throw it away. You have to come up with reasons for people to answer your questionnaire. Most people recognize that you are seeking questions to help yourself, but if they see it's also a way of improving your service to them, they will gladly respond.

There are a few easy tricks to writing effective questions:

○ Avoid ambiguous questions. There should be only one way to answer each question. For example:

I first heard of the medical center from:
☐ TV   ☐ Radio   ☐ Newspaper   ☐ Friends
☐ Yellow Pages   ☐ Professional Recommendation
☐ Other (Please Explain)_____

○ Keep questions short (fewer than 20 words) and simple to understand.
○ Keep similar questions together, in a logical progression. Save the most difficult questions until last.
○ Leave enough space for the respondent to answer easily.
  Refer to the sample questionnaires used by professionals shown in this chapter (#3–#6) for additional ideas.

Setting a Deadline

Don't let your research extend over a long period of time. A realistic deadline should be set so that decisions can be made at a specific date. Speed in completing a study is an important ingredient in research. So get everyone in your organization to cooperate to see that the study is completed on time.

How Large a Sample?

When all your preparation for research has been completed, you eventually come to the question of how large a sample you will need to make the survey valid. Sampling is the process of choosing a limited number of respondents from a larger number. The larger number is called "the universe." If the sample is properly selected, the results of the survey will be true of the entire universe. A valid sample is one whose selection is systematic and unbiased. The size of the sample is a highly subjective decision, dependent on many factors, but for the purposes of this chapter we will attempt to simplify it. As one researcher said, "There is no sample that is too small. You just have to realize that there is a margin of error."

Surveys of the United States conducted by one of the largest research organizations, Yankelovich, Skelley and White, use a random sample of 1,200 individuals. They are carefully selected to reflect the entire population of 230 million. One person out of every 200,000 people is selected; this random sample produces a ±3 percent error factor. When the organization surveys the New York metropolitan area, it uses a random sample of 1,000 to represent 15 million people. This should be a tip-off: It isn't the size of the sample that is important, it's how carefully the individuals are chosen to represent the entire universe.

Types of Samples

There are two types of samples: the probability and the nonprobability. Neither method is better than the other; however, your individual situation will dictate what sampling method to use. Whichever, it should be representative of the total population.

AD# 3

FIELD REPRESENTATIVE REPORT

DOCTOR _____   CODE NO. _____

1. Professional Bldg. _____ House _____ Apt. _____ Other _____
2. No. of Dentists   Full Time _____ Part-time _____
3. Employed: Assts. _____ Recpt. _____ Hygienists _____ Office Mgr. _____ Bkpr. _____ Secy _____
   Other _____
   Comments on above: _____
   _____
   _____

4. Is four-handed dentistry used: _____
5. Sterilization method: Autoclave _____ Cold _____ Other _____
6. X-ray Units: No. of _____ Short Cone _____ Long Cone _____ Panarex _____ Other _____
7. Radiation Protection: Lead Lined Walls _____ Lead Apron _____ Other _____ None _____
8. Method of Developing Radiographs: Auto. _____ Non-Auto _____
9. Nitrous-Oxide availability: Yes _____ No _____ Cost per visit: _____
10. Covering Dentist: Emergency: Name _____
    Office _____ Tel. No. _____
    Vacation: Name _____
    Office _____ Tel. No. _____
11. Answering Service: Yes _____ No _____
12. Patient Waiting Time _____ Minutes
    Comments: _____
    _____

13. Post-Examination Fee Schedule Presented: Yes _____   No _____
14. Laboratory on premises: Yes _____ No _____
    Comments: _____
    _____

15. Name(s) of present Laboratorie(s) _____

16. Condition of Equipment: A   B   C   D   F
17. Cavitron?   Yes _____ No _____   18. Electrosurge   Yes _____ No _____
19. Use of Master Charge?   Yes _____ No _____   Visa?   Yes _____ No _____
20. Waiting Room: Appearance   A   B   C   D   F
                                   5   10   15   20   +
21. Operatories: No _____   Appearance   A   B   C   D   F
22. Parking Facilities: Yes _____ No _____   Appearance   A   B   C   D   F
    Comments: _____

23. Practice Type: Low Inc. _____   Blue Collar _____   Middle/Upper _____ / _____
                     Upper _____   Medicaid _____
    Comments: _____
    _____

DOCTOR: A   B   C   D   F
Field representatives comments:
_____
_____
_____   Date _____
_____   R.D.H. _____
_____   Review _____

Dental Survey

To improve dental services to our patients, we would appreciate it if you would take a few minutes of your time and fill in the dental survey below. Thank you for your cooperation.

1. How did you choose Dr. _____ as your dentist?
   ___recommendation   ___read an article
   ___personal contact   ___heard him speak
   ___Yellow Pages ad   ___other _____
   ___newspaper ad   _____

2. I live within _____ miles of the office (check one).
   ___2 miles   ___3 miles   ___5 miles   ___over 5 miles

3. How do you feel about the explanations and information offered on a particular dental problem, fees, etc.?
   ___excellent   ___good   ___fair   ___poor

4. How do you find the appointment system in terms of promptness and accessibility?
   ___excellent   ___good   ___fair   ___poor

5. How do you find the appearance and comfort of the reception room?
   ___excellent   ___good   ___fair   ___poor

6. How do you find the professional equipment and offices?
   ___excellent   ___good   ___fair   ___poor

7. How do you find the professional assistants?
   ___excellent   ___good   ___fair   ___poor

8. How do you find the accessibility of the office?
   ___excellent   ___good   ___fair   ___poor

9. How do you find the parking facilities?
   ___excellent   ___good   ___fair   ___poor

10. What do you like best about the dental care offered? _____
    _____

11. What do you like least about the dental care offered? _____
    _____

Metropolitan Lawyer Referral Service

To help us improve our services to the public, we are asking you to fill out this questionnaire. The information you provide will be kept in strict confidence. Thank you for your time.

I first heard of the Metropolitan Lawyer Referral Service from:

___TV

___Radio

___Newspaper

___Friends

___Legal aid

___District attorney

___Public defender

___Courts

___Government or social agency—which one? _____

___Yellow Pages

___Orange information card—obtained where? _____

___Other—please explain _____

I decided to use the Metropolitan Lawyer Referral Service because of:

___Convenience and speed

___Price

___Reputation or recommendation

___No other alternative

___Advertising

___Other—please explain _____

When I called the Metropolitan Lawyer Referral Service, the person I talked with:

	Yes	No
Understood my legal problem	—	—
Explained the services and fees	—	—
Used language I could understand	—	—
Made a convenient appointment	—	—

My household income is ___less than $5,000　___$5,000–$7,000

___$7,000–$11,000　___$11,000–$15,000

___$15,000–$20,000　___more than $20,000

The last year of school I completed was _____

In a *probability sample,* everyone has an equal chance of being selected for interview. This may be done on a purely random basis, or every *n*th (10th, 20th, 50th, etc.) name on the available population list may be chosen until your sample is completed. Still another approach is to divide the population into homogeneous groups from which random samples are drawn in direct proportion to the group's representation in the entire universe.

In a *nonprobability sample,* each person has an unknown chance of being selected. It is generally regarded as less accurate than the probability method, but it is being used by most professionals at this time. Basic human judgment is involved in making the selection of sample members. It can produce valid results if it happens to be a reasonably accurate model of the entire universe.

In a small practice (fewer than a thousand C/Ps) the nonprobability sample should be used, since you can select people for questioning on the basis of convenience and the ease of interviewing in your office.

The population being studied (your overall practice) will be spread over a normal bell-shaped curve. The information obtained from any study will typically take the form of this curve. The true average will lie somewhere between two percentage points (plus or minus) on either side of the figure calculated. By planning the sampling process in advance, you can evaluate the data within certain margins of error.

One professional recommended that if you have a clientele of 1,000 a sampling of 100 would be adequate provided that it reflected the entire cross-section of your practice. When the Preventive Medicine Institute surveyed 20,000 patients, it used a sampling of 200. In most cases (particularly if you have a small practice), you will want to sample a good portion of your clientele. It is possible to alert your staff to make sure that they conduct an unbiased survey. Set a time limit; conduct your survey over one or two months. And remember, your sample should be representative of your practice.

Tabulating and Analyzing the Data

There are essentially two ways to tabulate data: by hand or by computer. Both have their time and place. You should use hand tabulation when you have a small sample and few questions, with a limited number of cross tabulations. Computers should be used when you have a large sample and many questions, with an extensive number of cross tabulations. Most of the research suggested in this chapter is designed for hand tabulation by a secretary or receptionist.

Strang Clinic
Initial Patient Motivation Study

TOTAL NUMBER OF PATIENTS ___

1. Have you ever had a complete physical exam?   Yes ___   No ___

2. How long ago?
   1 year ___   5 and over ___
   1–5 years ___   Never had exam ___

3. Where did you have the exam?
   A–Private MD ___   B–Hospital clinic ___
   C–Ambulatory clinics   D–Miscellaneous
      Life Extension ___   Canscreen ___
      HIP ___   Health fair ___
      Clinic ___   Service ___
      HMO ___   E–Never had exam
      VA ___
      Kaiser ___

4. Can you remember your reason for having the exam?
   Checkup ___   Insurance ___
   Symptoms ___   VISA ___
   Job required ___

5. Any particular reason for not returning there?
   A–More thorough exam desired ___
   B–Dissatisfied with MD ___
   C–Not convenient ___
   D–MD died/service no longer available ___
   E–Moved/no longer with company ___
   F–Miscellaneous
      Referred to Strang ___   Second opinion ___
      Job required ___   Wife recommended Strang ___
      Situation changed/all   Met Dr. Miller ___
      services in one location ___   MD has no time ___
      Not insured ___   Excess waiting at MD office ___
      No report sent ___
   G–No exam

6. Do you have a personal physician?   Yes ___   No ___

7. Have you ever used him/her for a complete physical?   Yes ___   No ___

8. Did you consider going to your personal physician for this exam?   Yes ___   No ___

9. Under what circumstances do you go to him?   Illness ___   Checkup ___

10. Have you ever gone to a physician for an exam where you had no symptoms or complaints?   Yes ___   No ___

11. What is your main reason for having this exam?   Symptoms ___   Checkup ___

12. Was there anything personally or in family or friends that entered into your decision to come?
    No ___   Illness or death in circle ___   Urged by relative/friend ___

13. What made you choose Strang Clinic for your exam?
    A—Personal recommendation
    B—Publicity
       Subway ___
       News ___
       Radio ___
    C—Other Recommendations   D—Miscellaneous
       Memorial Sloan-Kettering ___   Walked by ___
       American Cancer Society ___   Old Strang patient ___
       Religious order ___   Canscreen ___
       Dr. Miller ___   Female clinic patient ___
       MD ___

14. How long did you think about having this exam before you actually called to make the appointment?   Weeks: Months: Years:

15. What kind of benefits do you expect from this exam?
    A—Diagnosis ___   D—Miscellaneous
    B—Clean bill of health/peace of   Complete exam ___
       mind ___   Health advice ___
    C—Health Status ___   Correct problem area ___
                                                      Call attention to risk factors ___
                                                      Permission to exercise ___
                                                      Advice on preventive
                                                         measures ___

16. What does preventive medicine mean to you?
    A—Stop disease before it gets too   E—Miscellaneous
       far ___   Take medicine ___
    B—Good diet/exercise/no smoking ___   Reduce risk factors ___
    C—Diagnose problem areas ___   Follow doctor's advice ___
    D—Take frequent checkups ___   Avoid illness ___
                                                    Health guidance ___

Once data are gathered, examine them carefully. You should be able to reach certain conclusions about why differences exist between each segment of a question. This will require prior knowledge of the problems (and opportunities) and how these data can be used to solve them.

In order to act on your research findings, you need a decisive yes or no reaction to your questions. If the split is 55 to 45 percent, you might have to rethink the results. You might want to conduct another survey, wording the questions differently to reach a conclusion that you can act on.

In addition to specific recommendations, there may be alternative actions that can be taken on the basis of your research and observations. One medical center located in a large city surveyed its patients to obtain demographic information to be used in advertising. Much to the center's surprise, it found that 20 percent of the new patients were black. One of the recommendations to management was to hire more black professionals to reflect the increased percentage of new black patients.

FOCUS GROUPS

A focus group is a discussion group of eight to ten people led by a moderator. It is representative of the target audience you want to reach. The objective is to get the group to speak out freely and express needs, desires, attitudes, and opinions.

The moderator is highly trained and able to analyze the panel members' remarks, thoughts, and behavior. Using this information, the researcher is able to develop concepts for creating advertising campaigns, affecting consumer attitudes toward professional services, and positioning the service. Focus groups are often used to check the strengths and weaknesses, both verbal and visual, of a proposed advertising campaign. People can really open up and give researchers new insights into professional services and image building.

RESEARCH TIPS

o Research is like a computer: It is only as good as the information fed into it. Therefore, it is important that the right questions be asked.

o Research sheds light on a situation as it existed at the time the research was done, but the situation can change dramatically in just a few months.

o Research must be interpreted carefully, realizing the potential for error.

o Focus groups can be very effective for testing concepts and ideas before identifiable market segments. They will help prevent disasters and improve you chances of success.

○ Don't try to survey anyone that's in a hurry or under duress. They may be too pressured to give useful answers.

○ Smart advertisers maintain daily, weekly, and monthly response charts to determine peak and poor response periods.

○ The better you pinpoint who your potential C/Ps are, the better your advertising response is likely to be.

For more information on the role of research and reasearch firms, contact the American Marketing Association and the Marketing Research Association, Inc. (see the listing in Appendix 3).

CHAPTER 5

Positioning Your Practice

ONE OF THE MOST misunderstood and misused terms in advertising today is *positioning*. Professionals refer to it constantly and even employ the strategy, though many of them don't really know what it means.

The term was first used in an advertisement that appeared in *The New York Times* on April 7, 1971. The ad was written by the inimitable adman David Ogilvy, and in it he outlined his 38 points for creating advertising that sells. The first point Mr. Ogilvy called "the most important decision." He went on to say, "The results of your campaign depend less on how we write your advertising than on how your product is positioned."

Since that advertisement appeared, "positioning" has become the battle cry of companies large and small. It is mentioned in articles, seminars, and lectures—hardly a day goes by in the advertising world when you don't hear a reference to positioning.

CONSIDERATIONS IN POSITIONING A PRACTICE

Stated briefly, positioning is examining the professional marketplace and determining opportunities for your practice that no one else is taking advantage of. To be successful today, a practitioner has to be marketing oriented. You must know everything that is happening in the professional marketplace. You'll need to take a situation analysis, as detailed in Chapter 3, to obtain information on the consumer, the competition, your area of specialization, and recent trends. Then analyze these data and transform them into a marketing/positioning strategy. The information will determine what kind of personnel you will hire, the specialty and image you will want to project, and the message you will want to run in all your advertising.

The Consumer

In building a practice, you need to determine what kind of clients/patients (C/Ps) you want to attract. Will they be low-, middle-, or high-income consumers? What is their education, age, sex, and attitude toward professionals? What kind of life-style do they lead? The better you know your target audience, the better chance you will have of creating a persuasive advertisement that will attract it and move it to action. You have to understand what your target audience considers relevant to its needs, desires, and problems.

Many professionals, using secondary research available from associations, have targeted their practices to middle-income consumers who are hard pressed financially because of inflation. They have stressed reasonable fees in their advertising and positioned themselves as the professionals for middle-income groups.

The Competition

Many professionals start advertising with little thought to the competition in the marketplace. They don't emphasize their experience, expertise, or knowledge, or the qualities that make their practice different. They advertise with no position in mind, and as a result they are usually disappointed with the outcome.

To cope with today's crowded and competitive professional marketplace, you must create a place in your prospect's mind. One way to do this is to relate your practice to competitors in the field that have already established themselves in the community. You have to create a position for your practice that is not being filled by other professionals. You have to accept what is already there and build around it. You can't ignore your competitors' position in your area. For example, you may practice in an area that is dominated by professionals who advertise low fees. To compete with these professionals on a price basis is the road to ruin. You'll have to devise a marketing plan that takes advantage of services and benefits not being offered by these low-fee professionals.

Your Specialty

This can be the determining factor in positioning your practice. If it is truly unique, then you can use it to distinguish your practice from the rest. However, if you are a generalist, you might select one area of expertise and use it as the basis of an advertising campaign. For example, one legal clinic advertised how it can solve consumer debt problems. It abandoned a broad-based advertising approach to position its practice to a narrow—but highly profitable—segment of the market.

THE BATTLE FOR THE PROSPECT'S MIND

Two leading exponents of positioning, Jack Trout and Al Reis, wrote: "Positioning is used in a broader sense to mean what the advertising does for the product in the prospect's mind."* And it is in the consumer's mind that the positioning battle takes place.

It appears that advertising isn't working the way it used to. The reasons for this are twofold: First, we live in a media-saturated, overcommunicated nation; and second, the proliferation of similar products and services has confused the public.

Consider the fact that the United States is the world's largest user of advertising. With only 5 percent of the world's population, we consume 54 percent of the world's advertising output. The per capita consumption of advertising in the United States is about $230 a year. A barrage of messages are constantly competing for the consumer's mind.

Each day, thousands of new professionals start to advertise. Add to this the many thousands who have already established names for themselves. The human brain has a limited capacity for remembering these names. When new names are introduced, consumers learn them at the expense of other names that they were familiar with.

MARKET SEGMENTS

One way to establish a position is to concentrate on one segment of a total market. You can provide a specialty that currently doesn't exist or is not being advertised. It is not sufficient just to advertise a shopping list of fees and expect to attract clients. In order to be successful, you must create a unique position in your prospect's mind. For example, in my interviews with professionals:

o Dr. Allen Gutstein of Universal Dental Centers said, "As more and more dental clinics started to advertise low fees on Long Island, fees became somewhat comparable. And if fees are similar, a patient has to have a reason for choosing one clinic over another. So you have to create a position for yourself in the market that will make the patient come to you as opposed to going to your competition. Filling the need, for example, for more convenient hours, seven days a week, is why we're successful."

o The legal clinic of Jacoby & Meyers was one of the first professional firms to use positioning. "In our first TV spot, we positioned Jacoby & Meyers as a respectable law firm specializing in serving the middle class at a reasonable cost," said Robert Hodges, the adman who worked on the ad campaign. Hodges was using American Bar Association data that revealed that the vast majority of Americans do not avail themselves of legal

---

*Al Reis and Jack Trout, *Positioning: The Battle for Your Mind*, New York, McGraw-Hill, 1980.

services because they overestimate the cost of lawyer fees. More important, "they didn't know where to go to get competent legal advice."

○ A private health center in New York City advertises under "Urologist–Surgeon" in *The Village Voice*. The center offers medical care to gay men for prostatitis, venereal diseases, and diseases of the kidney or bladder as well as comprehensive general medical care. It is establishing a position for a segment of the market that is affluent and seeking specialized medical care.

○ Dr. Frederick Seltzer said, "My position in all my advertising is to bring home to people that preventive dentistry is continuous; in the long run, good dentistry saves you money. It doesn't have to be a horrendous experience. Certainly not in my office."

○ When F. Lee Bailey and Aaron J. Broder advertised their expertise in handling "wrongful death and personal injury cases arising out of aircraft disasters," on the front pages of *The New York Times* and other newspapers, Mr. Bailey was reported as saying his reason was to counter the public feeling that "I touch nothing but murder cases at $100,000 a clip. Advertising is a way to establish an area of expertise [positioning] where the public does not expect it to be" (*The New York Times*, April 23, 1979).

○ Many smaller accounting firms have built thriving practices by positioning themselves as specialists, for example, for real estate agencies, banks, savings and loans associations, hospitals, insurance companies, hotels, or restaurants.

REPOSITIONING IN THE 1980s

One of the oddities of positioning is observing how marketers of professional services are changing their positioning to meet the opportunities in the years ahead. Repositioning comes about when a marketer looks at the marketplace and the competition and reacts to how they have changed since the last time the service was positioned.

Capitalizing on repositioning, Jacoby & Meyers ran TV spots in the third phase of its ad campaign in which it abandoned a broad appeal for legal services at reasonable cost and switched to a narrow position stressing specific types of legal cases. The firm concentrated its advertising on divorce and criminal matters—two areas that represented nearly 50 percent of its case load. It dropped all reference to cost and emphasized know-how instead. Subsequent television advertising stressed the competency of the firm, using research on legal clinics provided by a major university.

Above all, trend-setting professionals recognize that consumers and their attitudes are in a constant state of flux. This is due to many factors: The population is growing older; soaring inflation is putting strains on the family pocketbook; a rising divorce rate and delayed marriages are producing more single households; families are smaller; one out of two adult women are now working; and a greater emphasis on self is affecting all human behavior.

More and more practitioners are targeting their advertising to this changing marketplace. They are repositioning themselves and their practices in a way that is unique and different from the competition. And more importantly, they are filling a genuine consumer need.

CHAPTER 6

Developing an Advertising Plan and Budget

Now that you have taken a situation analysis and researched your particular problem, you are ready to write an advertising plan. The situation analysis and research provided you with all the information needed to position your practice, plan a strategy, and set realistic objectives and goals.

All advertising starts with a plan. Whether you do it yourself or hire an advertising agency, you must have a carefully prepared program for a specific period of time. In most cases it will be for one year, but it can also be for six months.

Arnold Siegel wrote in the *California CPA Quarterly* (March 1979):

> In our attempt to create an accounting firm that could prosper in the current environment, we initiated a methodical and fairly arduous process of long-range planning. We began by examining and identifying our special strengths. We found that certain markets were tailor-made to our skills, experience, and backgrounds. To identify these markets, we asked ourselves: "What can we really do well and what is unique about us?" We felt our most unique attribute was our ability to speak our clients' languages. We also took a hard look at how much growth we wanted to achieve and how quickly we wanted to achieve it.

WHAT THE PLAN CONTAINS

Unless you are part of a large group practice, you will be responsible for your own advertising plan. This includes:

- *Getting the facts.* Through your research, you will be able to identify problems as well as opportunities.
- *Setting objectives and goals.* Where do you want to be one year and five years from now?

○ *"Positioning" your practice.* What makes your practice unique compared with the competition in your area? Is it a low fee, a unique specialty, or personalized service?

○ *Determining a budget.* Every professional will have his or her own method for determining a budget. It will be based on objectives and tasks to be accomplished.

○ *Selecting media.* Once you've determined a creative approach, you need to select the right media to expose it to the right people—with impact. The right people, determined by your research, will be your target audience.

○ *Creating a message.* This is one of the most important aspects of all successful advertising. What you say and how you present it are vital to the effectiveness of an ad campaign, as well as to the building of your image.

○ *Evaluating your ad program.* Whether on a weekly, monthly, or yearly basis, you should determine the effectiveness of your advertising.

If you are just starting a practice or would like to revitalize one, you should have well-defined objectives and goals. All professionals who undertook an advertising program had clear-cut objectives and goals. They knew what they wanted and in what time frame and drew up a plan to accomplish this.

Today these professionals are increasing their client/patient flow and solidifying their current C/P base. They are making their practices very organized businesses and are using consistent advertising as an integral part of their practices. And these are goals that you can set for yourself.

SETTING GOALS

Goals are the desired *long-term* results of your overall marketing plan. They are supported by strategies that state specific short-term objectives. Objectives are stepping-stones to attaining long-term goals.

Whenever possible, define your goals in quantitative terms so that they can be measured. There are many monetary and nonmonetary goals. For example:

1. Build a $150,000-a-year practice within ＿＿＿ years.
2. Achieve ＿＿＿ percent awareness and recognition in the community in ＿＿＿ years.
3. Become a national (or statewide) company in ＿＿＿ years.

Set your goals high enough so that they give you and your staff something to reach for. But make sure you don't set unreasonable goals. You want everyone to work for a goal that can be attained.

SETTING OBJECTIVES

Objectives are short-term goals. After you determine your goals, make a list of all the objectives of your strategic marketing plan. These are the secondary goals that will help you determine where you want to be a number of years from now. They must be consistent with your overall marketing plans.

After listing your objectives in order of importance, develop plans to achieve them. Set specific targets to reach by dates that you determine. Each objective should move you in the direction of your long-term goals and be a motivator for future growth. Every plan can have major and minor objectives.

The objectives you set for yourself should be realistic and achievable. For instance, if you are going to start an advertising campaign that reaches the population of an entire metropolitan area, make sure to have offices that are centrally located to take advantage of the increased C/P load.

When the legal clinic of Jacoby & Meyers launched an ad campaign of TV spots in the New York metropolitan area, it simultaneously opened 11 offices in the important surrounding counties. The firm wasn't going to waste its money by not having a sufficient number of conveniently located offices to accommodate the client flow produced by the advertising. "It's the only way to make the advertising economical," mentioned one attorney involved in the legal clinic. A continous C/P flow is one of the major objectives of all professionals.

Like long-term goals, short-term objectives should be defined in quantitative terms so that they can be measured and evaluated. They should be clear cut, well defined, and flexible enough to allow for changes in the future.

Here is a list of objectives that a professional might consider:

1. Increase the number of new C/Ps each week, month, or year by ___ percent.
2. Increase monthly volume by ___ percent.
3. Increase yearly income by $ ___.
4. Increase community awareness and recognition by ___ percent.

Examples of Professional Objectives

While writing this book, I found that professionals had many different objectives for advertising. But the major objective, was to build a practice with new C/Ps. Even though a good deal of the advertising was educational in nature, these professionals were out to increase their C/P flow.

Objectives can change from year to year, or even after a few months, because they reflect what's happening in the marketplace. If a clinic opens in your area, cuts fees, and launches an ad campaign, you might consider taking counteraction to let people in your community know the value of the services you render. In addition, as state regulations change, new dimensions are introduced into the marketing of professional services. Therefore, be flexible with your objectives. If they have to be changed, do so right away.

Here are some typical objectives cited by practitioners who launched advertising campaigns. Most of the information was obtained from personal interviews. Although many of the professionals quoted below are currently altering their objectives to reflect the changing nature of their practices, the major objective of seeking new C/Ps has remained the same.

o "The first objective in our advertising campaign is *awareness*. And when top management and financial executives start to select auditors for the first time, or if they are going to change auditors, we want them to think of us and give us a try. We are seeking new clients." Deloitte Haskins & Sells.

o "Our objective was to make the public more aware of the legal referral service and to encourage people to use these services. It's a service to bring lawyer and client together." Metropolitan Lawyer Referral Service.

o "Our objective has been to increase patient load while educating the public. A lot of people just do not know where to go for cosmetic surgery. So many people do not have general practitioners with whom they have rapport. They don't want anyone to know that they are seeking cosmetic surgery. They don't know where to turn. Our advertising approach has been educational. Of course, there is an income coming in from it as a result." Creative Surgery Center.

o "Most lawyers who advertise are interested in new clients, big clients, major cases. Our concern at Bailey & Broder was that F. Lee Bailey was associated with criminal law and the only way the public would learn that our firm is in aviation accidents and not limited to the criminal field was to advertise. We've been practicing for eight years and the public wasn't *aware* of this at all—that we have aviation-related clients." F. Lee Bailey and Aaron J. Broder.

o "The most important result we wished to achieve was that our peers in the accounting profession approve of our ads. Failure in this area presented the greatest risk and success the greatest benefit. . . . It was our intention to attract clients who do not have a CPA or those who already decided to terminate the relationship with their current CPA. As a small firm, our marketing strategy was directed toward developing new business for ourselves, not entering a struggle over an already exploited and finite existing market." Siegel, Sugarman & Seput (*California CPA Quarterly*, March 1979).

○ "The American Dental Plan is trying to sign up every dentist in New York State. Our goal is to be a national company. We would like to have every dentist participate in the program. We are also offering our dental plan to companies, as well as federal and state employees." American Dental Plan.

○ "We estimated after being in practice a while that the number of people we would be seeing in the course of a given year in terms of patient visits would average about 5,000 per practitioner." Universal Dental Centers.

○ "Within five years, Jacoby & Meyers plans to have offices in all major metropolitan areas. We have already been instrumental in creating a new system for giving the average citizen adequate access to legal services at reasonable fees. We expect to handle 50,000 clients this year and double the number of New York offices, expand in California, and enter another urban market in a third state." Jacoby & Meyers.

○ "We were facing a serious problem. Our patient load had declined alarmingly from 75 patients a day in 1974 to 35 patients in 1975. With this serious decline, the clinic was now facing an operating deficit. We had to do something. Our objective was to raise the patient flow to 80 per day. So we decided to advertise to persuade people to come in for an examination (as well as to educate the public)." Preventive Medicine Institute/Strang Clinic.

DETERMINING AN ADVERTISING BUDGET

Once you finalize your objectives and devise a plan for action, you should determine your advertising budget. This is probably the most puzzling aspect of advertising—what should you spend on an advertising program? John Wanamaker, the pioneer mass merchant, said, "Half the money I spend on advertising is wasted. And the trouble is I don't know which half." But before you can begin to plan an advertising strategy of any dimension, you must know how much you are prepared to spend, and picking a figure out of a hat is not the answer.

Most firms and individuals will allocate an amount that they think is reasonable—and that they can afford—and hope that they make a sufficient impression in the marketplace to attract a steady flow of C/Ps. But there really are many ways to arrive at an advertising budget, and you have to choose one that you can live with. There are generally too many variables to make a hard-and-fast rule about budgets that applies to every professional.

Here are some important considerations for establishing a budget:

1. What media will reach your target audience?
2. What is the cost of the media and for what time period?
3. What is the reach (or circulation) or the media?
4. How much time or space do you have to buy and in what frequency to make an impression on the target audience?
5. Is there an alternative way of reaching your target audience (e.g., direct mail, transit advertising)?
6. What other expenses need to be considered—for example, art and production costs, public relations and advertising fees, photography, signs and billboards?

Methods of Planning a Budget

You can plan a budget any way you desire. Here are some suggestions.

The task method. This is based essentially on what task or series of tasks you want to accomplish. The budget is determined only after considering how you can best obtain these objectives. In this appraoch, you must know competitive market conditions, your target audience, and other factors that influence the advertising budget. The expenditures will be determined by the cost of publication space, broadcast time, production charges, promotional literature, postage, etc. But no matter how much money you have available, there will never be enough to accomplish all your objectives. Therefore, you are going to have to make compromises. Adman David Ogilvy wrote, "I have come to think that nine out of ten advertising budgets are too small to do the job assigned to them." He recommended that you "concentrate what money you have in your most lucrative markets or confine your advertising to one income group."*

Priorities must be given to the tasks that you want to accomplish. Evaluate them and determine which ones are most important. Is it to attract new C/Ps immediately, or to create an awareness of your practice? Is there a competitive situation that requires a separate advertising budget? Whatever the priority, the task method is usually revised to meet the changing guidelines and objectives of a program.

---

*David Ogilvy, *Confessions of an Advertising Man*, New York: Atheneum, 1963.

The percentage of gross Income method. The setting of an advertising budget as a percentage of gross income is probably one of the most popular methods used in business. This figure can run from a fraction of 1 percent to over 15 percent, depending on the industry and product being advertised. A 1980 study of leading U.S. corporations by Schonfeld and Associates Inc., a Chicago-based consulting firm, revealed the following figures of advertising expenditures as a percentage of gross sales for different industries:

Industry	Percentage
Drugs	6.4
Nursing/personal care	2.2
Finance	1.7
Services, engineering, and architecture	0.4

These figures, derived from financial statements of publicly held firms, are on the low side since they reflect companies with many diversified product lines. The figure most commonly used by small business for advertising is somewhere around 5 percent of forecasted gross sales. This method arrives at a set dollar amount without considering the objectives of your program. The budget may be totally inadequate for your goals. However, this method is very popular because of its simplicity. Here's an easy formula for determining the percentage of gross volume:

$$\$150,000 \quad \times \quad .05\% \quad = \quad \$7,500$$

(forecasted gross volume)   (percentage of forecasted gross volume)   (advertising budget)

The empirical method. This flexible method uses various experimental procedures to determine the budget. Interest in this type of budgeting has been growing because it is based on feedback from your target audience as opposed to assumptions and guesses. Only through testing which creative appeals, media mix, and time periods pull the best results can you arrive at optimum spending levels. When you find significant results from these tests, implement them immediately. Don't wait till next year to use what you have learned. Conditions could change considerably. Use the results today!

The media requirement method. In this approach, the practitioner estimates the amount of media coverage needed to reach a predetermined number of C/Ps with a selling message. This should be done as carefully as possible with whatever data you have available regarding seasonal attitudes of C/Ps and the best periods for advertising. For example, one large preventive medicine center found that patient activity slumped badly in December no matter what it did. The center determined that people were far more concerned with Christmas than with their health. For this reason, it discontinued all advertising during the holiday period and resumed with a strong campaign in January and February.

Living Within a Budget

It is important to review a budget periodically to determine if you have stayed within your limits for each time period. This requires discipline and good business sense. You will be beseiged by media salespeople trying to sell you on their publication or station. You need determination to say NO once you are committed to a program. As your practice matures, keep your eyes and ears open to special media opportunities that enable you to buy time and space at lower than rate-card costs. To do this, you must know your media representative on a personal level.

Listed below are some budgeting techniques used by professionals, as obtained from personal interviews and other sources. The techniques vary from practitioner to practitioner. You need to find a method that you can apply to your own situation; these are provided as examples only.

○ "Our advertising agency conducted a study and made a presentation to us that included different levels of advertising expenditures. They recommended a campaign that we ultimately adopted. We feel it gave us the most coverage for our advertising dollars. If it was less coverage, it would be less money, but we wouldn't be reaching a sufficient percentage of our audience. We could have doubled or tripled our budget and put ads in every newspaper in the country. But that would be wasteful. We decided to limit our advertising to national financial publications." Deloitte Haskins & Sells.

○ "The majority of our budget is spent on radio. We also use newspapers. We have found from experience that radio, particularly the morning drive time, provides the greatest number of inquiries. These people hear our message and when they arrive at work they call us (during the day) to schedule an appointment. Evening drive time pulls a lesser response as does newspaper advertising." Metropolitan Lawyer Referral Service.

o A successful cosmetic surgeon in California reported spending "somewhere in the area of 5 percent of gross income" for advertising. Dr. L. Lee Bosley (*Medical Economics*, August 6, 1979).

o "We determined that the clients who engage us should generate billings that would cover the cost of the campaign. The analysis follows:
1. If they remain clients for a year, and if their billing materializes as projected, our new clients will generate gross annual billings of approximately $50,000.
2. Our budget for the campaign was $25,000. Of this, $16,000 was spent on media and $9,000 on creative and production costs.
3. Consequently, projected gross billings will come to twice our [overall advertising] costs and three times our media budget." Siegel, Sugarman & Seput (*California CPA Quarterly*, March 1979).

o "Our advertising expenditure has effectively been able to generate income immediately to the point where we have become self-sufficient after a short period of time. If you're spending $10,000 on advertising and you're only getting $8,000 back as a result, then maybe you should do only $8,000 in advertising." Universal Dental Centers.

o "My attitude is, the only way to make money is to spend money. Nothing happens for nothing. So I decided to spend $45 per week on small-space newspaper ads. That's about $180 a month. And I did it week after week. I set a gross income objective and doubled it. . . . Continuous advertising has paid off." Dr. Frederick Seltzer.

o "When you start, you have to set a dollar amount and guide yourself by the response. If you spend between $25,000 and $50,000 and say this is an investment in your advertising program, you have to be prepared to see what kind of response it gets. If it's successful, you may want to cut back a little. It depends upon how much your practice is capable of handling." Creative Surgery Center.

o "We picked a certain dollar amount for our budget with a number of things to accomplish. We wanted the advertising to sell, make a lasting impression, get as much reach and frequency as we could afford, and build credibility with the public." Universal Dental Centers.

o When Jacoby & Meyers opened 11 new offices in New York in 1979, it simultaneously scheduled a radio and television campaign budgeted between $350,000 and $500,000. The spots were broadcast on at least five TV stations.

CHAPTER 7

The Media Strategy

ONE OF THE MOST important functions of all advertising is to make sure your message is presented to and noticed by the right audience. You can have a truly creative and unique campaign, but in the wrong media, it will have little impact.

Summing this up, the Magazine Publishers Association offered a formula for success in advertising:

$$rm^1 + rm^2 = R$$

What this formula represents is the *right message placed in the right media (or magazine) brings RESULTS*. The proper selection of media means bringing your message to the greatest number of potential clients/patients (C/Ps) at the lowest possible costs—and with continuity.

But what are media? They are the vehicles that will deliver your message to your target audience. The most widely used media include newspapers, magazines, radio, television, direct mail, transit, outdoor, and the Yellow Pages.

Purchasing media time or space is the most expensive component of your advertising campaign. The actual costs for producing advertising represent a small percentage of your overall budget. In many cases, the amount allocated for production ranges from 10 to 20 percent of the total budget. The rest will be used for the purchase of media space and time.

So it is extremely important to know which media are going to reach the greatest target audience. One thing you don't need is a lot of wasted circulation—that is, distribution to people who are not logical prospects for your service. You want results! And the way to get them is to know your media objectives.

SETTING MEDIA OBJECTIVES

One of the first questions most practitioners ask is "Where shall I advertise?" This will depend on a number of factors, from the type of C/Ps you want to attract to the image you want to project. "Before you start to advertise," said one dentist who was setting up dental clinics in discount stores, "you've got to define your market. You've got to know who you want to reach and what you want to reach them with."

Below is a list of the most important objectives and considerations of a media plan.

1. *Determine what is to be accomplished.* Decide in advance what you want to achieve with your media plan. Try to be specific. Determine what percentage of your target audience you want to reach and how often.

2. *Be consistent with your objectives.* Your media decisions should be a component of your overall advertising plan and consistent with your marketing objectives. You want to stay within the guidelines that you set for yourself. If you want to attract a specific audience, make sure that your media plan reflects this.

3. *Evaluate the creative requirements.* You should consider the creative requirements of your campaign and how adaptable each medium is in presenting your message. If your strategy demands visualization, then you will have to consider print or television. If you have a long story to tell—with price lists—then you must consider print or direct-mail advertising. If your advertising needs a demonstration, then your best vehicle would be television. If you can explain it in words alone, then by all means use radio. Each medium has advantages and disadvantages; you have to determine where your message will have the best chance of success.

4. *Consider the competition in your area.* Study the advertising and other techniques they are using to attract C/Ps. Don't try to imitate them. If you are competing with clinics or low-fee practitioners that are spending large amounts of money on advertising, then you will have to create a unique position in the marketplace for your practice. You might also have to select media other than those used by the competition, since you will be seeking a different audience. If a good alternative medium is available, use it. On the other hand, if you have a practice with definite advantages over your competition and if a direct comparison demonstrates the benefits of your service, then you may profit from placing your advertising in the same media that your competition is using.

5. *Establish your budget.* Take a realistic look at your proposed budget. The depth of your media plan will depend on the financial resources available. Large ads repeated often in a wide variety of publications may

be desirable to reach the greatest audience, but not realistic when you consider the limitations of your budget. If your budget is too small to make an impact against the weight of competing ads, it may be wise to concentrate your dollars in media where the most productive market segment lies. Quite often, it is possible through careful selection and better use of the media to create a greater impact than your big-spending competitors.

MATCHING THE MEDIA TO YOUR MARKET

The key to matching media with your market is to know who your prospects are, where they live, when they will be most receptive to your advertising, and how often and in what manner to reach them. This information will help you create the message as well as identify the people you are trying to communicate with. Three different methods are currently being used by media planners in selecting media:

Demographic matching. Demographics refers to the statistical study of populations. Practically all newspapers, magazines, radio, and TV stations can give you a breakdown of their audiences in terms of age, education, sex, income, family status, occupations, and place of residence. Using this method of media selection, your prospects and the media are matched to deliver the right audience at the lowest possible cost. What you are trying to do is to reach the largest number of prospects who fall within your audience profile guidelines. Many sophisticated professionals use demographic matching once they have identified their prospects.

- A large dental clinic identified its target audience as: male and female; income of $10,000–$30,000; aged 30–55; high school graduates with 20 percent having some college education; white-collar and blue-collar workers, office/clerical workers, skilled operators, and technicians.
- A legal referral service identified its audience as: blue-collar, low- to middle-income; first-term legal users; male and female; aged 25–49; with many falling into the black and Chicano ethnic groups.
- A large medical clinic identified its prospects as: male and female; 25 percent suburbanites, 75 percent city residents; income of $25,000–$35,000; median age, 51; high school graduates with 35 percent having attended college.

The user approach. Independent research organizations have conducted surveys of print and broadcast media to determine the consumption and buying patterns of readers and listeners. They have taken into consideration, not only use, but the volume of use of products and services. (Most advertisers will concentrate their media dollars where they see the greatest potential for return, and this is with the heavy user of a service or product.) This information is readily available from the individual stations, magazines, and newspapers. However, little information currently exists on the use of professional services by consumers. In the future, with the aid of the computer, we can expect to see this information readily available to encourage professionals to advertise.

Psychographic matching. In addition to such demographic factors as sex, age, and income, such intangibles as life-style, attitudes, and personality will affect the use of a service. This is called psychographics, which is a blend of the demographic and psychological characteristics of the buying audience. It takes the marketer a step closer to matching media with the actual prospect.

WHERE TO GET INFORMATION ON MEDIA

You can get an abundance of information from the media if you just ask for it.

Working with Your Media Salesperson

If you would like to learn a great deal about local media in your town or city, start with your newspaper, radio, or TV advertising salesperson. Salespeople can give you a lot of valuable information about recent trends in professional advertising, costs, availability of time and space, demographic characteristics, and product or service use.

The larger stations and newspapers have the ability to identify their audiences in terms of demographics and even psychographics. The research available today is designed to help you locate your most logical prospects. The media are able to identify high-volume purchasers of services, and in many cases this group will buy out of proportion to the total audience size.

In addition, most media salespeople will reveal statistics to try to convince you that their newspaper or station is the best buy in your area. They will point to the large circulation or the wide listening audience; they will show you the market coverage of a specific age group, such as 25–49 year olds; they will point to product usage data or the high income of the audience; or they may just show you how their station delivers the most prospects at the lowest cost.

All the facts may be true. It will take some sharp analytical skills to wade through the information and determine what your own special requirements are. If you want some help finding weaknesses in the statistics, call in a competing newspaper, radio, or TV station representative. The competitors will show you flaws in the research that were not apparent and then give you their own data on why they are the better media buy. Eventually, you will have to evaluate all the media and reach a conclusion on what vehicle will serve your interests best.

The Computer in Media Analysis

As new information is correlated from such research organizations as A. C. Nielsen, Arbitron, and Simmons Market Research, it is being recorded on computer tape for use by advertisers. This makes it possible to utilize the incredible speed of the computer for comparative media analysis. The larger radio and TV stations can supply you with the latest data instantly. The computer has contributed a great deal to media planning by facilitating comparisons between stations, on circulation, costs, and audience statistics. For example, computer runs done by WCBS Radio in New York City (see Figure 1) show: (1) an audience analysis of adults 25–34 on an hourly and daily basis for ten major stations; (2) a comparison of three stations, showing cost, number of announcements, reach, frequency, gross impressions, gross rating points, and cost per thousand; (3) an analysis of *The New York Times Magazine,* showing cost, number of lines, reach, frequency, ad impressions, gross rating points, and cost per thousand; (4) an analysis of a media mix of radio and newspaper, showing the reach, frequency, gross impressions, gross rating points, and cost per thousand. (All costs shown are estimated.)

Because the computer has been used in supplying the latest data, its role as a key marketing tool has increased dramatically in the last 20 years. It has enabled the marketer to define his target audience carefully and set achievable objectives. Advertisers have come to expect a greater return on their investment in media. They want to know what the media will deliver and the cost-efficiency, and they want a plan for using the media most effectively.

Standard Rate and Data Service (SRDS)

This is the standard reference used by practically all advertising agencies for media rates and other information. SRDS publishes a series of editions on a monthly (or biannual) basis so that all the rates and data are

1

```
          CBS RADIO        ARB AUDIENCE ANALYSIS      CUMULATIVE    (00)

MARKET-NEW YORK          APR-MAY '79           ADULTS 25-54    AREA - TOTAL

            MONDAY-FRIDAY              SATURDAY                 SUNDAY

       6-10  10-3  3-7  7-12  6-10  10-3   3-7  7-12  6-10  10-3   3-7  7-12
WABCA  9449  5897  7432  4447  3043  3413  2327  1064  1909  2661  1229  1097
WCBSA  9251  3593  4953  3581  2716  2257   867  1005  2277  1811   738   896
WINSA  8125  2496  3076  3671  2903  1874  1170   484  2402  1862  1258   707
WOR A  6616  3123  3017  3409  2903  2092   938   471  1568  1800   566   396
WNBCA  5550  3761  4943  2456  1275  1959   976   523   611  1486   691   722
WHN A  4964  3547  4449  2691  1598  2096  1446   843   933  1417   849   726
WKTUF  4564  4693  5828  4514  1421  2642  1789  2206   900  2208  1399   835
WBLSF  4497  4073  4264  3552  1913  2515  1393  1555   792  1601  1268   903
WNEWA  2947  2765  3103  3053  1976  1307   646   823  1016  1582   356   453
WCBSF  3907  2786  2893  3134  1301  1601  1154   937  1060  1783   366  1006
```

2

```
         CBS RADIO RADNEWS DETAIL ANALYSIS:  RADIO SCHEDULE
         --- ----- ------- ------ ---------  ----- --------

NEW YORK    METRO ARBITRON APR-MAY 79 ADULTS 18-49 (000) POP= 7,450.9

STAT   FORMAT    COST    ANN  REACH#  REACH%  FREQ  GIMP      GRP    CPM
----   ------    ----    ---  ------  ------  ----  ----      ---    ---
WCBSA  NEWS    $3,000    27   563.1    7.6%   2.0 1,210.0     17.6  $2.29
WOR A  TALK    $2,600    23   292.4    3.9%   2.3   912.7     12.2  $2.95
WKTUF  DISCO   $1,500    16   911.2   12.2%   3.1 2,854.8     38.3  $.53
                     RADIO SUMMARY DETAILS
                     ----- ------- -------

                      # OF           REACH
               COST    ANN  REACH#     %    FREQ  GIMP     GRP     CPM
               ----    ---  ------   -----  ----  ----     ---     ---
ALL STATIONS   $7,100   66 1,729.3  23.2%   2.9 5,077.5    68.1  $1.40
```

3

```
         CBS RADIO RADNEWS DETAIL ANALYSIS:  NEWSPAPER SCHEDULE
         --- ----- ------- ------ ---------  --------- --------

NEW YORK    METRO    TGI (MMI) 77    ADULTS 18-49 (000)  POP= 7,450.9

                  # OF LINES   AD     REACH    AD     AD
NEWSPAPERS   COST ADS PER AD  REACH#   %   FREQ IMPRESS  GRP     CPM
----------   ---- --- ------  ------  ---- ---- -------  ---     ---
TIMES       -3 $11,450 01    350 1,057.1 14.2% 1.0 1,057.1  14.2  $10.83
                     NEWSPAPER SUMMARY DETAILS
                     --------- ------- -------

                  # OF  AD     REACH     AD      AD
             COST ADS REACH#     %    FREQ IMPRESS  GRP    CPM
             ---- --- ------   ----- ---- -------  ---    ---
ALL NEWSPAPERS $11,450  1  1,057.1 14.2% 1.0 1,057.1  14.2 $10.83
```

4

```
         CBS RADIO RADNEWS SUMMARY ANALYSIS  TOTAL AD READERS/LISTENERS
         --- ----- ------- ------- --------  ----- -- ------------------

               ARBITRON  APR-MAY 79          TGI (MMI) 77
             NEW YORK     METRO ADULTS 18-49 (000)  POP= 7,450.9
                    # OF
             TOTAL  ADS/  REACH  REACH
             COST  SPOTS    #      %    FREQ  GIMP     GRP     CPM
             ----  -----  -----  -----  ----  ----     ---     ---
NEWSPAPER  $11,450    1  1,057.1 14.2%  1.0  1,057.1  14.2  $10.83
RADIO       $7,100   66  1,729.3 22.2%  2.9  5,077.5  68.1   $1.40
MEDIA MIX  $18,550   67  2,503.4 33.6%  2.5  6,134.6  82.3   $3.02
```

Figure 1. Computer runs supplied by WCBS Radio in New York City.

current. Each edition gives a breakdown of all services, rates, deadlines on contracts, closings on production material, circulation, and other information that an advertiser needs to plan and schedule advertising. The separate volumes listed below are available on a subscription basis:

Business Publication Rates and Data
Community Publication Rates and Data
Consumer Magazine and *Farm Publication Rates and Data*
Direct Mail List Rates and Data
Network Rates and Data
Newspaper Rates and Data
Print Media Production Data
Spot Radio Rates and Data
Spot Television Rates and Data

Many large public and university libraries with business sections carry recent editions of SRDS. For more information, write to the Standard Rate and Data Service (see Appendix 3).

DEVELOPING A MEDIA STRATEGY

Media planners are coming up with new ways to use media creatively. Many are employing innovative approaches that go beyond the basics of solid planning, execution, and postevaluation. They are experimenting with media, and the results have clearly shown the effectiveness of developing a media strategy—just as you would develop a unique position. Some of the elements of strategy development and creative media use are discussed below.

Before you start planning a media strategy, you should be familiar with the language. A Glossary appears at the back of this book. Some of the words and phrases apply only to print advertising, while others apply to broadcast, and some apply to both.

Developing a Simple Media Plan

The first approach to media planning is to concentrate all your media dollars in one or two vehicles (newspapers, radio, TV, or magazines) that reach your prime audience. By spreading yourself thin in different media, you will only dilute the impact of your message. By developing a simple media plan, you will maximize your communications efforts.

The ideal media plan would call for advertising throughout the year with a *continuous* campaign. (See Figure 2.) This certainly would produce

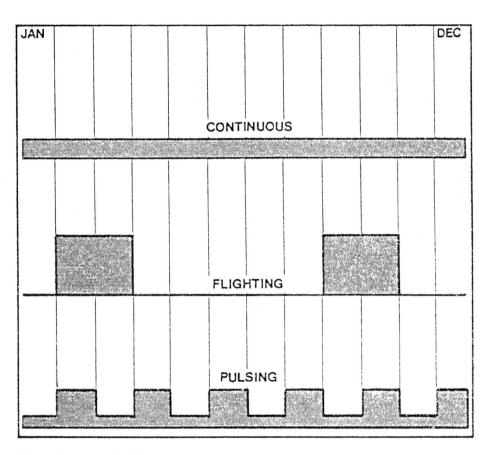

Figure 2. Methods of scheduling an advertising campaign.

the continuity and frequency that is needed if your message is going to be remembered. This may not be practical, however, since your ad budget may be small.

In this case, you will have to be innovative and use *flighting*—that is, concentrate your advertising in short periods. This can be particularly effective if you are trying to establish a position in the marketplace for your practice. Consider running a heavy volume of advertising initially for a short duration. This will produce greater recall of your message.

Another method of scheduling advertising is called *pulsing*. It is a continuous program to keep your name in front of the public with periodic bursts of advertising in heavy volume. It is actually a combination of continuous and flighting advertising.

In addition, if you want your message to have greater impact, consider compressing your advertising flight. For example, you may have a flight planned on radio or TV with 250 one-minute commercials over a 13-week period. If you squeeze the schedule into six weeks, the impact and recall factor will be greater. You will get the same reach and frequency, but it will be bunched up into a shorter period of time. In many cases, you can use this flighting technique during key consumer usage periods.

How to Increase Recall

The sharp growth of advertising has had an impact on consumer recall of advertising messages. According to Starch, one of the major research organizations, about 25 percent of magazine readers can associate a black-and-white page ad with the particular brand being advertised. The Burke research organization reports only 20–25 percent of television viewers can recall anything about the commercials they watch.

One thing that all media planners agree on is that in order to build recall and awareness of your advertising message you need continuity and frequency in your advertising program. In fact, studies indicate that as the frequency of your advertising message increases so does the percentage of recall.

Figure 3 shows how recall of advertising messages is affected by the

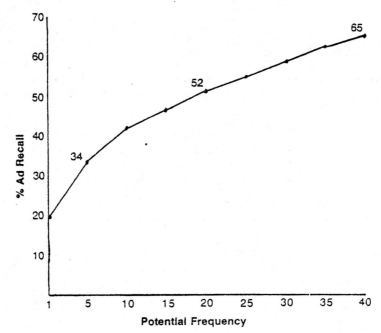

Figure 3. Estimated recall by ad frequency for nighttime TV audience. (Reproduced by permission of Manoff Geers Gross.)

frequency. The figures are for a nighttime TV audience; the recall factor is higher at night than in the daytime. One exposure to a TV commercial in the evening produces a 20 percent recall factor. A higher level of frequency, five exposures, will produce a recall factor of 34 percent. At ten exposures, the recall factor is 43 percent of the audience.

Reach, Frequency, and Gross Rating Points

The terms *reach, frequency,* and *gross rating points* are used widely by media planners and station representatives. They are extremely important because they indicate how effective your media plan will be in reaching your target audience.

Many stations will give you a computer printout when they submit a proposed schedule. Included will be the size of your target audience, the numerical and average reach, the frequency, the gross rating points, and gross impressions. The schedule may cover a period of one or more weeks, depending on your budget and objectives. The figures listed will tell you the size of the audience you are reaching with your message and how often these people are seeing your commercial.

Reach is the total number of people in your target audience who will see or hear your advertising message. A high reach over a four-week flight can deliver 60 percent of your audience. A low reach will be in the 20 percent category. Reach can be expressed as a number (1,454,000 adults age 18 to 49), as a percentage (27.7%), or both.

Frequency is the total number of times your target audience will see or hear your message within a given period. A high frequency can be six or more times; a low frequency can be two times or less. The average frequency for a schedule of spots will be listed as a number (such as 3.7).

Rating refers to the percentage of people or households in a specific area who are watching or listening to a particular program. It is usually expressed in terms of points. Thus a proposed commercial for a specific time period may deliver 7 rating points. This means that the spot is reaching 7 percent of the total households. When you add up all the rating points in your media plan over a specified period of time—say, a week—you obtain your gross rating points.

The relationship between reach (R), frequency (F), and gross rating points (GRPs) is expressed by this formula: R × F = GRPs. If you have a media plan that has a reach of 80 and a frequency of 4 over a two-week period, you will have 320 GRPs, or 160 per week (80 × 4 ÷ 2 = 160).

Theoretically, 100 GRPs means that you are covering 100 percent of your audience, but this is not really true, since GRPs include a duplicated audience—that is, people who have been exposed to your message more than once. Thus many media buyers will tell you that in order to make an impact in a short period of time you have to buy 150 GRPs or more in a one-week flight.

How many individual commercials or GRPs will you need to achieve your objectives? There is no magic number. The figure will depend on whether you are introducing a completely new professional service or one that is already established and has a certain amount of consumer awareness. Keep in mind, too, that advertising works differently on people at different times. The same message exposed to the same person on two different occasions may elicit very different responses, depending on the person's state of mind each time. The effect will also depend on the station's programming and the nature of your message.

Timing Your Advertising

In the summertime, you will see a large volume of advertising for beer, soft drinks, air conditioners, and a whole host of other products related to hot weather. These manufacturers know that the major share of their business will be done in a two- or three-month period.

Similarly, many professionals have a very definite cyclical pattern to their client flow, and advertising will produce a greater response at certain times of the year than at other times. It is apparent that it makes more sense to advertise when most people are receptive and in the market for your service.

December is an extremely bad month for most professionals; however, one cosmetic surgeon thought that this was an excellent time to advertise because many people schedule surgery during the Christmas holiday. A dentist who was running a consistent ad campaign, when asked about timing, said, "A toothache doesn't know seasons. When you get one, you need a dentist fast. And that's when I want them to think of me." The Strang Clinic found that the worst month for scheduling examinations was December; the best months were April, May, and June.

Likewise, you may find that certain days of the week will produce a greater response to your advertising than other days. Jacoby & Meyers found that Monday, Tuesday, and Wednesday were good days to run on television. They never ran on Friday or over a weekend. And in the selection of time periods, many professionals air their radio commercials during the time when people are driving to work. They want to attract a working audience rather than teenagers.

To sum up, even if you know your target audience and the C/P activity pattern of your practice, you will still have to evaluate the results of your advertising and experiment with media. Don't be afraid to make changes in your media plan in the initial stages. If you find that your advertising is not working, you'd better call a halt and review the total program. Don't be afraid to break with tradition and do the unusual in the selection of media. For example, when there is no cyclical pattern to your practice, a study of your competition may reveal opportunities for running a low-budget ad campaign at a time of year when there is less media clutter. Most radio and TV stations offer lower rates in the first and third quarters of the year, and if you can take advantage of these rates, you can make a greater impact at a lower cost.

Repetition of Print Advertising

If you're running a print advertising campaign, you have probably asked yourself how often you should change your advertisement. This will depend on a number of factors, particularly if your objectives change. However, if they remain the same and no competitive situation is forcing you to change your message, then you might want to repeat your ad for many months—even years—if it is pulling a significant response.

In fact, "advertisements that are repeated usually obtain consistent reader interest ratings." This statement is from a study by the McGraw-Hill Laboratory of Advertising Performance of 50 ads that were repeated in up to seven different issues of one business publication. The ads obtained excellent readership scores and sustained this performance with four, five, six, and seven insertions in the same publication. One company repeated an ad 41 times over a five-year period and found that inquiries were greater in recent years than in the early years of the campaign.

What Size Ad to Run

One of the most difficult decisions most advertisers must make is what size print ad to run in a magazine or newspaper. A study of newspaper readership by the Starch INRA Hooper (1970–1976) organizations concluded that larger ads don't deliver relatively higher readership. The results of the study are shown in Table 1. Note that the readership scores are higher for men. If you are trying to reach a male audience, this fact should be considered in your media strategy. If you are trying to reach a female audience, you will have to contend with the lower newspaper "noted" readership scores.

If your budget is limited, it would be better to seek continuity and repetition with small ads than to spend your entire budget on one large ad.

Table 1. Readership and ad size.

Size of Ad	Size/Cost Index (full page = 100)	Starch "Noted" Readership Index	
		Men	Women
Full page	100	100	100
1/2 page	50	87	66
1/4 page	25	75	58
1/8 page	13	52	50

Noted = reader remembered seeing the ad.

In fact, when I experimented in running two different advertisements for a client (a half-page and a full-page ad) in the same publication, the half-page ad pulled a greater response than the larger ad. The smaller ad featured a different message, which indicates that the creative approach used is just as important as (if not more important than) the size of the ad. According to the Newspaper Advertising Bureau, creativity can actually *double* the average readership "noted" score. It is also possible to design a small ad that can dominate a page because of its bold graphics and intriguing copy.

The Media Environment

The shrewd media buyer knows that a medium is more than a vehicle for carrying a message. The media environment is also extremely important. If you are advertising in a newspaper, you might want to place your ad in a special section related to the service that you are offering. The ads run in special sections, such as health, business, or real estate, will have an edge over ones seen in a neutral or unfavorable environment in terms of both the way they are perceived and the response they generate.

Many plastic surgeons have found that advertising in the Living Section of *The New York Times* pulls an excellent response. Others have experimented with *Playboy* magazine, recognizing the new attitude of men toward self-improvement. Many accountants advertise in the financial section of newspapers. Lawyers specializing in real estate advertise with display-classified ads in the real estate section of local newspapers. On radio and TV, professionals advertise on specific programs that pull excellent results. Jacoby & Meyers found that afternoon soap operas pull a large number of divorce and Social Security cases, while violent programs (like "Perry Mason" and "The FBI") pull criminal cases. On radio, many professionals advertise on programs that offer advice on real estate, finances, and human relations.

To sum up, each medium has a definite style and personality. The media planner must determine the value of the medium as a vehicle for delivering his message to appropriate target groups. There is a psychological rapport between the medium and the audience, and you can use it to your advantage.

Rating the Media on a Cost per Thousand Basis

"The proper use of media means putting your message where it will get into the minds of the largest number of prospects at the lowest cost," wrote adman John Caples.* Most advertising media buyers will compare the cost per thousand of various media and show you why a particular radio station, magazine, or newspaper is the best buy for reaching your target audience.

Cost per thousand is the advertising cost of reaching a thousand units—households, readers, viewers, and so on—with a particular media vehicle or media schedule. It is computed by dividing the advertising cost by the number of households or viewers and multiplying by 1,000. If a newspaper ad costs $600 and reaches 15,000 homes, the cost per thousand homes is ($600/15,000) × 1,000 = $40.

In 1979 *Advertising Age* magazine rated the media in terms of cost per thousand efficiency. The breakdown by various media according to 1980 estimates is shown below. The lower the number, the more efficient the medium. The figures are based on a 1967 index of 100.

Spot radio	164
Magazines	166
Network radio	178
Spot TV	201
Outdoor	220
Newspapers	226
Network TV	245

Media rates are normally determined by the size of the audience that each medium delivers. The bigger the audience, the more you can expect to pay. Rates are also based on the quality, exclusivity, and purchasing power of the audience. For example, a magazine that delivers top corporate executives would cost more per thousand than a magazine that delivers blue-collar workers.

---

*Willard Pleuthner, ed., *460 Secrets of Advertising Experts*, New York: Thomas Nelson & Sons, 1961.

In short, it would be a mistake to buy media on just a cost per thousand basis. You also have to determine whether the medium is delivering your prime prospects efficiently and in the proper editorial or programming environment.

The Media Mix

Media mix is using more than one medium to get your message across. You might use newspapers and direct mail, or transit advertising and radio, or billboards and radio, or magazines and television, or any combination of these—or even all of them.

What it comes right down to is that today's better-educated consumer gets information that guides the ultimate purchasing decision from many sources. You can reach a larger target audience of C/Ps and prime prospects by using a media mix. However, this should not be considered unless you have a budget that is large enough to sustain such an advertising program. Don't spread yourself thin in many media so that you will not make an impact with your advertising message.

The reason that advertisers use a media mix is because many people favor one medium over another. For example, according to the *Magazine Newsletter of Research* (January 1979), consumers who are heavy readers of magazines tend to be light viewers of television. These people get their information from magazines when they make a buying decision. One advertiser found that, by taking his television budget and dividing it equally between television and magazines, he was able to reach a segment of the market that was previously neglected.

Another study tested various combinations of television and newspaper advertising, using different percentages of each. The results of the survey indicated that different combinations of media had different effects on sales. By using a greater percentage of one medium over another, sales would rise dramatically. For example, one lawyer who had set a dollar budget for advertising changed his media mix from 75 percent newspaper and 25 percent television to just the opposite: 75 percent television and 25 percent newspaper. It doubled his clients and expanded his market.

Media as a Component of Time Management

Two things that all professionals have to offer is knowledge and time. Any time management consultant will tell you that it is extremely important to have your calendar filled with appointments. If you have time that is not being utilized, then you should consider advertising to increase the volume of your practice. But if your advertising produces such a huge response that you can't handle the surge of new clients, then you have really wasted your money. Some practitioners find that they can expand their practices easily by bringing in consultants and part-timers without enlarging their present facilities. You have to control the flow—never exceeding the capabilities of your practice.

Adman Robert Hodges of Horlick Levin & Hodges learned this concept in handling the advertising for Jacoby & Meyers. He said in a personal interview:

> We conceived of advertising as an instrument of inventory management . . . like an airline, a cruise ship, or TV station, a law firm has a huge facility with people that just sits there and costs up a storm whether anybody is buying it or not. Once past a certain fatal moment, units of inventory cease to exist as a salable commodity. And the cost of the perished inventory plunges straight down to the bottom line. . . .
>
> Our [Jacoby & Meyers] problem, once an attorney was on the payroll, was to fill up his calendar with the kind of cases he was hired to handle. That attorney occupied an office, had a desk, a telephone and support staff and he got paid whether his calendar was full or not.

Jacoby & Meyers worked with the agency and learned how to control its professional time inventory. And time inventory management is of crucial importance in the marketing of professional services.

Negotiating with Broadcast Media

The first step in any negotiations with local broadcast media is to meet in person with your station representative. Tell the rep your objectives, your target audience, your budget, and what you hope to accomplish. Then ask for a package plan that will help you realize your objectives.

When your station rep returns with a number of different package plans, he will be able to give you a detailed computer printout showing the number of people reached, the frequency, the rating points for each commercial, and the Gross Rating Points for the total proposal. The computer runs will also show you what stations are producing the greatest number of impressions for the lowest possible cost.

At this point, don't be shy about negotiating the best possible deal for yourself. Rate cards, package plans, and media schedules do not always mean what they say. And it is a known fact that some media buyers can negotiate a better deal for less money than inexperienced media people. In fact, the president of a large media-buying service (a firm that specializes in buying media for advertising agencies and clients) conceded that on the same day two buyers could call the same station and end up with two different budgets for the same exact time.

Media/scope magazine asked a number of media buyers this question: "How large a part does negotiation play in your buying?"

One of the answers was: "Considerable. In an industry where lack of prime availabilities, restrictions, and limitations appear to grow faster than advertiser's dollars, it is necessary to negotiate continually for the best possible efficiency and positions."

In short, this means that you should try to get the best time availabilities for your commercial in the selected time periods. One thing you don't want is to buy a package of spots during the morning drive and find that they were all aired at 5:00 A.M. or 9:45 A.M. You want to get a good rotation of your spots during the entire time period.

Advertising executive Otto Kleppner summed it up when he wrote the following about negotiating:

> In advertising parlance one assumes negotiating means cutting rates, but in practice it comes a lot closer to the literal meaning. One negotiates for a price. One negotiates for positioning. One negotiates for market information. One negotiates for competitive information. One negotiates for promotion and merchandising. One negotiates for possible new ways to use media. One negotiates for better availabilities. One negotiates for good makegoods. Negotiation, obviously, plays a large part in the buying function.*

---

*Otto Kleppner, *Advertising Procedure*, Englewood Cliffs, N.J.: Prentice-Hall, 1966.

CHAPTER 8

All About Media

NEWSPAPERS, magazines, radio, TV, outdoor and transit advertising, direct mail, and the Yellow Pages are all effective media if used correctly. Each exposes your message in a unique way to a specific audience. And the rates can be predetermined, so you can evaluate which ones will help you achieve your objectives at the lowest possible cost.

Listed are trends, facts, advantages, and disadvantages of different advertising media.

NEWSPAPERS

Most professionals who advertise use newspapers. They have discovered that it is a great medium for reaching the local market. Whether in a large city, a suburb, or a small town, newspapers provide information on where to get professional services. In some states, newspapers are the only medium in which professional associations and societies permit advertising.

The *American Bar Association Journal* (July 1979) reported that newspapers were the major medium used by lawyers, and those who were advertising were experimenting with small boxes in classified columns. These ads were generally placed by individual lawyers or partnerships with small practices. Twenty-nine states reported that newspapers were the prime vehicle for lawyer ads.

Newspapers are a mass circulation medium, containing news of interest to everyone within a specific geographic area. It is a distinctively regional medium, with very limited distribution outside the defined area. Some newspapers, like *The New York Times*, have a large national circulation, but this is the exception. A large national circulation will do the practitioner little good if he is looking for a local clientele.

Furthermore, newspapers are the most important medium for local advertisers. The vast majority of ads carried pertain to local businesses. Newspapers are the ideal medium for letting consumers know what is available in the marketplace and where to buy it within a certain distribution area.

Newspaper Facts and Trends

Today there are almost 1,800 daily newspapers in the United States that reach a combined circulation of 62 million each day. This figure represents a five-year high in daily circulation. On any given day, seven out of ten adults read a newspaper, according to the Simmons research organization. This means that 104 million Americans read a newspaper every day. Eighty-four percent of the adult population read a newspaper in the course of the five weekdays. And newspaper readers are in an "upscale" audience—they have above-average incomes and education levels.

In addition to daily papers, there are close to 7,000 weekly newspapers with a combined circulation of almost 38 million. Newspapers reach every town, village, and city in America, no matter how remote. Most suburban and rural newspapers are weeklies that report news of their local communities. The news and ads they carry are not found in the big metropolitan dailies or on radio or television. Many of these papers are kept for a longer period of time than daily newspapers.

There are also specialized papers of interest to professionals. Among them are foreign-language, religious, and ethnic newspapers and newspapers that reach special- and common-interest groups. Foreign-language newspapers are usually found in large cities where there is a sufficient concentration of people of the same cultural background. Some professionals have found that ads placed in these newspapers appealing to specific ethnic groups with the right message will pull a large response. Further, there are newspapers that appeal to such groups as unions, students, and businesspeople with stories of interest to their constituents.

Equally important are Sunday newspapers and magazine supplements. There are close to 700 Sunday newspapers with a combined circulation of 54 million. Though there are fewer Sunday papers than daily papers, they enjoy wide circulation. In fact, Sunday is a day that the family traditionally spends reading the newspaper, usually for a longer period of time than on weekdays.

Many of these Sunday newspapers have magazines that are distributed in the papers. The magazines enjoy very high readership, since they are often the first section that people turn to. These supplements provide the professional with an opportunity of getting a large local circulation with the high-quality reproduction of a magazine.

Some of the Sunday magazines are published by the individual paper, and space can be purchased from the newspaper salesperson or representative. In other cases, Sunday magazine supplements are syndicated, being published in quantity and distributed through many different newspapers. These supplements may be published on a statewide, regional, or national basis. Two of the leading syndicated Sunday supplements are "Family Weekly" and "Parade."

From time to time, many newspapers will publish special sections on health, finance, business, real estate, etc. These sections lend themselves to professional advertising and should be considered when they are offered to you.

Buying Newspaper Space

Even though you are buying space, in actuality you are buying readers who are potential clients/patients. Evaluate newspapers on the basis of the quality of the audience delivered and the cost per thousand.

There are two different newspaper formats. The standard size is up to nine columns wide and 280–300 lines deep. The tabloid size is five or six columns wide and 200 lines deep. These measurements vary from paper to paper, since no two papers are exactly alike. Check advertising column sizes before you start your campaign. If you submit artwork, many papers will resize the ad to fit their format at little or no cost.

Newspaper space is sold two ways: by the agate line or by the inch.

The agate line. In the large-circulation daily newspapers, space is sold on an agate line basis. An agate line is equal to 1/14 of an inch in depth by one column in width; thus, 14 agate lines equal one column inch. A column in most newspapers is about 1 5/8 inches wide. As mentioned earlier, however, column widths vary considerably from one paper to the next.

Here is how to determine the cost of an advertisement: If the line rate of a newspaper is $1 and the ad that you want to run is two columns wide by 150 lines deep, the cost would be $300 (150 lines × 2 columns × $1 = $300).

There is a direct relationship between the newspaper line rates and circulation—particularly in the large daily newspapers. This relationship may not exist, however, for the small-town weeklies that deliver a highly localized audience.

The column inch. Another way that space is measured is by the column inch. Most newspapers with small circulations use this method of determining cost. If you run an ad that measures three columns wide by 10 inches deep, it will be a 30-inch ad. If the rate per column inch is $12, then the cost of the ad would be $360 (30 inches × $12 = $360).

Newspaper Discounts

Newspaper advertising rates may be quoted several different ways. There is the one-time rate, called the "open rate." It is the highest possible rate and does not reflect any discount.

Newspaper rates are subject to quantity discounts, which are given on the basis of the total linage contracted for or purchased over a one-year period. There are also frequency discount rates. If you sign a contract to run 26 or 52 times within a given year, you will enjoy a lower agate line charge.

The New York Daily News, with close to 1.5 million in circulation, offers the following line and frequency discounts on the weekday paper:

	Line Cost
One-time rate	$13.94
5,000 lines	$13.45
10,000 lines	$13.31
50,000 lines	$12.96
100,000 lines	$12.41
52 insertions	$13.45

Note that the quantity of lines will determine the cost. Also, the frequency discount for 52 insertions is limited to a minimum of 300 lines.

Many smaller newspapers will offer discounts starting at about 1,500 lines to encourage local advertisers. The best thing to do is to meet with your salesperson and discuss how you can take advantage of the newspaper discount structure.

If you do not fulfill your contract to purchase a specified amount of lines or frequency of ads, you will be short rated. A short rate is the difference between the contract rate and the actual rate earned, when the contract rate is higher. For instance, if you contract for 1,000 times at $1.10 per line and you actually earn the $1.25 rate because you run only 500 lines, you will be billed an additional $75 (15¢ × 500 lines = $75).

In addition to frequency and quantity discounts, newspapers offer different line rates based on what you are advertising. Many newspapers offer different rate structures for professional, financial, classified, and nonprofit advertising. Find out what category you fit best; you may be able to save money.

You can also buy space on the basis of position in the newspaper. If you buy what is called ROP (run of the paper), the ad can be placed anywhere and you will pay the normal line cost. However, if you want "preferred position," you will have to pay a premium. In this case, your ad will appear on the page that you have selected. Premiums charged for preferred position may run anywhere from 5 to 50 percent above the ROP rates.

If your practice is targeted to specific groups, you should consider the editorial environment. Readership studies show a relationship between the size of the response and the editorial. An ad placed in the proper editorial section (e.g., sports for men, women's pages for females) will do about twice as well as the same kind of ad placed in a neutral editorial environment.

There are times when you may be able to get specific positioning with no additional charge. A request like this may be honored by the publication if you are an important advertiser. This does not apply to classified ads, which generally carry lower rates.

Classified ads present a unique opportunity for professionals, because readers turn to the daily classified section when they have a specific need for a job, a house, or a professional. Most newspapers offer professional classified sections, and you can have your ad listed under your profession and specialty. Classified ads are also referred to as "tombstone" ads. The line rates for these are lower than for regular display ads. This permits the professional to advertise on a continuous basis at a very low cost.

Regional or Zone Editions

There are many large-circulation, big-city newspapers, such as *The Chicago Tribune, The Houston Chronicle and Post, The Los Angeles Times,* and *The New York Daily News,* that offer zone or regional editions.

The New York Daily News offers 18 different zone sections, for counties like Manhattan and suburban areas like Long Island. This gives you the opportunity to buy space in a large-city daily paper at a fraction of the cost of the full-run edition, and you reach just the area you want, so you don't have any wasted circulation. In addition, many papers will publish special weekly regional sections, which are inserted into the Sunday paper. Again, this gives you the versatility of reaching just the area you need, while advertising in a large-circulation paper.

The Wall Street Journal is a particularly effective vehicle for professional advertising. Many accounting and law firms advertise in this national newspaper to reach business leaders and corporate decision makers.

Space in the *Journal* can be purchased by geographic regions; so if you are located in Texas, you can buy the southwestern edition only.

Advantages of Newspaper Advertising

○ Newspapers provide the best local coverage of the consumer marketplace. They offer a depth of penetration that no other print medium can match.

○ Newspapers have wide-range appeal. Most adults read at least one newspaper every day.

○ To the readers, the ads in a newspaper are just as important as the editorial matter. In fact, advertising in newspapers is news about the marketplace and may be as interesting and useful to readers as the editorial. According to Response Analysis Corporation, 72 percent of readers say they look forward to reading the advertising in newspapers, and 63 percent say they would find the paper "less satisfying" without advertising.

○ Newspapers are a medium that talks about today. They give you the urgency and immediacy of what is happening now.

○ Newspapers offer timing and space flexibility. You can get an ad into print in 24 hours if necessary, and you can use as much space as you need to tell your story and list your fees, services, and specialties.

○ A newspaper is an ideal vehicle for presenting advertising messages aimed at influencing public opinion, because it is a forum for the exchange of information and opinions. Advertising like this often generates as much discussion and reader interest as editorials or feature articles.

○ Newspapers are an ideal medium for advertisements with clip-out inquiry forms. They carry about three-quarters of all such coupon advertising. Many professionals are experimenting with coupon ads in newspapers to pull leads.

○ Newspaper readership is relatively constant throughout the year despite summer vacations and Christmas holidays. There is a small drop in readership in the summer months (July and August), while there is a slight increase in October and November.

Disadvantages of Newspaper Advertising

○ Newspapers have a relatively short life. They have characteristic pattern of "in the house one day and out the next."

○ A newspaper reader spends only 34 minutes on the average reading a newspaper, and only 18 percent (or 6 minutes) of this is spent reading the ads.

o In a newspaper filled with 200 or more ads, the small ad may get lost. It also tends to get poor placement on the page.

o Because of the coarse quality of newsprint, the reproduction is extremely poor. This is particularly true in the large-circulation daily newspapers that use letterpress printing. In the smaller news weeklies that use offset lithography and a better grade of paper, the reproduction is better, but still limited in terms of reproducing photographs with clarity.

o Newspaper sizes, rates, and discount structures are not uniform.

o Newspapers can add more pages to accommodate more advertising. The increased volume of advertising means your ad faces a good deal more competition in fighting for the reader's time.

SHOPPING PAPERS

Shopping papers, or "shoppers," are not newspapers but advertising vehicles for promoting local businesses in a town, village, or shopping mall. In many places, these shoppers are called "Pennysavers." They are all distributed free, and circulation will be hard to verify since they are not audited like a newspaper.

In some cases, these shoppers contain some local news or columns, but that is not the reason people read them. They are popular because they contain ads that direct the reader to a variety of products and services at low prices. Specials are offered on food, tires, dentistry, and legal services.

Many professionals whose practices are geared to low fee and high volume are using shoppers successfully. They recognize that these papers pull results. However, shoppers are not the place to build an image in a community. The poor reproduction and surrounding environment will work against any professional trying to build a prestigious practice.

Space in these publications is sold by the agate line or by the column inch. The best thing to do is to request a rate card. Find out if the shopper has a section for professional services. It would pay to be in this section, away from all the cut-rate retailers and home repair firms.

Measuring the merit of these publications will be difficult for several reasons. First, some shopping sheets are sent in the mail addressed to "occupant." In many cases, people throw them out, since they have little or no editorial content and are regarded as junk mail. Second, some shoppers are dropped at doorsteps by distribution organizations. This method of home distribution can be unreliable, because there is no way to check to see if the shopper was delivered.

The way to find out the value of these publications is to call a professional who advertises regularly in one—someone who is not a competitor of yours. Ask what success he has achieved in the shopper and get additional input on how to create practice-building ads in these publications. Shoppers can be an offbeat way to reach a localized circulation at an extremely low cost.

MAGAZINES

Today there is a magazine published for every interest, profession, trade, and business. If you want a magazine for architects, investment advisers, physicians, insurance brokers, bankers, real estate agents, or health care professionals, you will find it. There are magazines for everyone. And of course, there are the mass circulation magazines that offer news, gossip, and feature articles of interest to men or women.

More and more professionals are discovering magazines as a medium not only for national advertising but for local advertising as well. In 1979 companies increased their investments in magazine advertising by a billion dollars. And more importantly, advertisers are shifting funds previously earmarked for television and other media to magazines to increase reach and frequency.

Magazine Facts and Trends

Today there are 725 consumer magazines in the United States that you can select from to carry your advertising message. They reach 127 million adults, or 90 percent of the adult population. Each has its own particular personality and character and is an integrated part of the reader's life and life-style.

Magazine circulation has grown by 73 percent since 1950. This growth is reflected not only in the mass circulation magazine but also in the special-interest magazines that have entered the field in unprecedented numbers. The upward trend in the number of people reading magazines continued in 1979. Magazines have met the challenge of TV by developing specialized editorials for narrow-interest audiences, while TV coverage has taken a broad approach to viewers.

Magazines involve the reader, who is seeking information and ideas within a stimulating and enjoyable environment. Such involvement is rewarding in terms of filling needs related to interests and activities both inside and outside the home. Today's consumer is constantly seeking knowledge and ideas for self-improvement in a personally satisfying and enjoyable way, and magazines are the perfect source for this information.

Nearly everyone reads magazines. Nine out of ten adults read an average of eight different issues per month, or a couple of magazines each week, and there are 3.6 adult readers on the average for every copy of a magazine. The average reader spends 93 minutes reading every issue.

Magazines have been growing in importance with upscale consumers. They have a high percentage of readers within the most rapidly growing segments of the marketplace—18–44 years olds, suburbanites, white-collar workers, high-income persons, and the college educated. The typical magazine reader is young (34.9 years) and married, lives in a single-family home in the suburbs that he or she owns, and has a household income 24 percent above the national average.

Regional Editions and City Magazines

One of the reasons for the rapid growth of magazines in the past 20 years is the increase of city, state, and regional magazines. There are magazines for specific locales—such as *New York, Chicago, New West, Texas Monthly, Houston City, Southern Living,* and *Philadelphia*—that have news and facts of interest to residents of those areas. In addition, there are theater and sports programs, college alumni magazines, and organizational magazines that appeal to an audience narrowly defined either by geographic location or by participation in a social, religious, or fraternal organization.

Just as important as the growth of city magazines has been the growth of regional editions of mass circulation magazines. Every major mass circulation magazine offers regional and metro editions. *Time,* for example, offers regional editions in New England, the East, the Southeast, the Southwest, the West-Central, and the East-Central. It also offers spot market editions for Boston, Chicago, Los Angeles, New York, Cleveland, Miami, Minneapolis–St. Paul, Philadelphia, Pittsburgh, St. Louis, San Francisco, Atlanta, and many other large cities, as well as many small-city market editions and state editions. *Time* also publishes special demographic editions for business, high-income zip codes, students and educators, top management, and physicians.

These magazines are attracting more and more ads by local businesses, retailers, professionals, and others. They are going beyond their role as a medium used to create brand awareness to a medium employed to build immediate sales and business. Regional advertising has also grown by 77 percent since the mid-1960s and now accounts for one out of every five dollars spent on magazines. In two years (1975–1977), the top retailers in America increased their advertising investment by 380 percent. Magazines are fast becoming a local medium for advertisers.

Buying Magazine Space

Space in a magazine is usually sold by the page or fraction of a page. The actual cost is based on the ad size and the circulation of the magazine. An advertiser can buy a full page, one-third page, one-half page, or even one-sixth page. The sizes available vary depending on the format of the magazine. Frequency and quantity discounts are available to advertisers who complete a contract for a specified number of ads within a given period of time. Rates and discounts vary from magazine to magazine, so it pays to arrange a meeting with your magazine salesperson. The sales rep will give you a media data file and rate card and explain all the services that the magazine can offer you.

You can also buy special positions in a magazine at an additional cost if they are available. The inside front cover (called the "second cover"), the inside back cover (called the "third cover"), and the back page (called the "fourth cover") all carry an extra charge for preferential positioning. Many direct-response advertisers prefer the first page opposite the second cover, because they find it pulls more responses than an ad that runs elsewhere in the magazine. This space is given to advertisers who make a commitment to the publication for a major campaign. There are other pages in the magazine where you can attract attention because of the editorial. If you are advertising an accounting firm, you would want to be in the financial section. A physician or dentist might want to be in the health section. And a lawyer would choose to be near the legal pages.

Color ads carry a higher price·than black-and-white ads; you can add one to four colors. The charge is different for each magazine. If you want to bleed the ad—that is, run it to the edge of the page, eliminating the white border—there will be a 10–15 percent additional charge.

Magazines base their rates on a circulation that they guarantee to deliver. If they fail to deliver the circulation, they give a rebate to the advertiser; however, this rarely happens. If the circulation goes above what is guaranteed, the advertiser receives the additional readership free; this is called "bonus circulation."

Table 2 shows how the cost of a full-page ad in *Time* is affected by the circulation.

Consumer publications have their circulations audited by the Audit Bureau of Circulations (ABC), while business and professional publications

Table 2. *Time* magazine rates for a full-page black-and-white ad (1981).

Edition	Circulation	One-Time Cost ($)
National	4,250,000	49,335
New York	425,000	7,020
Los Angeles	265,000	5,040
Chicago	190,000	3,630

have their circulations audited by the Business Publications Audit of Circulations (BPA) and the American Business Press (ABP). These organizations validate the circulations of magazines and newspapers, so look for the publication's affiliation with these organizations.

There are also such organizations as Media Networks Inc. that make it possible to buy space in magazines on a market-by-market basis with the same accuracy expected of other media. They make the selective audiences of national magazines available to local advertisers at affordable rates.

Media Networks Inc. (600 Third Avenue, New York, N.Y.) publishes full-page sections of advertising for each of the magazines that belong to the network. These preprinted units are then bound by participating magazines into copies sent to subscribers in predetermined zip code areas. Your ad becomes an integral part of the magazine in the chosen zip code areas.

Media Networks Inc. was designed for the local advertiser who did not want to use the large-circulation magazine. It offers nine different demographic audience breakdowns and 125 precisely defined markets. For example, you can buy what is called the men's network in 329 different markets. This includes *Esquire, Gentlemen's Quarterly, Playboy,* and *Sports Illustrated.* If you buy a black-and-white page in Pittsburgh, you get 66,697 circulation at a cost of $2,400. If you buy the executive network, the following magazines are included: *Business Week, Dun's Review, Nation's Business,* and *U.S. News and World Report.* The circulation in San Francisco is 124,681 and the cost is $6,100.

Advantages of Magazine Advertising

- The magazine editorial environment can add to the effectiveness of your advertising message. Magazine ads tend to be compatible with and even enhanced by the editorial environment of the magazine.
- The average reader spends 93 minutes reading a magazine. Forty-

three percent of the readers tear out one or more ads from every issue to save for later reference.

o Consumers find magazine advertising informative, believable, and helpful in making buying decisions. Magazines generally emphasize product information, quality details, and performance. Fifty-two percent of the readers prefer magazines to carry advertising.

o The average advertising page receives 1.5 different exposures per reader. The second exposure to an ad significantly increases the memorability and positive effects of the ad.

o The average magazine is kept accessible for 28.7 weeks; 2.5 percent of the readers of each copy send for information on a service or product.

o Magazine readers are exposed to 89 percent of all the ads in a magazine.

o There is only a slight seasonal variation in magazine readership, ranging from 2 percent below average in the July–September period to 2 percent above average in the October–November period.

o If you run a direct-response or coupon ad in a weekly magazine, you can expect to pull 95 percent of the inquiries within six weeks. In a monthly magazine, 94 percent of the inquiries will come within six months (see Table 3).

o Magazine reproduction is excellent in most cases. You can use photographs, illustrations, and four-color artwork in your advertising. Magazines will use fine screens (120-line or more) to reproduce photographs on coated paper stock for the best results.

Table 3. Percentage distribution of responses for ads appearing in weekly and monthly magazines.

Weekly Magazine		Monthly Magazine	
Weeks	Inquiries (%)	Months	Inquiries (%)
1	54	1	54
2	25	2	22
3	7	3	8
4	4	4	5
5	3	5	3
6	2	6	2
Later	5	Later	6
Total	100	Total	100

Source: Starch.

Disadvantages of Magazine Advertising

○ Magazine ads must be planned ahead, since the contract closing and production material deadline can be anywhere from 21 to 60 days in advance of publication.

○ Technically, there is no limit to how many pages a magazine can have. Some magazines, like *Playboy*, have over 200 pages in many issues. In these larger issues, the competition for the reader's time is even greater; about 50 percent or more of the space is devoted to advertising and the rest to editorial.

RADIO

Radio is one of the most powerful media in the world. It penetrates every country, city, town, village, and community. It is also one of the most popular vehicles for delivering an instantaneous message. Professionals everywhere are experimenting with this exciting, flexible, and creative medium. They recognize that radio is an extremely economical way to deliver a message. It can be used to create an image as well as to generate direct responses from potential C/Ps. If you want to build a practice, here is a medium that when used properly can do it for you.

Radio Facts and Trends

When it comes to sheer numbers, nothing can compare to radio. There are about 9,000 FM and AM stations in the United States. Many of these stations have powerful signals that can reach an entire metropolitan area—and many miles beyond. And there are similar stations with weak signals that cover only a highly localized area. The signal strength is important, since the station's rates will be based on the size of the audience. Decide whether you want to reach a wide audience or a small community. One thing that you don't want is to pay for a lot of wasted circulation.

Most FM and AM stations carry a wide variety of music programming—contemporary, country, rock, disco, and ethnic. Less than 10 percent of all radio programs are news and talk formats. FM stations represent the fastest growing segment of the radio industry; about half of all radio stations are now FM.

Virtually all homes in the United States—98.9 percent—have at least one working radio. The average home has 5.7 radios. There are over 450 million sets in use, and each year 55 million new ones are sold. Close to 25 percent of new radios sold are for auto use.

The car is the major form of transportation for America's 80 million workers; 85 percent of them drive to work. And radio is an extremely important medium for reaching people in cars. There are 110 million cars with radios. This represents 95 percent of all autos. Radio reaches seven out of ten adults within the course of one week, whether they are driving to work, to the supermarket, or between cities.

Radio audiences grew 63 percent between 1967 and 1978. Every day over 31 million individuals listen to the radio. The average adult listens for 3 hours and 26 minutes each day. Radio is the dominant daytime broadcast medium.

Buying Radio Time

Most professionals who advertise on the radio have discovered that it is a highly selective and fragmented medium; it reaches different kinds of people with different kinds of programming. The kinds of programs available will vary depending upon your locale. If you are in a large city or suburban area, there will be a wide variety of stations and programs. Each station attempts to be unique, to attract a particular audience. Some of the different types of popular programming are:

All news
Talk show
Call-in dialogue
Contemporary music
Progressive rock
Classical music
Ethnic
Beautiful music
Country music
Variety

Many stations have a combination of two or more of the above, and offer this programming on FM or AM.

All stations should be evaluated on the size and quality of the audience delivered. The price you pay for a commercial will depend on the number of people the station reaches; their age, income, life-style, etc., and the selling power of the station's personalities.

Many radio stations limit the time for advertising to 18 minutes in one hour. They may not increase this ratio no matter how great the demand for air time. So when a station has no commercial time available, you will not be able to get on the air. Thus, if you are planning a radio campaign, it would pay for you to work well in advance. Meet with your station representative and discuss availabilities for announcements and the costs. Discuss the support that the rep can give you, and try to obtain as much information on your proposed media buy as possible, including the characteristics of the station audience, reach, frequency, cost per thousand, and gross rating points.

Many small-town and suburban radio stations have scant data available on their audiences. Most of these stations do not participate in Arbitron research on listening audiences. Therefore, they will hand you information that may be highly biased or outdated. Ultimately, you will have to decide whether to use these stations on the basis of your own instincts and the importance of the station to the community.

The Radio Advertising Bureau offers these additional suggestions on buying radio time:

1. Don't rely completely on your own taste. Your C/Ps may prefer station formats that do not appeal to you.
2. Study audience surveys available from local stations to see which stations are strong with which customers.
3. Listen to all the stations in your market and add your judgment to the ratings and station research that you have reviewed.
4. Give stations as much advance notice as you can on your schedules. This will enable them to give you their best availabilities.
5. Finalize your weekly or monthly buy with a signed contract and written instructions about how many spots are to run, on which days, and what copy is to be used for each spot. This is particularly important when you have more than one schedule running at the same time.
6. Listen to your spots on the air, and encourage your staff to listen, too. Involve your people with their advertising.
7. Keep track of the results of your radio campaigns on your weekly planning sheets, and try to figure out the elements that made the campaigns successful.
8. Plan your next campaign to take advantage of past experience with stations' pulling power, time slots, and impact schedule.
9. Plan radio advertising on a long-range basis for continuity in your campaign and to secure the best availabilities from your stations.

In addition, you should have goals for reach and frequency. Determine what percentage of the target audience you want to reach and how often you want them to hear your message.

Commercial time and availabilities. There are three different time units sold in radio: the 60-second, 30-second, and 10-second commercial. If you study the radio station's rate structure, you will find that the 30-second rate is about 75 percent of the 60-second rate, and the 10-second rate is approximately 50 percent of the 30-second rate. It is no wonder that most advertisers select the 60-second announcement: It has greater impact and value. It gives you sufficient time to tell your story and also separate your message from the programming and other commercials.

Daily time grids. Once you select a station, consider what time periods are most desirable for reaching your target audience. One group of lawyers found that the Monday to Friday morning drive time (5 A.M. to 10 A.M.) was the best time to air its commercials. It pulled a large response from the listening audience (see Figure 4).

Study the station's rate card, and note the grid—that is, the way daily time is broken down into different classifications. The terminology and time classifications used by each station may be different, but they will be

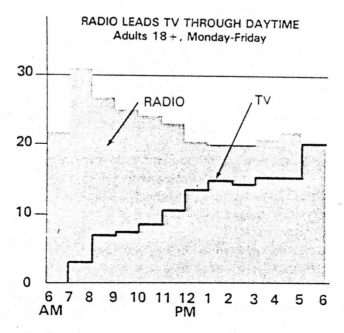

Figure 4. A comparison of radio and TV daytime audiences.
(Radio Advertising Bureau.)

similar enough for your to make reasonable comparisons and judgments.

The Radio Advertising Bureau offers the following time classifications to give you a sense of how most rates are determined:

Day Part	Times of Day
A.M. drive (AMD)	5 A.M.–10 A.M., Mon.–Sat.
Daytime (DAY)	10 A.M.–3 P.M., Mon.–Fri.
P.M. drive (PMD)	3 P.M.–7 P.M., Mon.–Fri.
Evening (EVE)	7 P.M.–12 P.M., Mon.–Sun.
Overnight (OVN)	12 P.M–5 A.M., Mon.–Sun.
Weekend drive (WKD)	10 A.M.–7 P.M., Sat.–Sun.
Sunday A.M. (SUN)	6 A.M.–10 A.M., Sun.

The morning drive time (5 A.M.–10 A.M.) is the most desirable and is sometimes called AAA time. It is also the most expensive. A commercial in this time slot can cost as much as $450 for one minute on a major radio station or as low as $15 on a small suburban station. Afternoon drive times (3 P.M.–7 P.M.) are also expensive, since they reach people returning home from work. Costs will drop considerably for daytime and evening broadcasts. In brief, advertising rates will differ depending on the time of the day the commercial is aired. In most cases, the time periods that have the highest rates deliver the largest audience.

Radio stations also offer lower rates during certain times of the year. The first (January–March) and third (July–September) quarters of the year are the least expensive. The second and fourth quarters are the most expensive and have limited time availabilities. If you can take advantage of the seasonal low points in advertising volume, you can achieve a greater impact with the same budget.

Special package plans. Most radio stations offer a variety of package plans for different budgets. They want to show you what different expenditures for radio will buy. Stations want you to buy a combination of spots during the day and evening, and they prefer a volume commitment. In fact, some stations will include a number of bonus announcements for completing a weekly or monthly contract. They will give you free commercial time, generally during the evening or late-night hours, to make it worth your while.

Other stations will offer a Total Audience Plan, which gives you a package of announcements that will reach all of the station's listeners in a specified time period. This is important if you want to make a significant impact on a particular segment of the market.

Advantages of Radio Advertising

- Radio delivers the news first in the morning, and it is the major source for daytime news.
- Ninety-six percent of adults are satisfied with what they hear on radio—whether it is news, music, or talk programs.
- Radio is an extremely economical medium; it offers the lowest cost per thousand of all the media.
- Radio reaches seven out of ten adults in a one-week period. The average man (aged 18+) spends 3 hours and 24 minutes listening to radio. The average woman (aged 18+) listens to radio for 3 hours and 29 minutes each day. Radio reaches more adults in a week than any other medium.
- Radio is a great medium for building frequency. If you want a memorable radio campaign, you have to repeat it—and radio permits this because of its low cost and wide reach.
- Radio is able to target special demographic groups and life-styles. It is able to reach different kinds of people because it is highly fractionalized.
- Radio has impact levels close to TV. Research has indicated that among adults (aged 18+) average recall scores proved radio to be 77 percent as effective as a 30-second TV commercial. For commercials heard on car radios, the recall was virtually the same as for TV commercials.
- People who listen to radio tune in stations, not programs. A radio listener finds a pleasing station and settles with it for a while. In contrast, TV viewers watch programs, not channels.
- Most listeners do not regard radio as a consumer of time. While listening you can be doing other things, such as driving, working, studying, and reading.
- You can produce a radio commercial at little or no cost. Many stations will write your spot and have an announcer read it with no extra charge to the advertiser.

Disadvantages of Radio Advertising

- Your message is limited to approximately 150 words for a 60-second commercial.
- Radio advertising—like all broadcast advertising—is retained in the

listener's mind only. The listener cannot clip it out (as in print advertising) and save it for future reference.

o In order to build recall of your advertising, you need frequency. Your commercial must be heard by each listener several times to make an impression.

o There is a limited number of commercial availabilities in any given hour. If a station is sold out, you will have trouble getting your commercial on the air.

o Since many people listen to radio while doing other things, they do not pay full attention to the programming or the commercials.

o Radio audiences are difficult to measure because of their transient nature and out-of-home listening.

o Radio is a highly fragmented medium. Your target audience may be split up among many radio stations, with none having a clear-cut share of a particular audience segment.

TELEVISION

Television advertising, like the medium itself, has grown dramatically over the past 30 years. It is the newest of the major media and certainly the most powerful. It has revolutionized our lives and the way we communicate—and it is an important factor in the marketing of products and services.

The major advertisers spend billions of dollars on national television advertising because they recognize that it is a medium of demonstration. Nothing can compare with the way television combines sight, sound, color, drama, and action, and it delivers the message to people in their homes with all the force and persuasiveness of face-to-face selling. It can produce the image you want to project and move people to react to your message.

At present, professionals are spending millions of dollars on local TV advertising. They recognize that it is a medium that can not only build volume but also educate the public. One legal clinic in New York City, after experimenting with newspapers, turned to spot TV advertising. Its objective was to increase the number of clients by offering reasonable fees for legal services. The clinic ran a straightforward spot that highlighted affordable fees as its most salable attribute. The result was overwhelming: The firm picked up 150 new clients.

Another legal clinic, Jacoby & Meyers, has grown tremendously since the early 1970s by using television. Gail Koff, a partner with the firm, said, "TV advertising is really the only way we have for letting clients know about the availability of our services. It has been the most successful medium for us in terms of cost-efficiencies and making people aware of our services."

Television Facts and Trends

There are over 700 commercial broadcasting stations in the United States. These stations are divided into three different groups: network stations owned by CBS, ABC, or NBC; network affiliates that carry a certain amount of programming offered by the major networks supplemented by their own programs; and independent stations that have their own programming or purchase programs from independent distributing organizations.

These TV stations broadcast a signal from a centrally located point within a market (or geographic) area. There are some 200 such markets within the United States, encompassing over 3,000 counties. A. C. Nielsen refers to these TV markets as designated market areas (DMA), while Arbitron refers to them as areas of dominant influence (ADI). Both terms are interchangeable with the phrase "TV market." A good deal of information is available about these markets, including demographic data, consumer purchasing patterns, and media comparisons.

Television has an almost universal presence in American households: 98 percent of all homes (76.3 million households) have at least one television set. This is an increase of 20 percent since 1970. It is estimated that 50 percent of all homes have two or more TV sets, and 83 percent have at least one color set. There are 145.7 million TV sets in use, and every year about 16 million new sets are sold.

One of the greatest challenges to TV today is the growth of cable television. There are close to 4,000 systems serving about 14 million homes. Cable TV has had a remarkable growth; about 18 percent of all households now subscribe to a cable service. Cable TV penetration continues to be strongest in the nonurban areas. As such services continue to grow and flourish, the American public will no doubt change its viewing patterns and the impact will be felt by broadcast TV. Advertisers are now experimenting with this medium, using it for direct marketing of a variety of products and services. They recognize that more and more people will be shopping at home because of the convenience and the soaring number of working women who have less time to shop. The TV set can be the vehicle to provide shopping information and other facts to a cable TV audience.

TV Viewing

TV viewing in the United States has risen steadily over the past three decades—from an average of 4 hours and 35 minutes per day in 1950 to 6 hours and 28 minutes in 1979, according to A. C. Nielsen. The number of people watching TV varies considerably during different times of the day. The morning, afternoon, and late-night hours have relatively small audiences. In the evening, between 8 P.M. and 11 P.M., TV viewing reaches its peak. After 11 P.M., as people go to bed, there is a sharp drop in viewers.

In addition, TV viewing levels have seasonable variations. November, December, January, February, and March are high viewing months, whereas July and August are low viewing months. The drop in viewing in the summer occurs mainly during the afternoon and early evening hours.

TV viewing varies considerably by income, education, gender, and age. For example, men with incomes over $25,000 view TV an average of 123 minutes per day, while men with incomes under $10,000 view TV for 182 minutes each day. In fact, the higher the income and education level, the less time spent watching TV. People with occupations described as professional/technical view TV the least when compared to non-white-collar workers, among whom TV viewing is strong.

Furthermore, TV is the major source for news in this country. In a survey conducted by TIO/Roper, 67 percent of respondents selected TV as the medium for getting the most news.

TV programming and ratings. The most popular programs on TV are situation comedies; they attract the largest viewing audiences during prime time (8 P.M.–11 P.M.). They are most popular with young women, children, and teenagers. Feature films continue to pull a high male audience as do sports events. TV specials, such as "Roots," have been a vital component in network programming, since they pull large audiences. News and public affairs programs represent 25 percent of all programs and are an important part of a station's mix.

The ratings that are assigned to each program are determined by the A. C. Nielsen and Arbitron research organizations. They use electronic recording devices in selected homes, telephone interviews, and diaries mailed to a random sample of families to measure audience viewing patterns. The two organizations measure local audiences four times a year—in February, May, July, and November. (Nielsen also measures national audiences every week, 52 weeks a year.) These periods are called "sweeps" by people in the industry. Programs are given ratings on the basis of these measurements. A rating is a percentage of total households watching television. A 10 rating in Cincinnati with 635,000 TV homes means that 63,500 sets are tuned in to that program.

Advertising agencies and stations use this information in planning TV buys. These ratings are used by media planners to select specific programs during which to advertise. You must recognize when buying television time that 80 percent of all TV viewers tune in programs rather than stations.

Buying Television Time

Like all advertising costs, television commercial costs are determined by the size of the audience—in this case the audience that is watching a particular program during a specific time of the day. The larger the audience, the more you can expect to pay (see Figure 5). Advertisers will pay a premium to advertise during the nighttime slot. If you want to buy TV time less expensively, consider daytime, early evening, and late-night time periods.

Television, like radio, can be used to reach specific target audiences. Media buyers recognize that different programs and time periods attract different audiences, so they match the viewers to their client's market and buy on the basis of audience demographics and other data supplied by the station, as well as their own research. Your spots should run at the time your target audience is tuned in.

Television day parts. Television stations divide the day into several parts, which the industry calls "day parts." The number of people watching will go up and down depending on the time of the day, the day of the week, and the month of the year. Prime time—the highest viewing time—is the 8 P.M. to 11 P.M. slot. It peaks on Sunday night—the most popular night for viewing television—and hits a low on Friday and Saturday nights. The 7:30 P.M. to 8 P.M. period, the high point of the early evening slot, is known as prime access time. Since there is no industry standard for TV time periods, I have listed the most commonly used day parts in Table 4.

Commercial time lengths. In buying television announcements, you have a choice of different commercial lengths used by local advertisers. The 10-second commercial can focus on one item or service, a price, and one

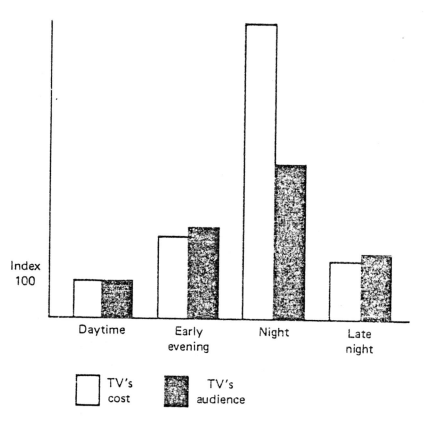

Figure 5. A comparison of TV audience size (adults 18 and over) and commercial costs. (A. C. Nielsen, February 1977; TV Bureau Spot Television Planning Guide, 1977–1978.)

reason to get people to respond to your message. The 30-second announcement is the most popular with local advertisers, representing 84 percent of all commercials. If your goal is to give specific details about your service or company, this length gives you the opportunity to present your message with impact. It allows plenty of time to present benefits and facts about your practice. When you have to present a lot of information, the 60-second commercial gives you the time to involve people in your message. Announcements longer than 1 minute are used about 1 percent of the time. This length is popular with direct-response advertisers who want to give a great deal of facts and ordering information about a service or product.

Table 4. Commonly used TV day parts.

Day Part	Times of Day	Audience
Morning	7 A.M to 10:00 A.M.	Attracts upscale adults.
Daytime	10:00 A.M. to 4:30 P.M.	Attracts women at home, mainly housewives.
Early evening or early fringe	4:30 P.M. to 7:30 P.M.	Attracts women, men, and teens.
Prime access	7:30 P.M. to 8:00 P.M.	Attracts women, men, and teens. Great for building frequency.
Nighttime (prime time)	8:00 P.M. to 11:00 P.M.	Attracts a large family audience. Delivers a mass audience—fast.
Late-night fringe	11:00 P.M. to 1:00 P.M.	Attracts an upscale audience of men and women.
Saturday and Sunday daytime	8:00 A.M. to 2:00 P.M. 2:00 P.M. to 5:00 P.M.	Attracts children in early hours. In later hours attracts predominantly men—2 to 1 over women and children.

Meeting with Your Station Representative

When you are thinking of running an advertising campaign on local TV, the first step is to meet with station representatives. See as many reps as possible. They can give you a tremendous amount of information and provide you with sources for producing your commercial. The reps will ask you about your objectives, your target audience, and your budget. They will want to know when you would prefer to run the campaign. Be prepared to give them these answers, so that they can give you a package plan that meets with your needs and goals.

The rep will come back with a written proposal, containing a list of the availabilities (called "avails") offered to you. He will also show you the cost of each commercial and a recommended package plan of announcements for a specific period of time. A variety of other information will also be supplied, including the number of homes reached, number of people in your target audience, frequency, rating points, gross rating points, cost per thousand viewers, and cost per rating point.

When you buy a package of TV spots, it is a good idea to buy several "fixed" spots. These are spots that will be aired at specific times on the days you select. They might be tied in with the late-night news or another program that delivers a particular audience. You will pay a premium for the commercials, but they will be well worth it, because those spots cannot be preempted. The regular announcements that you choose to run during different time periods can be preempted. The station has the right to reclaim the time they have sold to you and give it to another advertiser who pays a higher rate. If your spot is taken off the air, you will not be charged for it and the station will offer you other available time slots. You are under no obligation, however, to take the alternative time slot if it doesn't meet with your media objectives.

There, are also "run-of-station" (ROS) spots. These spots are aired at the station manager's discretion, any time during the day when time is available. The disadvantage of ROS spots is that you never know when they will be broadcast. And if you are targeting your message to a particular audience, you will be wasting your money.

At this point in the negotiating process, you may find some time periods or programs do not meet with your objectives. You can make any changes you like, and more importantly, you can negotiate costs and the rotation of your spots (see the section on negotiating with the broadcast media in the preceding chapter).

Buying time on TV is a little like buying stock. The price you pay depends on the supply and demand at a specific time of the year. There are no rate cards. Stations have a limited number of commercial minutes to sell, and the greater the demand, the higher the price you can expect to pay. If you want to get on a very popular show, it is going to cost you more.

Television time charges, like those for radio, are lower in the first and third quarters of the year. During the summer and after Christmas, prices drop, and you can get some great media buys. In addition, if you are in a city that has more than one station, you might be able to get concessions on rates by making a major commitment to one of the stations. It is possible to negotiate a lower package cost for spots, particularly if you are the first professional to use the station, since the station can use your campaign as a model to attract other professional advertising.

Once your schedule is finalized and signed, it becomes a contract. The station rep will be able to show you the final rating points, reach, and frequency of your schedule. The rating points, as explained earlier (see the section on reach, frequency, and rating points in the preceding chapter), represent the percentage of your target audience reached by one commercial. When you add up all the rating points in one week, you get the total percentage of your target audience reached with your announcements.

In addition, request the following information from your station representative: (1) the exact time the spot appears, with a notarized schedule, and (2) identification of the spot, with the copy notarized. If the station errs on any of your commercials—because of faulty transmission, cutting the commercial short, leaving off a tag line, or whatever—you will be entitled to a "makegood." The makegood is a free spot—so ask for it.

Advantages of TV Advertising

o Television is one of the most effective media for reaching a mass audience; 98 percent of American households have at least one set.
o Television is the ideal medium for demonstrations. It has the advantages of sight, sound, color, and action.
o Television permits you to reach a target audience by carefully selecting programs and time slots.
o Television is the major source of all news for Americans, and they consider TV the most up to date and authoritative of the media.
o Television commercials, according to a survey conducted by R. H. Bruskin, are the most influential of all major media advertising.
o Television reaches a more varied audience per day than any other medium.
o Television viewing is at an all time high. The average household views 6 hours and 28 minutes of TV every day.

Disadvantages of TV Advertising

o There is a significant amount of commercial clutter as advertisers fight for the viewers' attention. Between 1956 and 1978, the use of 30-second commercials increased 73 percent.
o As more and more advertisers seek exposure on TV, stations are moving to shorter commercials. The result is a lot of disjointed messages.
o Many programs are not suitable vehicles for professional advertising, because they are offensive to some segment of the viewing audience.
o If you have only one location, there may be a lot of wasted circulation with television. It doesn't pay to advertise on TV unless you have a unique practice or many offices.
o Television advertising is costly in terms of both station time and production. This is particularly true in large metropolitan areas, where these costs may be prohibitive.

○ There's a reaction time lag in commercial viewing. People don't react immediately to the first message. It may take several impressions before the viewer acts.

○ There may be a shortage of commercial time during certain periods of the year, and you may have trouble getting good time slots.

○ You need a good deal of advance planning before you get on the air. Commercials can take weeks, if not months, to produce.

○ Like radio commercials, television commercials are retained in the viewer's mind only. There is nothing to refer to later on, and this severely limits what you can say.

YELLOW PAGES AND OTHER DIRECTORIES

Unlike the other media discussed, directories actually serve as buyer's guides. Consumers turn to them when they are planning to purchase something. Some people turn to the Yellow Pages because they have seen your advertising and have forgotten the location and telephone number of your practice. Other people haven't been influenced by any advertising but have a need for professional services and are using the Yellow Pages as a source to determine which firm or individual to patronize. In either case, your ad in the Yellow Pages guarantees that your message will be noted.

The Yellow Pages is one of the major media for professional advertising. One dermatologist who advertised in the Yellow Pages said, "The listing cost $12 a month, and it was very effective. People feel that if it is in the Yellow Pages, it's official."

Directory Facts and Trends

The Bell System, with 23 operating divisions, is the largest publisher of directories. However, there are hundreds of independent telephone companies and publishers that produce directories of all kinds. There are over 6,000 directories in the United States, from specialized ones for health care or business to general directories for towns, counties, and cities.

The Yellow Pages is the fifth largest advertising medium, and the fastest growing print medium. In 1977, advertisers invested $1.3 billion in Yellow Pages advertising, twice as much as was invested in outdoor advertising.

Nearly everyone uses the Yellow Pages—84 percent of adults consult it when they are considering a purchase (82 percent men and 85 percent women). Yellow Pages users tend to be under 50 with incomes over $15,000 and above-average educations.

Buying Space in the Yellow Pages

The first thing to do in planning a Yellow Pages campaign is to determine what coverage you want in your local market. It might pay to broaden your market by advertising in neighboring directories. Many people in surrounding communities might be willing to travel the extra distance to obtain specialized professional services.

A recent Yellow Pages directory for Nassau County in New York contained over 140 ads for physicians, lawyers, accountants, and dentists. They ranged in size from one-half page ($4'' \times 10\frac{1}{4}''$) to a half-inch listing ($\frac{1}{2}'' \times 2''$ wide). The half-inch listing allows for just your name, address, telephone number, and two lines of general information. Display ads are more versatile and are sold in fractional page units ($\frac{1}{2}$, $\frac{1}{4}$, $\frac{1}{8}$, $\frac{1}{10}$ page); they permit you to design an ad using your own graphics.

The rates charged for Yellow Pages advertising will vary depending on the circulation of the directory and the size of the ad. You will have to sign a one-year contract and be billed on an annual or monthly basis.

It would be advisable to meet with your Yellow Pages representative and discuss a program for your practice. Decide what categories you should be listed under, the ad message and size, and where you would like to advertise. The representative will be able to give you advice based on his experience and guide you on what other professionals are doing.

If you would like additional information on directories, write or call the National Yellow Page Service Organization (see Appendix 3). It will supply you with information about your local Yellow Pages. It also has demographic information and rates available on all directories.

Advantages of Yellow Pages Advertising

- o The Yellow Pages is the ideal medium for reaching your prospects at the precise moment they are in need of a service. It reaches people when they are ready to buy.
- o It works for you all year round.
- o Yellow Pages advertising is economical. It costs comparatively little to be listed in the Yellow Pages.
- o When consumers need a professional in a hurry—and they do in most cases—they will turn to the Yellow Pages.
- o The ads attract attention and single you out from the other professionals listed.

Disadvantages of Yellow Pages Advertising

○ The Yellow Pages is not the place to build a professional image. These ads are directory ads and list the benefits and features of your practice.

○ Reproduction is normally poor in directories, and you may be limited to reproducing line art only. Photographs, in many cases, will not be accepted.

○ You must contract for a full-year program. If you move or merge your practice, you will be billed until the end of the contract.

○ You have to work well in advance so that you can make the deadline for the annual directory.

OUTDOOR ADVERTISING

Except for a few professional organizations, outdoor advertising has been all but ignored by professionals. This is probably because outdoor advertising has always been considered a supplementary medium—and not one that is familiar to professionals.

However, there are professionals who are using the medium—and doing it effectively. The Minnesota Dental Association has long pioneered the use of outdoor advertising for consumer education. Sandra K. Nelsen, account executive for the association, told me in a personal communication.

> You can exert more control over your campaign in the outdoor medium. It is possible to know how many boards you can expect to post, their posting locations, and how long you can expect the message to remain posted. In other words, you can preplan and schedule your campaign, which is not possible in other media. . . . Our experience confirms that our dental messages in these media [outdoor and transit] are always seen, talked about, and remembered.

Outdoor Facts and Trends

Outdoor advertising has become a highly standardized, regulated, and disciplined medium. There are some 250,000 sign structures with uniform dimensions available in 9,000 communities throughout the nation. Of these boards, 40,000 are painted, 135,000 are illuminated, and the remainder are printed posters.

Outdoor advertising soared to a record $700 million in 1979. Yet, it represents only 1.6 percent of total advertising expenditures in the United States, making it the smallest of the advertising media.

Until recently, the industry suffered from a lack of research that left media buyers guessing about what audience they were reaching. Today, the industry has a vast amount of data available that indicates who views billboards. The number of exposures per sign is based on audits conducted by the Traffic Audit Bureau. The audit is accomplished by making a count of motor vehicle and pedestrian traffic at sign locations throughout a market.

Outdoor advertising reaches more prospects, more often than advertisements in other media. It reaches more of the educated than any other medium and is unmatched in size, impact, and buying potential. Table 5 lists the highlights of a study conducted by TGI in 1975. Included are reach and frequency by sex, income, and education.

Buying Outdoor Space

Each outdoor sign is owned and maintained by a company, or plant. The sign is located on land owned or leased by the plant; the space is rented on a monthly or yearly basis to the advertiser. There are two different types of standardized outdoor signs: the poster panel and the painted bulletin. These are discussed in detail in Chapter 12.

The poster panel is an outdoor sign that will take a printed advertisement. It is distributed by the plant. There is space on the panel for three different poster sizes: the 24 sheet, the 30 sheet, and the bleed poster. There is no difference in the monthly rental charge for the different poster sizes. Furthermore, you will have to supply each plant with printed posters.

The painted bulletin is a larger sign and is produced by skilled artists from designs supplied by the advertisers. The method of selling painted bulletins differs from that of posters. Bulletins are usually sold one at a

Table 5. Reach and frequency of outdoor advertising by demographic characteristics.

Characteristic	25 GRP		50 GRP		100 GRP	
	R(%)	F	R(%)	F	R(%)	F
Men	73.1	8	80.8	15	85.8	29
Women	72.2	6	81.7	11	87.5	20
Income:						
$15,000 or more	80.0	9	85.8	17	90.3	32
Education:						
attended college	79.7	8	87.0	15	91.1	29

GRP = Gross rating points.
R = Reach.
F = Frequency.

time for longer durations than printed posters. They can also be sold in packages. While some painted bulletins are fixed in location, others are moved from site to site in what is known as a rotating plan. Under this plan an advertiser can have several different bulletin designs and rotate them periodically in the same market.

The Junior 8 poster, located at eye level, was created to be close to where the traffic is and to satisfy the point-of-sale requirements of large and small advertisers. The size of the standard Junior 8 poster is 6' × 12', with a copy area of 5' × 11'. It can be used for mass coverage of market or for pinpointing advertising in specific areas. You can target any audience using Junior 8 posters: high or low income, students, businessmen, racial or ethnic groups, etc. These posters are printed and posted by "plants" in a similar manner as the larger billboards. Junior 8 posters are purchased in packages by advertisers who select locations or an entire market. The advertisers have the flexibility to reach a target audience with pinpoint accuracy.

In most markets, poster panels are sold by the month in packages determined by gross rating points (GRPs). A 100 GRP package will provide enough billboards to deliver 100 percent of the total population of a market in one day. A 50 GRP billboard package will deliver one-half of the population in one day, while a 25 GRP purchase will deliver one-fourth of the population.

Poster panels used to be sold in packages called "showings." A 100 showing was similar to the 100 GRP package, delivering 100 percent of the total market in a given day. This was changed in 1973 when the outdoor industry standardized its unit sales from market to market.

What does outdoor advertising cost? Table 6 gives typical charges for

Table 6. Outdoor advertising costs for San Diego and Cincinnati (1981 rates).

City	GRP	Number of Panels	Cost per Month ($)
San Diego	100	80	22,200
	50	40	11,100
	25	21	5,805
	10	8	2,240
Cincinnati	100	76	21,360
	50	38	10,680
	25	19	5,340
	10	7	2,002

two cities—San Diego and Cincinnati—as supplied by Foster and Kleiser, one of the largest outdoor advertising organizations in the United States.

Dealing with Your Outdoor Sales Representative

If you are contemplating outdoor advertising, meet with your sales representative. The rep will guide you in designing a poster and choosing sites that meet your advertising objectives.

When you have made a final decision to use outdoor advertising, you will have to sign a contract. The contract will cover a period of 1 to 12 months and will include posting and maintenance charges. If you rent a painted bulletin, the costs of painting will be covered in your monthly charge. The bulletin may be repainted on a semiannual or yearly basis depending on your location. The outdoor company is responsible for keeping your poster or sign looking good, the lights burning on an illuminated sign, the area cleared of litter and weeds, and the supporting frame clean and neat. Paper posters may have to be replaced every two months because of weather conditions. All items should be spelled out in your contract.

Advantages of Outdoor Advertising

○ Outdoor advertising reaches 87.2 percent of all adults in the average market, with a frequency of 31 times a month. People who view billboards are young, affluent, and educated.
○ Outdoor advertising serves as a reminder to consumers when they are out of the home.
○ Outdoor signs can be purchased individually or in a variety of packages.
○ Outdoor advertising is flexible. You can zero in on your target audience with precision by selecting specific locations. You can buy advertising space in a region, state, city, or section of a city.
○ Outdoor advertising allows you to concentrate your message in areas frequented by different age, income, or ethnic groups.
○ Outdoor advertising is a great medium for reaching working women, who now make up over half of the outdoor audience.

Disadvantages of Outdoor Advertising

○ Outdoor advertising is considered a secondary medium and is normally used to support the major media.
○ Unlike advertising in newspapers or on radio and TV, outdoor advertising can take weeks to make an impact on a geographic area.

○ You are severely limited in how much you can say in outdoor advertisements. To be effective, you should use only six or seven words at the most and should keep the graphics simple.

○ Many people regard outdoor advertisements as environmental blights and are offended by this type of advertising.

TRANSIT ADVERTISING

Transit advertising includes the cards and signs found on the inside and outside of buses, trains, or subways. It also includes the posters and illuminated signs found in railroad stations and airport terminals.

Transit advertising is a very efficient way to reach a target audience. You can place your advertising aimed at specific groups on appropriate bus routes and train lines, and you can advertise during the months of the year when the chances of success are greatest.

Many professionals have discovered transit advertising and are using it effectively. One legal clinic pulled close to 150 new clients with a one-month transit advertising campaign. The Preventive Medicine Institute/ Strang Clinic has been particularly successful with advertising in the New York subways. The Strang Clinic attributes this to the average length of a ride (about 25 minutes) and the repeated viewing of the message. In one month, a person can be exposed to your message 30 times, building greater awareness and recall.

Transit Facts and Trends

With gasoline prices going up, ridership on mass transportation is soaring. Bus ridership has increased dramatically, and every month 7 million new riders start using buses. In 1980, about 35,000 buses carried 6.5 billion riders nationally—a new record. A recent survey in Columbus, Ohio, showed that 40 percent of all respondents will switch to the bus from cars if gasoline reaches $2 per gallon.

The average length of a bus ride varies from city to city. Table 7 shows a range from 46 minutes in Washington, D.C., to 27 minutes in New York and Minneapolis. In addition, the demographics of the average rider differ from city to city. The percentage of riders with family incomes over $15,000 is 59 in Minneapolis, while in New York City it is 35.

The recall of your messages is extremely high in transit advertising. The average copy recognition score was 54 percent of the riders in New York City subways and 53 percent in buses. This is attributed to the fact the riders are a captive audience for over 25 minutes each day as they travel to work. They can't avoid seeing your message in a one-month

Table 7. Comparison of bus-riding times and demographic characteristics for four cities.

Characteristic	Washington	Minneapolis	Atlanta	New York
Average Length of Ride (min.)	46	27	28	27
Family Income $15,000+ (%)	49	59	39	35
Some College (%)	53	34	28	37
Professional/Managerial (%)	33	44	24	36
Female Adults (%)	63	65	54	56
Actually Read Advertising (%)	85	70	75	87

Source: TDI/Winston.

campaign. Transit advertising delivers a large number of gross rating points and a very high frequency. In fact, in one month. bus advertising delivers a reach of 87.1 percent with a frequency of 20 times (see Figure 6), and it will do this at a very low cost per thousand.

Displays on the outside of buses also deliver a large audience with a high frequency. These signs are comparable to outdoor advertising, since they are seen on the move and must have a simple, powerful message. While these signs do not have a captive audience, they gain attention

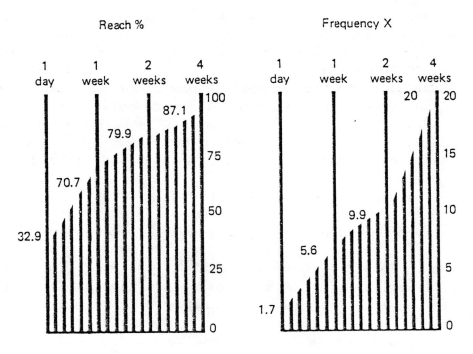

Figure 6. Reach and frequency of bus advertising. (Transit Advertising Association.)

through constant exposure and repetition. A recent study conducted by Telcom Research, Inc. found that king-size posters deliver all the visual impact of a 30-sheet poster, with an 85.7 percent reach and a frequency of 18.4 times.

Buying Transit Advertising

If you want to buy car cards inside a bus or train, you will find that they come in a variety of shapes and sizes. On the outside of buses, posters are called displays, and they also are available in a wide variety of sizes, shapes, and locations. Displays can be located on the top, front, rear, and both sides of the bus. Some signs are illuminated. (See Chapter 12 for a more detailed discussion.)

You can buy transit car cards, signs, or posters on the basis of coverage. The terms used for coverage vary from operating firm to operating firm. Some use the word *showing* or *run*. Whatever word is used, contracts will be written on the basis of the market reached. A 100 showing is one poster or card in (or on) every vehicle in a market. A 50 showing is half that number of cards and a 25 showing is a quarter of that number. The contract period will range from one month to one year, depending on the duration of your campaign.

If you want to reach a particular market, operating firms can select routes that carry a large number of passengers with the desired demographic characteristics. Cards can be placed in those vehicles most likely to be transporting the people you want to reach. There is no additional charge for specifying routes and targeting your audience. Table 8 shows the cost of an interior bus card for four selected cities in 1981.

Station transit posters are available, too, in various sizes (see Chapter 12). Space is sold also on the basis of coverage—intensive (100 percent), representative (50 percent), and minimum (25 percent) showings. The quantity of posters needed to cover a market will differ from city to city depending on the number of stations available.

Table 8. Cost of an interior bus card (11″ × 28″).

City	Number of Vehicles	100 Showing ($)	50 Showing ($)
Detroit	860	4,300	2,150
Atlanta	800	4,000	2,000
Oakland	800	4,000	2,000
Chicago	3,000	15,000	7,500

Source: TDI/Winston.

When you buy car cards, posters, and displays you will have to supply the printed advertisements just as in outdoor advertising. The cards will be posted according to your contract and monitored by the operating company. You will also have to supply the operating company with some extra cards, to replace posters that are damaged through normal use.

The Transportation Advertising Association provides advertisers with market math research reports that indicate what bus transit advertising delivers to regional and local advertisers. The association can provide you with computer printouts for 102 cities. The typical computer page shows the total adult population; breakdowns by sex, age, and income; reach and frequency for a 100 or 50 showing; and the cost per month.

Advantages of Transit Advertising

○ Transit advertising delivers an extremely low cost per thousand—about 50 cents for 1,000 impressions in a major market.
○ Transit advertising can saturate a market and build awareness quickly—even in a few days.
○ Transit advertising dominates in the daytime, when it is not in competition with other media. It goes where the people are.
○ Transit advertising offers a wide reach and a very high frequency.
○ Inside car cards have a captive audience for about 25 minutes every working day; certainly enough time for your ad to make an impact.
○ Transit advertising is flexible. You can run it for one month or an entire year, and you can buy one route or an entire city.

Disadvantages of Transit Advertising

○ Transit advertising is regarded as a supplementary medium and limited in terms of what you can say.
○ Posters and cards can be damaged by the weather or vandals.
○ No matter how your contract is written guaranteeing you distribution, you are at the mercy of the operating company's personnel and mishaps can happen.

CHAPTER 9

Creating the Message

WE'VE NOW COME to the phase of advertising that is probably the most interesting—and one of the most difficult: creating a message that will have impact and bring results. This requires a great deal of thought, time, and work.

Julius Phoenix, Jr., of Deloitte Haskins & Sells, said in a personal interview: "Having never advertised before, there was kind of a mysterious feeling about it. When we started to work with our agency, we found that it was no mystery at all. It's like most other things. It's hard work. You sit down, roll up your sleeves, and start thinking . . . and work!"

Creating effective professional advertising isn't easy. Most of the ads tend to look alike, and very little effort is given to the copy or layout. Professionals have been imitating each other, and in most cases, the results have been dismal. No thought has been given to creating a unique position. A good concept and a strong and interesting visual presentation can attract attention, keep the readers' interest, and move them to action.

Before you get involved in advertising, decide who is going to do the work. There are four ways to proceed, as outlined below.

Doing it yourself. Whether you choose this approach will depend on two factors: the amount of time you have available and your writing skills. If you have a busy practice and family obligations that are time consuming, think twice about doing it yourself. You will never be able to turn out good ads on a continuous basis. Chances are that you will have to drop the program because of the demand on your time.

However, if you have a flair for writing and are willing to put in the hours after work writing ads, then do it. One of the most effective advertising campaigns was produced by Dr. Frederick Seltzer, a dentist who had no advertising training but a great deal of writing skill and a natural instinct for public relations. Dr. Seltzer knew the value of continuous advertising and ran a weekly ad in his local town newspaper for close to two years.

Working with an ad agency. If you have a large practice or firm you probably can afford it, so consider working with an advertising agency. (Refer to the chapter on how to select and work with an ad agency.) An agency that wants to work with professionals can provide you with a variety of services, including art, production, media, research, marketing, and planning. Some even have public relations departments.

Working with freelancers. There are many talented art directors, copywriters, and media planners who will work with you on a freelance basis. Many of them are employed full time in top ad agencies and moonlight to pick up a few extra dollars. Some advertise for clients in local advertising publications (like *Adweek*) or in newspapers. Most of these freelancers will work closely with you, but you'll have to direct them—and your guidance is extremely important. Don't attempt to do this unless you have a good idea of the benefits of your practice and are able to communicate this to the freelancers you will be working with. You should also know who your potential clients/patients (C/Ps) are.

If you get involved in directing your own ad program, you will be signing contracts with the media, checking schedules, making sure the production materials meet deadlines, checking proofs, and eventually paying all the bills.

Using creative services. Many newspapers and magazines have art and copy departments for producing advertising. These departments use staff people, and in most cases, the services are provided free. In addition, many radio and TV stations employ copywriters and production personnel to help them produce commercials. They will supply announcers and recording facilities at little or no cost to you. The reason they provide all these services is that they are interested in selling space or time and want new advertisers. The disadvantages in using these sources is that they tend to be retail oriented and lack the expertise in creating unique image-building professional advertising campaigns.

THE AIDA FORMULA

Before you start creating your message, you should recognize different levels of the "communications spectrum": unawareness, awareness, comprehension, conviction, and action. The flow of your copy should move the C/P through these different levels, so that the end result will be that he comes through your office door.

The copy and visual aspects of your advertisement should accomplish the following objectives:

Attract Attention. If you don't attract attention, the prospect will turn the page or ignore your advertisement.

Create Interest. Involve readers in the benefits of your practice so that they become totally interested in your message.

Stimulate Desire. Create a desire on the part of the potential C/P to try your practice.

Move to Action. Convince the C/P to take action immediately by making an appointment with your office or requesting additional information.

Some admen have summed up these different aspects with the simple acronym AIDA—Attention, Interest, Desire, and Action. It's an easy way to remember the different phases of a successful ad.

SELECTING YOUR MEDIA

Before you can even attempt to create a message, you must know where you intend to advertise. Each medium has advantages and disadvantages for delivering a message. These are discussed in detail in Chapter 8. You must know the benefits as well as the limitations of the media, so you can create a message that has impact.

The selection of media will be based on two factors: your advertising budget and the cost-efficiency for reaching your target audience with continuity.

Choose the category of media you want to use. If you select newspapers, determine which specific newspapers you want to advertise in, what size ads you want to use, and how often you will run them. If you choose radio or TV, you must decide on the station, time period, and length of the commercial (10, 30, or 60 seconds).

You can obtain much of this information from media salespeople. They will be happy to supply you with demographic information about their audiences. They can also supply you with details on other professionals who have advertised with them. And if you request it, they will submit an advertising plan of many commercials (at an attractive cost) designed to reach a large share of your audience. For example, a radio station will put together a weekly package of one-minute radio spots that will give total audience coverage. The station will be able to tell you the reach (the number of people listening) of the total campaign and also the frequency (how many times the commercial is heard by each listener).

BRAINSTORMING

One of the ways to arrive at a unique concept is by brainstorming. It's a method that was introduced in the early 1950s, and it is still one of the most effective methods for arriving at a solution to a difficult creative problem. Brainstorming sets people free to produce great ideas. As the brilliant adwoman Shirley Polykoff said, brainstorming is "thinking it out square. Then saying it with flair." If you have the greatest ad in the world and the basic concept is wrong, it will not pull people into your practice.

Brainstorming involves several individuals, including the copywriter, art director, and account executive. In many cases, it may be an assistant who comes up with the great idea that makes a memorable campaign.

In the process of brainstorming, you will determine what copy approach to use and what kind of illustration. You will also have to determine the purpose of the ad, to whom it is being directed, and the competitive conditions that exist in the marketplace. In short, you need the research described in earlier chapters in order to plan and create a successful advertising message.

Rough layouts (called "roughs") will be made from the ideas that are conceived during the session. They will help you visualize what the finished ad might look like. There are endless ways to write copy and create a dramatic visual concept. In fact, if you give the same information to a hundred copywriters and art directors, the chances are that you will get a hundred different copy and art approaches. It's highly individual and requires a great deal of skill and talent.

WHAT MAKES SUCCESSFUL ADVERTISING?

There are two basic steps that make for successful advertising: (1) seek out your potential C/Ps; and (2) motivate them to make an appointment with you.

Good advertising seeks out the logical prospects—the target audience. A prospect is a person who at a given moment in time has a need for professional services and can afford to pay for them. If you haven't identified and located your prospects, your ads will not be successful no matter how creative they are.

Seven other essentials of making a great advertisement are:

1. *Create the concept.* The most important component of any advertising campaign is the basic concept. It's the idea behind your campaign that

will make it work. Adman David Ogilvy wrote, "Unless your ad is built around a great idea it will flop."*

2. *Sell benefits.* As any adman will tell you, don't write about the features of your practice, write about the benefits to the reader. Selling benefits not features is one of the fundamentals of all advertising. "Each advertisement must say to each reader, 'Buy this product and you will get this specific benefit,' " wrote adman Rosser Reeves.** Another adman, Elmer Wheeler, summed it up this way, "Don't sell the steak; sell the sizzle."†

Most professionals are so totally immersed in their daily activities that they forget that they offer real benefits to their C/Ps. Benefits are what the public really wants, not a lot of technical jargon. The benefits you offer will affect the way C/Ps perceive your practice.

One way to determine the benefits of your practice is to make a list of the individual features and the benefits of each. For example:

Features	Benefits
Specialized knowledge of wills and trusts.	Your family, not the government, will get the bulk of your estate.
Knowledge and use of nitrous oxide and hypnosis.	Dentistry can be a pleasant and painless experience.
Full medical testing facilities for a checkup.	You can stop worrying and start living.
Knowledge of financial statements and corporate and business tax returns.	You can be assured of total commitment to improving your firm's profitability.
On-premise denture facilities and staff.	In 24 hours, we'll make you look and feel like a new person with natural-looking dentures.

3. *Keep it simple.* Simplicity in advertising is the key. The average reader doesn't have the time or the patience to figure out what you're trying to say. The direct, simple approach is the best one. Study your ad and limit it to one major selling idea. Don't try to say too many things in one ad. You can include supporting facts, but keep the message simple to hold

---

*David Ogilvy, *Confessions of an Advertising Man.* New York: Atheneum, 1963.
**Rosser Reeves, *Reality in Advertising,* New York: Random House, 1961.
†Willard Pleuthner, ed., *460 Secrets of Advertising Experts,* New York: Thomas Nelson & Sons, 1961.

the reader's attention and convince him. Shirley Polykoff summed it up in *Advertising Age* (June 4, 1979), "Creativity has always been the knack of expressing a single idea or simple concept in a fresh, new way."

4. *Stay interesting*. In the glut of advertising today, you must keep the readers' attention. It's a challenge to hold your reader throughout the ad. The copy must flow and totally involve the readers, and finally move them to action.

5. *Be believable*. For advertising to be effective, it must be credible. If your potential C/Ps mistrust your advertising, you've wasted your money. How can you create this believability? By understanding and knowing your prospects and communicating with them in a manner that doesn't insult their intelligence.

6. *Be informative*. Consider what else the prospects need to know in addition to the benefits they will receive from your practice. The more information there is in the ad supporting your basic message, the harder the ad will work for you. Most people read advertising for information, so why not educate them about the need for professional services?

7. *Build an image*. Your advertising is a link connecting you and your C/Ps. It should not only convey a message that will attract C/Ps but establish an image for you in the community. Image is determined not only by advertising but also by such factors as the C/P's first-hand experience with you, word-of-mouth communications, and your public relations efforts.

Advertising Is a Two-Way Dialogue

Although advertising may seem impersonal, it really is a dialogue between two people—a sender and a receiver. In successful advertising, a practitioner is saying to the reader (or listener), "I understand your problems. I know how frustrated you are in finding a professional who can take care of your needs. I want to help. I think you'll find my practice competent, considerate, and fair. And I'll give you the facts so that you can decide for yourself."

Good advertising is that simple. It's always remembering that the person who receives the message knows the difference between warm, friendly advertising that talks about benefits to the reader and an ad that says, "I'm here. Take me."

Adman Bob Stone advises the copywriter to find the product's (or service's) dramatic differences and link them to your prospect's needs and wants. And you must communicate in a one-on-one style that's readable and believable.

CHAPTER 10

Creating a Print Ad

PRINT ADVERTISING was the forerunner of all advertising, and despite the popularity of television, it's still one of the most powerful media. There is nothing more compelling than words. They have created religions, started revolutions, instigated wars, and even brought down empires and presidencies. Just look at the enduring effects of the great literary works and you realize the power of the printed word.

Nothing is tougher than writing a print ad. Aldous Huxley recognized this in his essay "On the Margin": "It is easier to write ten sonnets good enough to take in the most inquiring critic, than one effective advertisement that will take in a few thousand of the uncritical buying public."

NEWSPAPER AND MAGAZINE ADS

Though the basics for making a great ad are the same for all print ads, there are differences between magazines and newspapers that may affect your creative efforts. Each one has advantages and disadvantages.

Newspapers are immediate and newsworthy. They give you a sense of urgency. Knowing the pulling power of this medium, local businesses invest billions each year in daily newspaper ads. Newspaper advertising is really news about the local marketplace and seeks an immediate response from the reader.

Magazines, on the other hand, do not have the immediacy of newspapers, or the wide circulation in all markets. However, they are read for longer periods of time, and people save magazines. The ads continue to pull responses many months after publication.

Most professionals currently use newspapers to reach clients/patients (C/Ps) because they recognize the opportunity to tie in their ad messages with news and current events in the local marketplace. They know that newspapers are flexible and provide a unique opportunity to build an image.

Although newspapers enjoy a wide popularity, they have limitations.

The average person spends only 6 minutes a day reading the ads, and in each paper there are anywhere from 50 to 500 ads (not counting classified) competing for the reader's time. In order to get your message across with impact, you must be creative.

Types of Newspaper Advertising

There are three different types of newspaper advertising: display, classified, and display-classified. Each type is designed for a specific section of the paper.

Display advertising, also called ROP (run of the paper), will appear in any section of the newspaper that you specify: local news, sports, health, entertainment, business, home, or personal living. You can create an ad of any size and select any typeface or illustration. You have complete control. You also have an opportunity to tie in the ad message with news of what is happening in your town.

Classified advertising is useful when newspaper readers are looking for a particular product or service. Many papers have a professional services section: Ads for dentists, physicians, accountants, lawyers, psychologists, chiropractors, and so on are grouped by category. These ads are smaller and are generally measured by the number of agate lines; there are 14 agate lines to the column inch. Some newspapers charge by the column inch, while others charge by the line. Classified ads are all-type ads and use the same typeface for each ad. There are no illustrations, and the only creativity is in your copy.

Display-classified advertising is a combination of the two types just described. This type of ad is designed to appear in the classified pages but uses such devices found in display advertising as illustrations and bold type to attract attention. These ads are generally small, but larger than the typical classified ad. They attract attention on a page of classified ads because of their bold graphics and design.

Classified ads. If you think that it requires little talent to create an effective classified ad, think again. A great deal of thought and effort should be given to your advertising message.

The *headline* of the classified ad is the single most important part of the ad. If it attracts the reader's eye, he'll continue to read the rest of the copy (see the section on creating headlines later in this chapter). The headline should offer the C/P a real benefit.

A *value* must be illustrated in persuasive, factual, and easy-to-read copy. Keep your copy to the point. Your typical reader wants to know what is in it for him. Classified ad readers want all the facts. Factual ads pull far better than ads that leave out the details. Avoid abbreviations at all costs. The ad will have more impact if you spell it out—and it will be easier to read.

List your firm's *name, telephone number, and address* prominently. They must be easily read or no one will call. Also give the name of a person in your firm to call. People like the security of knowing a specific name to ask for.

It is best to submit typed copy to the newspaper to avoid mistakes. If you call it in to an ad representative, spell out the difficult words and include punctuation. Don't assume that the representative will spell things correctly. Also ask the person to read the ad back to you, including the punctuation, capital letters, etc.

Some typical ads for professionals that might appear in the classified section follow.

CRIMINAL LAW FIRM
SMITH & JONES
$20 Consultation Fee
The $20 fee entitles you to one-half hour consultation with an attorney specializing in criminal law. If further legal services are desired, we will quote you a fee. The fee charged in any case will depend on the particular circumstances of your case. If you do not want any additional legal services, there is no obligation.
PHONE: 666-7000
(ask for Mr. Baines)
2160 Queens Blvd.,
Suite 2100, Woodside, N.Y.

DENTISTRY WITHOUT PAIN
If you neglect your teeth because you're afraid of dentists, your worries are over. This office uses the most advanced techniques to deliver painless dentistry. Call us now to discuss your particular problem. We want to make your dental visit a pleasant experience.
DR. JOSEPH THOMPSON
3875 Wilshire Blvd.
Los Angeles, CA
TEL: 687-2304

Display advertising. Unlike classified advertising, display gives you a great deal more flexibility. You can use any typeface; you can also use a photograph, illustration, or even cartoon. You are not limited to any specific ad size, so you can run a full-page ad or a fraction of a page. In fact, it is not uncommon for advertisers to run the same display ad created for newspapers in a magazine. They recognize that a good print ad will produce results no matter where it is placed.

The basic elements of a display ad are the headline, copy, illustration (or photograph), and advertiser's logo (or signature). All these should be combined in a layout that will attract attention and get the reader to act.

The ads shown on the following pages illustrate a variety of approaches used in newspapers and magazines. The ad for the American Dental Plan (#7) appeared in *The New York Times Magazine*. It uses a direct-response technique with lots of copy highlighting consumer benefits. The Minneapolis and St. Paul District Dental Societies ran an ad in local newspapers and regional magazines (#8). The ad sought to obtain referrals for members as well as to inform the public about gum disease. The ad for the law firm of Froehlich & Richter, P.C. (#9) has appeared in local newspapers on Long Island. The firm offers a 36-page booklet of information for law clients, which can be obtained by sending in the coupon featured in the ad. (If you run a coupon ad, make sure the paper doesn't run another coupon on the back.) Froehlich & Richter uses a computer to track all responses and to determine which papers actually produce clients. The ad for the Bosley Medical Group (#10) features an endorsement. The ad appeared in *Playboy* and other male-oriented magazines. The objective of the ad for the accounting firm of Laventhol & Horwath (#11) was to create greater awareness for the firm as well as to publicize the involvement of its partners. The ad appeared in *Fortune, The Wall Street Journal,* and *Business Week.*

Know the components involved in planning for an ad. If you understand their importance, you'll be able to create advertising that will build your image as it builds your practice.

Creating the Headline

The most important part of any ad is the headline. If you start off with a strong headline, you'll have a strong ad.

"On the average, five times as many people read the headline as read the body copy. If you haven't done some selling in the headline, you have wasted 80 percent of your client's money," advised David Ogilvy.*

The fact is the vast majority of people never get past the headline. They will glance at the ad, look at the illustration, and if it doesn't catch their eye, they will turn the page. A good headline should provoke the prospect to read the body copy.

---

*David Ogilvy, *Confessions of an Advertising Man,* New York: Atheneum, 1963.

Something worth smiling about...

Now you can receive quality dental care from a neighborhood dentist of your choice and save up to 70%

INTRODUCING
The American Dental Plan®

As a member of the American Dental Plan, you can actually save hundreds of dollars a year on your dental bills. These savings are made possible by a group of dentists in your community who are as concerned as you about the skyrocketing costs of health services.

We've joined forces to cut back fees without sacrificing quality care or individual attention to save you up to 70% on your dental bills.

You can select a dentist office from the hundreds of American Dental Plan dentists who have committed to this important cooperative effort throughout the five boroughs of New York, Long Island, Westchester, Putnam, Rockland and Ulster counties.

Simply enroll as an individual, couple or family and choose one of the two plans which best suits your needs.

The low annual membership fee is based on the plan you select:

Enrollment Fee Schedule:	Annual Fee	
	Plan "A"	Plan "B"
Individual	$37.50	$ 70.00
2 Individuals	$65.00	$130.00
Family (three to five)	$95.00	$165.00
Each additional dependent	– 0 –	$ 10.00

Under Plan B there is no charge for simple extractions and only a $1 charge per filling per surface (Silver Amalgam).

This annual membership fee entitles each individual to TWO complete dental CHECK-UPS per year – absolutely FREE. This includes:

* Complete Cleaning
* Full Mouth X-Rays
* Complete Oral Examination
* Office and Emergency Visits
* Fluoride Treatments for Children
* Gum Treatment (Scaling of Teeth)
* Preventive Dental Education
* Filling Out of School Forms

There is absolutely no charge for these services – no matter how many people you have in your family. And these free check-ups alone should more than cover the cost of the plan.

What's the catch? There is no catch! Since American Dental Plan acts as a continuing source of patients for American Dental Plan dentists, it's good business for them and good value for you. Your participating dentist is a private practitioner who is established and respected within his own community. You are treated in his private dental office. Not a clinic or department store. He has years of experience providing quality dental care to thousands of patients. Small wonder that more than 48 million Americans are already enrolled in similar plans throughout the country.

And you can't "get stuck" with a dentist you won't like. Because of our high Professional Standards, we are confident you will be very pleased with the dentist you select. But if not – for any reason – you are free to switch to any of

the more than 500 dentists on the American Dental Plan roster. The choice is always yours.

Even if you are presently covered by an insurance plan, with your enrollment in the American Dental Plan your savings will be greater. That's because most insurance companies do not cover the full cost of dental treatment.

For example, if you need a porcelain-fused-to-metal cap, you could pay $275. Your insurance may pay only $125. This leaves you a balance of $150. As a member of the American Dental Plan, the cost for the same porcelain-fused-to-metal cap is only $175. With your present insurance coverage of $125 your out-of-pocket payment to your American Dental Plan dentist is only $50. That's a cash savings of $100 to you.

Look at your dental bills. Compare your costs to the corresponding American Dental Plan fees below. See how much you will save if you enroll now!

Usual Customary Fees	Plan "A"	Plan "B"
Full Mouth X-Rays	$ 25.00	No Charge	No Charge
Oral Exam and Diagnosis	15.00	No Charge	No Charge
Teeth Cleaning	15.00	No Charge	No Charge
Emergency Visit	25.00	No Charge	No Charge
Simple Extraction	20.00	$ 10.00	No Charge
Fillings involving One Surface (Silver Amalgam)	12.00	6.00	$ 1.00
Two Surfaces (Silver Amalgam)	19.00	12.00	2.00
Porcelain Crown	200.00	105.00	105.00
Porcelain with Metal Crown	275.00	175.00	175.00

After you receive your membership card, simply call the dentist you have selected and make an appointment for your initial visit. There are no time delays or claim forms to be processed and you can charge your membership to any major credit card.

CALL TOLL FREE—800-325-6400
Ask for Operator 30
OR MAIL COUPON TODAY:
800 Third Avenue, New York, N.Y. 10022

AMERICAN DENTAL PLAN®   NYT
800 Third Avenue, New York, N.Y. 10022

Please rush me your Free Enrollment Kit with complete details about the American Dental Plan savings for singles, couples and families (including orthodontic services) and Directory of Dentists, without obligation.

Name _____

Address _____

City _____ State _____ Zip _____

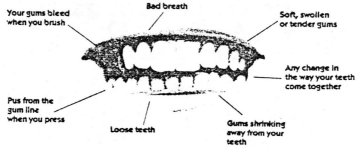

AN ANNOUNCEMENT FROM THE BOSLEY MEDICAL GROUP

Medical breakthrough reduces baldness

"I was a skeptic. Now I'm a believer, thanks to MPR and Hair Transplantation."

by Dr. Jeff Greenberg, SAN DIEGO, CALIFORNIA

"Too little hair and too much baldness. Hair transplantation would never work for me, or so I thought. On top of that, my friends and relatives kept insisting I looked fine the way I was.

Still, I knew there was room for improvement, and after one consultation visit to the Bosley Medical Group, I definitely decided to stop going through life as a bald man. But, being from a long line of skeptics, I didn't give BMG the go-ahead until I had checked out several other places.

AN A-1 RATING

The more places I visited, the more I became convinced that BMG was the *only* place to go. First of all, the Director, Dr. L. Lee Bosley, is Board Certified, and is a member of the American Medical Association (AMA). All of the other Bosley Medical Group staff physicians are also certified by the Boards of their respective surgical specialties, and are members of the American Medical Association (AMA). And most important in my particular case, BMG has developed a special procedure called Male Pattern Reduction (MPR),℠ that greatly reduces the size of the bald area. As it turned out, MPR solved my "supply and demand" problem. For another thing, the BMG Beverly Hills facility received my A-1 rating for cleanliness and what I call "quiet efficiency."

In fact, the Bosley Medical Group is so advanced in so many areas that I adapted several of their medical techniques to my own practice.

A TRUE BELIEVER

I was definitely committed to not being bald anymore, but at first I wasn't confident that I would ever again have a good head of naturally growing hair. As you can see from these pictures, I needn't have worried. Not only do I have to schedule regular hair cuts, but I find I can style my hair in many different ways.

Now I approach all my bald friends and patients with the zeal of a missionary, urging them to check out the Bosley Medical Group. Just one brief, no-charge consultation appointment and you'll know if you qualify for MPR (should you happen to need it) or Hair Transplantation. Not everyone does. But if being bald bothers you like it did me, don't spend the rest of your life worrying about it. Do something about it!"

CALL DON BRODER, COUNSELOR
(COLLECT)   213/651-0011

Ask for complete information regarding our special reimbursement plan to cover your air travel to Beverly Hills (Los Angeles).

---Or mail this request for information today---

Bosley Medical Group

L. Lee Bosley, M.D., Director
Certified Diplomate of the
American Board of Dermatology
8447 Wilshire Blvd. (at La Cienega).
Beverly Hills, Calif. 90211 · (213) 651-4444

Please send:
☐ HAIR TRANSPLANTATION AT THE BOSLEY MEDICAL GROUP
Includes over 40 close-up before/after photos of our patients, details on MPR℠ AND MICROGRAFT℠ procedures, cost, tax benefits and insurance coverage—and much more.
☐ COSMETIC PLASTIC SURGERY AT BOSLEY MEDICAL GROUP
Includes over 16 close-up before/after photos of our patients; details on all surgeries performed for enhancement of the face, eyelids, nose, ears, chin, forehead, breasts (enlargement or reduction) hip, abdomen, buttock, thigh, upper arm. Also information on skin treatments for wrinkle and scar improvement, tattoo removal, electrolysis and broken capillary treatment.

Name _____

Phone _____

Address _____

City State Zip _____
© 1980 Bosley Medical Group—A Medical Corporation   PlyBy/6/80

Hair Transplantation and Cosmetic Plastic Surgery are 100% tax deductible as medical expense.

Beverly Hills, 8447 Wilshire Blvd., (at La Cienega) 213 651-4444

You must recognize that on any given day the percentage of the public that needs a lawyer, dentist, or physician is pretty small, and this group (called a "thin market") is constantly changing. So you have to state your case in the headline with impact so that you can attract this small market to your advertisement.

Listed below are suggestions for making a great headline:

1. *Always tell the readers what is in it for them.* You should promise a benefit to your potential C/Ps. And when you write a headline, always use "you" not "we." Think of the readers saying to themselves "What's in it for me?" The answer will tell you what makes a great ad.

There are essentially two kinds of benefits: primary and secondary. For a dental patient, having healthy teeth is a primary benefit, but the secondary benefit is having a beautiful smile. It can make the patient attractive, socially acceptable, and successful in business. In many cases, the secondary benefit will have a greater impact on motivating a patient to take action.

2. *Include your name.* Remember, the average reader has only a few minutes to read all the ads, and five times as many people read the headline as read the body copy; so include your name as well as the benefits in the headline.

3. *Use strong words.* The great copywriters know that there are certain words that attract people. They have used them over and over again and know the results. They are flags that attract the reader's eye. These words include *how to, what, new, suddenly, announcing, introducing, it's here, amazing, revolutionary, easy, the truth about, compare, hurry,* and *quick.* These magic words have pulling power.

4. *Use the unexpected word.* One way to create an interesting ad is to use the unexpected word. For example, several years ago Volkswagen ran an ad with a photograph of the famous "beetle"; underneath it was a one-word headline: "Lemon." The ad, created by Doyle, Dane and Bernbach, became a classic because it showed how you can use the unexpected in advertising to achieve high readership. Curiosity is a powerful motivator, and if you include an element of surprise in the caption and relate it to a benefit, you'll have an attention-getting ad.

5. *Be consistent.* When you run an advertising campaign, strive to be consistent in your appeals and benefits. Advertising should reflect an attitude and a point of view. This can be summed up in a slogan that appears in all advertising, such as "It's about time" (Jacoby & Meyers).

6. *Choose your audience.* One way to attract your target audience is to display the words that will catch its attention. "If you want mothers to read

your advertisement, display mother in your headline," wrote David Ogilvy. One professional seeking an audience with foot problems ran an ad with the headline: "Foot sufferers. You could get permanent same day relief."

Writing the Body Copy

The body copy of an ad is a continuation of the same concept expressed in the headline. The form of the copy can vary depending upon the purpose of the ad and the copywriter. When writing your body copy, pretend that you are sitting down trying to urge someone to use your practice. Try to use convincing arguments and get straight to the point; make your arguments specific and factual. Be interesting, friendly, conversational, and believable.

There are many ways that copy can be written, and no one method applies to every situation. However, there are some basic principles of writing an effective ad:

1. *Decide how much copy.* Some admen feel that ad copy should be kept short because most people don't get beyond the headline. Research indicates, however, that long copy is read. That doesn't mean, of course, that you should write long copy for copy's sake. The copy should be long enough to give all the facts, and do it convincingly. Copywriter John Caples advised budding writers to write "a lot of copy and then boil it down. For example, if you want 500 words of copy, you should begin by writing 1,500 words. Then go over and cut out all the nonessentials. Omit unnecessary sentences and weak phrases. Make it telegraphic, fast moving, and packed with facts. A piece of copy is like a pot of broth—the more you boil it down, the stronger the flavor gets."* Shortening what you write almost always makes it easier to read and more understandable.

2. *Keep the copy flowing.* Once you get the reader's attention, keep the copy moving at a quick pace. Present your points in a logical sequence. Remember, the prime purpose of writing an ad is to move the prospect to action, not to prove that you're smarter than the reader.

3. *Use simple words and expressions.* Simplicity in advertising—in concepts, graphics, and copy—is the key to producing a great ad. Don't use phrases known only to a few. Use language that is conversational, as if you were talking to the C/P in your office. Such an approach leads automatically to the "you" and "your" message rather than the "me" or "we" approach.

---

*Willard Pleuthner, ed., *460 Secrets of Advertising Experts*, New York: Thomas Nelson & Sons, 1961.

Also use the words that will bring an image to the reader's mind—simple words that are very familiar, like *face* instead of *countenance*.

4. *Repeat important points.* If you want to convince your prospect, repeat key points. For example, you can say in your headline: FREE CONSULTATION. In the copy, repeat the offer by saying, "The initial consultation will cost you nothing." And summing up at the end of the ad, you can say, "Come in for your consultation today. It won't cost anything."

5. *Don't imitate others.* Copying some other practitioner in your area is the road to disaster. No one can build a practice by imitating the advertising of others.

Creating Slogans

Slogans are the catchy phrases at the end of ads or commercials that generally emphasize the most important selling point made in the copy. Sometimes, slogans become so strongly identified in people's minds with an advertiser's product or service that when they hear the name of an advertised brand they immediately think of the slogan, and vice versa.

Slogans should be short and to the point, so that they will be easily remembered. In many cases, you might want to include your name as part of the slogan, to gain greater recognition.

The accounting firm of Deloitte Haskins & Sells uses a slogan—"Beyond the bottom line"—very effectively in all its advertising. Placed near the logo, it represents the firm's attitude as reflected in its advertising campaign.

You might want to consider using a slogan in your advertising. It will give your campaign greater continuity from ad to ad and sum up your point of view in a graphic manner.

CREATING AN AD FOR THE YELLOW PAGES

Most professionals have recognized the power of advertising in the Yellow Pages. The people who use the Yellow Pages are seeking the answers to the five basic questions: who, what, where, when, and why. If you answer these questions with impact, the Yellow Pages can produce a significant amount of new business for you. The components of a good Yellow Pages ad are outlined below.

Your specialty. Most prospective C/Ps are looking for a professional who can help them with a specific problem, and they need to find one quickly. That's why many successful practitioners list their specialty at the top of the ad in the headline and tell how it will benefit the reader. All other important advantages of your practice should be listed too. Keep the copy to a minimum, and set it in large type (10 point minimum).

Your name and telephone number. Unless you are very well known in your community, don't use your name in the headline. It's a good idea to place your name and telephone number in bold type toward the bottom of the ad. If you are using a slogan in other advertising, consider using it in conjunction with your name. It will give greater impact and recognition to your Yellow Pages ad.

Your location and hours. Be sure to list your exact address and location. You might also want to include instructions on how to get there. The accessibility of your office can be an important factor in attracting C/Ps. Also list the days and hours your practice is open. For example, seven days a week and late-night hours are definite advantages.

Why you? With hundreds of Yellow Pages ads competing for attention, why should a prospective C/P use you? In order to answer this question, ask yourself what benefit you can offer your client. One dentist used the headline: "Why fear pain? We offer dental care in our office while you sleep." A lawyer ran an ad featuring his specialty, plus a unique offer: "Call for FREE bankruptcy information." You have to tell the readers how you are going to take care of their special needs, and you must assure them of your reliability and competence. This can be done by mentioning your background, membership in professional associations, and previous affiliations. If you take credit cards or belong to a third-party payment plan or any other insurance group, list this information. It's a definite benefit.

A simple design. Once you determine what you want to say, you have to design your ad so that it will attract potential C/Ps. Remember to keep the ad simple and to the point. Make sure it's uncluttered and easy to read and that one major point dominates the ad. This focal point should show how your specialty or practice can benefit the reader. Avoid using any photographs, since they reproduce poorly in the Yellow Pages. If you have a logo, consider using it for greater recognition.

Because your ad will be placed with the competition, it is extremely important to tell the potential C/P why he should deal with your firm. Look through the Yellow Pages in your area and clip out professional ads that you regard as effective. Using these ads, determine what message you want to convey and the size ad you need.

An attention-getting Yellow Pages ad includes a summary of your specialty and what makes it unique. In many cases, this is featured in the headline. Here are some sample headlines for different professions:

Lawyers
- No fee for first consultation.
- Specializing in matrimonial and tax law.
- Bankruptcy information *free* by phone.

Dentists
- Why fear pain? Why be afraid?
- Treat your teeth and budget to tender loving care.
- Family dentistry and personal care.

Physicians
- Why not look better? You can!
- Family practice—senior care.
- Internist—house calls available.

Accountants
- Business and management advisory services.
- All business financial services—competitive fees.
- Reasonable fees for accounting services.

After you have created your ad, decide where you want to run it. The logical place is in the appropriate professional section (Lawyers, Physicians, Dentists, and Accountants) of your community Yellow Pages. However, you might also want to broaden your reach with ads in the Yellow Pages of surrounding communities. This is particularly important if you have a unique specialty that is not readily available (e.g., a lawyer with a specialty in bankruptcy cases).

PRODUCING THE PRINT AD

After you have written the headline and the body copy, you are ready to design an attention-getting ad. In many cases, the artist will work simultaneously with the copywriter in designing a layout.

As advertising creative directors and copywriters know, it is not only what you say that is important, but how you say it. The presentation is extremely important in making your ad stand out from the great mass of advertising found in newspapers and magazines. You have to create a unique visual presentation. Whether you use an unusual photograph, illustration, or headline, to be successful your ad must attract attention and drive home the message.

But attracting attention for attention's sake is not enough. There are many easy ways to attract attention in an ad. You can just use a photograph of a sexy woman or some other provocative illustration, and it's certain to gain attention. But guess what will be remembered? The illustration, not your message. So remember, if you use an illustration, make sure that it relates to the overall concept of the advertisement.

Designing the Layout

The layout is a blueprint of what an advertisement will look like when it is completed. The layout gives you the opportunity to make any changes regarding the concept at an early stage of production. In many cases, the ad idea will be rejected at this stage, and the artist and copywriter will have to come up with an entirely new one.

The layout may be a rough graphic presentation, or it may be a carefully rendered piece of art (called a "comprehensive," or "comp" for short). In either case, it's used to get your approval before the ad goes any further. Making changes later on in the production process can be very expensive, so it is extremely important that all copy and art changes be made at this stage of development.

The designer of the ad will be concerned with the size and placement of the illustration, the placement of the headline, the advisability of using a subheadline, the typeface, and the placement of the logo. The designer's decisions will be based not only on good composition but on previous experience with what makes a good, attention-getting advertisement.

The illustrations, headline, subheadlines, logo, and signature will be neatly rendered in the layout, with the copy lettered in the recommended typeface. The body copy will be indicated with straight or wavy parallel lines drawn to give the feeling of the type. The layout will help your artist later on in planning the finished artwork that will be sent to the newspaper or magazine. It will tell what typeface will be used and how large it will be. It will also indicate what kind of illustration (or photograph) is suggested.

The layout person's task is arranging all the components of an advertisement to gain attention, hold interest, and quickly deliver the sales message to stimulate action. What you are trying to do is direct the reader's eye through the ad in a predetermined manner. There are many ways that layouts can be made; however, they all have three things in common: balance, flow, and unity.

The balance in an ad can be formal or informal. All the parts of the advertisement should be arranged so that they achieve a pleasant overall effect. You don't want the ad to look as though it was designed by an amateur.

The flow of an ad will help move the reader's eye in a logical sequence through the ad and direct it to your name, address, and telephone number on the bottom.

The unity of an ad is the relationship of the individual components to the entire ad. All the elements—headline, illustration, type, etc.—must be in harmony and related to each other and must reflect a feeling, mood, or attitude about the way you practice. It can build your image and prestige, or destroy them.

There are some basics that you should know about for creating a good print ad:

1. *Design a simple ad.* Don't clutter up the ad with too many items. Many beginners think that if they are paying for the space, they might as well use it, so they put everything in it but the kitchen sink. That's a mistake. Keep your ad simple, and it will produce results. Make sure that one element dominates the ad. It can be the headline or the illustration, but not both.

2. *Choose an appropriate size and shape.* If you are running your ad in a newspaper, you can choose several different sizes and shapes for the same number of lines. For example, if you want to place a 300-line ad, you can run it as one column, 300 lines deep. This will be a very skinny ad and very difficult for your designer to work with. Or you can create an ad that is 3 columns by 100 lines deep. The horizontal format might work better, but chances are that it will be placed at the bottom of the page. Or you can work with 2 columns, 150 lines deep. This type of format will be easier for your designer to work with and may get better positioning on the newspaper page. To create a successful ad, your designer must know the number of lines that you are running in the newspaper; let him recommend the configurations of the ad. Table 9 shows the various widths for advertisements, in columns, inches, and picas.

3. *Use typefaces that will attract attention.* There are literally hundreds of typefaces available today. A typeface is a style of type, such as Roman, Gothic, or Script. Some Roman typefaces include Bodoni, Caslon, and Garamond; Gothic typefaces include Futura, Helvetica, and Avant Garde.

Table 9. Column Formats for newspaper advertisements.

Display (8-column format)	Inches	Picas	Display (9-column format)	Inches	Picas
1 Column	1¾	10.6	1 Column	1⁹⁄₁₆	9.3
2 Columns	3⅝	21.9	2 Columns	3³⁄₁₆	19.2
3 Columns	5½	33.0	3 Columns	4¹³⁄₁₆	29.1
4 Columns	7⅜	44.3	4 Columns	6⁷⁄₁₆	39.0
5 Columns	9¼	55.6	5 Columns	8⅛	49.0
6 Columns	11⅛	67.0	6 Columns	9¾	58.9
7 Columns	13	78.0	7 Columns	11⅜	68.9
8 Columns	14⅞	89.6	8 Columns	13¹⁄₁₆	78.8
			9 Columns	14⅞	89.6

Sometimes by just changing a typeface, you can avoid an unpleasant connotation and create a degree of social acceptance. For example, big bold black Gothic letters convey a feeling of hard sell, while Roman letters convey a feeling of elegance and professionalism (see Figure 7).

Today, phototypesetters can set type many different ways so that you can create a unique feeling in your ads. One thing that many designers forget is that type should be easy to read so you can communicate your message. The body copy should be large enough so that readers don't strain their eyes reading it. It has been my experience that if you want your copy to be read, avoid setting it in less than 9-point type (except for classified ads). It's better to eliminate a few words than set it in a smaller type size, which is difficult to read.

Type is measured in picas and points. A pica is equal to ⅙ of an inch and is used to specify the width of a headline or the body copy (the text of an ad). The point is used to measure the height of the type. It equals ¹⁄₇₂ of an inch; therefore, the height of a capital letter set in 72-point type will be one inch.

It is possible to determine the exact point size of type before you order it from the typesetter. Your artist will tell you in advance what point size he or she is ordering for the body copy of the ad.

4. *Use a large illustration.* One large picture generally gains more attention than several smaller ones. Use a photograph that has a strong appeal and lures the reader to the ad. If you can, use a photograph that shows people, because ads that have people in them attract greater readership.

5. *Convert your illustration or photograph to line.* If you use a photograph, or halftone, you will have to screen it to run it in a newspaper. If you look at it under a magnifying glass, you will notice that the screened photograph is broken up into a series of large and small black dots. Since

Free Consultation!

Free Consultation!

Free Consultation!

Free Consultation!

Free Consultation!

Free Consultation!

Free Consultation!

Free Consultation!

Figure 7. Sample typefaces.

newspaper reproduction is extremely poor, you must use a "coarse" 65-line screen. Even so, screened photos reproduce poorly in newspapers. One way you can overcome this is to convert your photo to a special line technique. (There are many sources listed in the Yellow Pages under ve-loxes or photocopying that offer this service.) The result is an illustration that has a great deal more impact than an ordinary screened photograph. This does not apply to magazines; since the printing and paper is vastly superior to newspapers, photographs (or "halftones") can be used effectively. You would be wise to check the production specifications of the publication before you prepare your finished artwork.

6. *Don't mix typefaces.* It's the sure mark of a beginner and results in a confusing, hard-to-read ad. Use one basic face, and you can't go wrong. If you use Helvetica, stick with it. Helvetica is available in extra bold,

bold, medium, light, italic, condensed, and extended. But keep the number of these styles to a minimum, too.

7. *Create a consistent format.* If you are running an advertising campaign, your designer should create a unique, recognizable format. Each ad should be similar in overall graphics. This look includes typefaces, methods of reproducing the illustrations, the design format, and your logo. The key question is: If someone were to cover up the signature at the bottom of the ad, would readers recognize it as your ad? If the answer is yes, then your designer has created a unique presentation. What he has done is to build continuity in the readers' minds so that when they think of a professional they think of you. Another advantage of using a consistent format is that it can save you money in production costs. This is particularly true if all ads in your campaign are created at the same time.

8. *Consider running a second color.* Many newspapers permit you to run a second color in your ad. There is a flat-rate, extra charge for the second color no matter what size your ad is. However, if you want to attract attention and readership, a second color is a great way to do it. Don't overdo the use of color, though. Use it judiciously. Research shows that adding one color to your basic black increases the noting (notice by readers) about 48 percent; using four colors increases the noting by 78 percent.

9. *Use white space.* When you buy space in a newspaper, consider what many art directors have known for a long time: White space can be used as a means of attracting greater readership. The designer considers the blank space an important element in an ad. White space sets your ad apart from the competition and the editorial matter. It acts as a buffer between your message and all the clutter that surrounds it. For example, 24 or 30 point type with white space around it can be more easily read than 72 point type without white space. White space gives your ad dignity, class, and most of all, greater impact. If you can afford it, use it.

10. *Make your message easy to read.* Avoid large areas of reverse type (white type on a black background). Reverse copy is generally hard to read, but in a newspaper, because of the poor reproduction, it is especially hard to read. Also avoid running small type on top of photographs or on screened tints (called "benday"). The type will fill in, and readers will just turn the page rather than strain their eyes reading your message.

11. *Create a logo. Logo* is an abbreviation of the word *logotype*, and it has come to mean the advertiser's nameplate or trademark. Most logos use type in a graphic manner as a symbol of the firm. In some instances, an

illustration will be included as part of the logo. Whatever it is, a logo should be rendered in line art and have the ability to be reduced in size and still have impact. Using a logo is one of the most effective ways to build continuity and recognition in all your advertising. If you look at the way leading advertisers use logos, you'll understand how to attain recognition from ad to ad over a long period of time.

Preparing the Finished Artwork

Once your layout and copy are approved, you have to prepare the finished artwork for the publication. The preplanning is a guide for the production of the finished artwork. The type for the caption will be set according to your artist's instructions. Each word in the body copy will be counted and fit into the space that you have allowed in your layout. In some cases, copy may have to be edited or cut because there is just too much of it. It's better to do it at this stage and avoid costly charges for corrections later. Your artist will get a type proof on thin photographic paper from the typesetter that will be used in the production of the ad.

Photographs will have to be taken, or an artist will have to render an illustration according to the dictates of your layout. If you take a photograph, it may have to be retouched. Retouchers can do marvelous things with a photograph, including airbrushing things into it that did not previously exist or taking out unsightly things that ruin an otherwise good photograph.

All the components of the ad will be attached to an illustration board with a special wax or rubber cement. This is called the pasteup (or mechanical). The mechanical will be sent with the artwork (photographs or illustrations) to the newspaper. Remember to check all the artwork carefully before it goes to the publication.

If you are producing an ad for a magazine, you will have to prepare an offset negative. In this case, the artwork will be sent to a photoengraver to prepare the negatives for each publication.

If you decide to have the newspaper set the type and paste up the ad for you, there are certain things you should know. First of all, you will save money doing it this way. Newspapers will not charge you for this service, since they are interested in selling you space. However, the type and art facilities of newspapers are limited. The typefaces are few, and the art people are not interested in turning out an ad that will be truly unique. They are dealing with hundreds and hundreds of ads each day, so quality has to bow to quantity.

Layout and Copy Checklist

If you do decide to have the newspaper set and compose your advertising, *The New York Times* offers a checklist for preparation of layout and copy:

Preparation of Layout

- Be sure the size of your advertisement meets the mechanical requirements of the newspaper.
- Show at the top of each layout your name, the date, and the size of the advertisement.
- Do not mark your type specifications on the layout. This should be done on the manuscript of the copy.
- Letter in display heads and subheads.
- Show copy blocks with lines.
- Identify borders by number.
- Give a good, clean tracing or facsimile for the illustration areas.
- Position all components exactly.
- Indicate on the art the final size you wish the illustration to be.
- Mark each element on your layout—A, B, C, D, etc., or 1, 2, 3, 4, etc.—to correspond to positions similarly keyed on the manuscript of the copy.
- Remember, your layout is the blueprint the compositor follows in preparing your advertisement. A precise and detailed layout insures final reproduction of the ad according to your specification.

Preparation of Copy

- Put name of advertiser, date of insertion, and size of advertisement on the top of each page.
- Type all copy double spaced on standard 8½ by 11 sheets of paper (do not write copy on layout).
- Type copy on one side of a sheet only.
- Leave wide margins in which to write instructions, at least 1 ¾ inches on each side of the paper.
- Specify only typefaces shown in type book of newspaper.
- When you specify the type size, make sure by measuring the copy and by using the character-count charts found in type specimen books that the copy will fit in the space allotted for it on the layout.
- Key all sections of copy—A, B, C, D, etc., or 1, 2, 3, 4, etc.—to correspond to positions similarly keyed on the layout.

o Remember, the typewritten copy is the first and most important step in producing your ad. If your copy is complete, correct, and clear, the printer will be able to produce exactly what you want and not have to guess at what you mean.

Effective Advertising Checklist

Listed below are 12 questions. If you can answer them in the affirmative, you have a winning ad. These questions were supplied by General Foods, which uses them to measure the effectiveness of its print ads.

1. Does the ad demand attention?
2. Is the general character of the ad consistent with the long-term strategy and positioning of the product?
3. Is the first impression consistent with the purpose of the ad and with the strategy?
4. Is the ad interesting?
5. Are there one or more elements in the ad that will quickly catch the eye and the mind of the consumer?
6. Is the key benefit immediately apparent?
7. Do the headline and illustration work together to dramatize the benefits?
8. Is the key benefit presented in clear, simple, and understandable language?
9. Does the body copy effectively expand the message of the headline and illustration?
10. Is the copy easy to read and understand?
11. Is the copy interesting and persuasive?
12. Is it easy to know who sponsors the ad?

The Ten-Second Test

Now that your ad is completed, take the ten-second ad test. Study your ad for ten seconds, and not a second longer. If the objective of the ad is not immediately clear to you, then you better start all over again.

Send your copywriter and artist back to the drawing board. Make sure that when they create an ad, they remember what the prime objective is. What do you want the readers to remember and what action do you want them to take? Say this in the headline, the illustration, and the body copy.

CHAPTER 11

Creating a Radio
or TV Commercial

SHOULD YOU USE radio or television? "Why that's for the big guys," said one professional recently. "They have the money and know-how. How can I compete?"

The answer is simple, as more and more professionals are finding out. In fact, *The Wall Street Journal* revealed that in 1979 physicians and dentists doubled their budgets for TV advertising to $7.4 million.

At present, many practitioners all over the country are expanding their practices by using the electronic media. These are professionals who have unique specialties, such as cosmetic surgery, dentures, estate law, and business taxes. In many cases, they are in clinics that have high volume and low fees. Groups of professionals, such as bar associations, are also advertising and acting as referral agents to people who need services. These professionals recognize the impact of radio and television—as well as the differences between the media.

This chapter is devoted to the fundamentals of creating messages for radio and television and to production techniques.

DIFFERENCES BETWEEN PRINT AND BROADCAST MEDIA

There are many differences between the electronic media and print, but the biggest is that in broadcast you're limited to a certain segment of time to deliver a message. And nothing is more fleeting than a few seconds of time. There is no way a person can refer to the message later—unless he tapes it. So the only way you can make an impression in broadcast is through an effective message, delivered with impact, and repeated over and over until the basic selling idea hits home.

The average listener or viewer is subject to all kinds of distractions and interruptions. These interruptions are much more disruptive than when a person is reading an ad in a newspaper or magazine. The interrupted reader can always return to the printed page and lose nothing of the content of the ad. However, the person who is distracted when listening to the radio or watching TV is likely to lose the selling idea and the message becomes meaningless. Furthermore, viewers and listeners are subject to more interruptions than readers of print advertising. People are more likely to take a break during a TV commercial to go to the bathroom or have a snack than they are to put down a newspaper or magazine ad to do the same thing.

With print advertising, you can put as little or as much copy in the ad as you desire. You can put in all sorts of details, benefits, and features. You can even include a fee schedule that a person can clip for future reference. And consumers can choose to read the ad immediately or later, depending upon the time available, and they can read it at their own speed and reread portions that they don't understand.

Radio and TV are fluid media. They exist only on tape or film, or in a person's memory. You have just a few seconds to communicate your idea, so you have to make every word and visual image count. The only reason commercials exist is to communicate a selling idea from you to your target audience. It is not to entertain. If you leave the audience laughing or confused, the chances are they missed the major point of your commercial (unless, of course, the humor is completely relevant to your selling idea).

BEFORE YOU START

If you're considering advertising on radio or TV, start watching the media, paying close attention to commercials. Start observing the techniques used by different advertisers. This is the first step in producing an effective commercial. Keep a pad handy and jot down unique presentations, phrases, sound effects, and visual images.

You might also want to get the reaction of members of your family to commercials. Get them to discuss what they like about various types of announcements. Study what makes a commercial memorable. Is it the unique benefits of the service? Is it humor? Is it the believability of the spokesman? Start listening and watching, and you'll start to be discriminating about your own message whether you write it yourself or have an advertising agency create it.

You don't have to sit in front of the TV or listen to a radio for very long to spot the commercials that have no basic selling idea. They may use all kinds of production techniques to attract attention but fall flat because the concept is weak. The golden rule is that you can never substitute production techniques for a bad idea—no matter how talented your people are or how much money you spend.

REPEATING THE AIDA FORMULA

A broadcast commercial should follow the same basics for producing effective advertising as print advertising. Again I refer you to the AIDA formula mentioned earlier—Attention, Interest, Desire, and Action.

However, I would like to reemphasize one point about attracting attention. The attention-getting device must be related to the benefits of your service or it will detract from your basic selling idea. Attracting attention for attention's sake is certainly not the answer.

As adman Bill Bernbach said:

> If you stand a man on his head you'll get people to look at your ad, but you won't sell anything unless you're selling a product to keep things from falling from the man's pockets. . . . We work and sweat to be relevant, fresh, original, and imaginative. You can do things that are fresh, original, and imaginative, but irrelevant, and be a bad advertising man.*

Pollster Alfred Pollitz summed it up:

> What are some of the conclusions about effective advertising which have emerged from consumer studies and experiments. . . . One conclusion is that gimmicks, cleverness, witticisms, or ingenious and tricky word combinations do not add to, but rather subtract from, the effectiveness of advertising. . . . Efficiency in advertising seems to depend on the use of simple language—simple direct presentations of sales arguments—and the avoidance of tricky attention-getting devices unrelated to the product itself.**

You must start off with an idea of interest to the viewer or listener, with the promise of a benefit from using your service, and then present the idea in the most creative, freshest way possible.

WRITING FOR THE BROADCAST MEDIA

The heart of creating an effective broadcast commercial is the basic selling idea. "The basic selling concept, the compelling reason to buy, the unique angle—these are the guts of a commercial and the toughest part to formulate," wrote adman Hank Seiden. "They're worth their weight in gold and deserve 90 percent of the time spent on a commercial by the agency and the client. The remaining 10 percent should be the execu-

---

*Otto Kleppner, *Advertising Procedures*, Englewood Cliffs, N.J.: Prentice-Hall, 1966.
**Kleppner, *op. cit.*

tion."* So before you run off and start getting involved in commercials, create a strong basic selling concept.

Even though the basic principles for all advertising may be the same, the creative techniques used will be different. You have to familiarize yourself with both the similarities and differences between radio and TV before you can create for either medium.

Don't make the mistake of thinking that radio and TV commercials are the same except that one has a visual dimension. It is true that both are graphic media. One uses pictures that can be seen, while the other conjures up visual images in the mind of the listener. But just adding pictures to your radio sound track or just taking your TV sound and using it for radio will not work. You must create specific commercials for each medium.

Television is a medium of demonstration, whereas radio is a medium of imagination. This means that in TV you should be showing the reader the benefits of your practice through a strong visual presentation that creates credibility.

In creating radio commercials, you are trying to stimulate the mind of the listener. You have to use words, sound effects, and music that evoke graphic images in the listener's mind. And you can use a single voice, a dialogue, or the entire New York Philharmonic to get your message across.

Another difference between radio and TV is that people can be doing something else while listening to radio. They can be driving, working, doing homework, or eating. Listeners can be using all their powers of concentration or none of them. On the other hand, television is a medium where you have to devote all your attention to the tube to get the complete message.

THE BASICS OF EFFECTIVE RADIO AND TV COMMERCIALS

Before we go any further, let's review some of the basics that go into making an effective commercial:

1. *Know your audience.* What types of people are you trying to reach with your commercial? Are they young, middle income, college educated? Knowing your potential clients/patients (C/Ps) will help you create the right message. Furthermore, it can be extremely helpful in selecting stations, programs, and time periods that deliver the right target audience.

2. *Check the concept.* One ad agency creative director said, "All the money in the world cannot save a commercial that has no strong basic

---

*Hank Seiden. *Advertising Pure and Simple.* New York: AMACOM, 1978.

idea to begin with." So before you run off and start producing a commercial, check your concept. Every commercial should have a unique selling proposition. It comes from analyzing your practice, the marketplace, the competition, and the target audience. You will have to state it in 10, 30, or 60 seconds—depending on how much time you need (and can afford) to communicate your message.

3. *Keep it simple.* Throughout this book, I have constantly stressed one point that is essential to all advertising: Keep your message simple. Simplicity is the key to creating a message for radio and TV. You have only about 150 words in a minute commercial to say everything about your practice, so you have to make every word count. Keep it short—and stay with one major idea. In order to be remembered, you have to be single-minded.

Stick to one basic benefit. Repeat it in as many different ways as possible. You can use supporting facts, but always return to the original premise.

Your commercials will be successful only if they are to the point and not cluttered with many ideas. Your announcement is being aired with many others, sandwiched between programming that will divert attention away from what you have to say.

Therefore, resist the temptation to put everything about your practice into words. A good writer can say in 12 words what it takes a tyro 112 to say. Editing and cutting out meaningless words that detract from your message is essential. A typical one-minute radio spot might run 150 words, but if you cut out words, the delivery and presentation can be even more effective.

4. *Keep it conversational.* If you want to make a commercial believable, write the way people talk. It should sound natural and easy flowing, and on a one-to-one basis. Pretend that you're sitting in your office talking to a potential C/P about your practice. Use a friendly tone, and avoid all professional jargon that is unfamiliar to the average person. Use simple but descriptive words. Keep the sentences short. Avoid complicated thoughts. The sure way to tell beginners in the ad business is that they use words to try to impress other people rather than to communicate ideas to the listener or viewer. They'll use words like *termination* for *end* and *facilitate* instead of *help*. Opt for the simple, concrete, and specific word.

After you have finished, read the copy aloud a couple of times. You'll find that you can eliminate clumsy phrases and thoughts. Edit and cut your copy until it flows smoothly.

5. *Make it believable.* Believability is probably the most important component of all advertising. A 1978 study by Yankelovich, Skelly & White revealed that 70 percent of Americans were concerned with questions of truth, distortion, and exaggeration in advertising. If your target audience believes your message, then you've accomplished one of the aims of your advertising. Talk to people in a straight manner, and don't insult their intelligence. Be honest with your potential C/Ps and try to understand their needs and desires—as well as their fears. Because of the immediacy of broadcast commercials, believability can be destroyed by a bad concept or poor presentation. Present your practice in terms of believable benefits.

6. *Repetition counts.* Most successful advertisers use repetition to build identity in the marketplace. They realize that there are two major points that should be repeated over and over again:

Your name or company name.
Your basic selling concept or benefit.

Advertisers recognize that mentioning their names as often as possible builds recognition. The reason for this in broadcast advertising is obvious: The first time your name is mentioned, most people do not hear it. The second time it appears, it barely registers with the audience. The third time, people may hear it, but they're not sure. By the fourth time, the name may finally register with the listener or viewer. And if your name is unusual or has a foreign derivation, spelling it out can double the impact. Many advertisers have done this with great success.

If you are launching a new advertising campaign and you want to build awareness, mention your name as often as possible and tie it in with your selling theme or slogan. When the name becomes associated with the basic concept, the two will eventually become interchangeable. For example, when you hear the slogan "We try harder," you immediately think of Avis. The two have become synonymous.

If you're a large company like Kodak or General Electric and have already established an image and created awareness, then the spot can be just as effective if your name is mentioned once or twice. However, such sparse use of your name should be attempted only when you have built familiarity with your audience over an extended period of time.

7. *Make it memorable.* When you consider that only 16 percent of all viewers can identify the sponsor of a TV commercial, you realize why you have to make it memorable. Your commercial should not only attract at-

tention but get the audience involved in your message. You will have to strike a chord in the presentation that will be remembered by potential clients.

So if you produce a commercial, stick to one basic theme. It might be affordable fees, convenience, or your unique specialty. Also, if you use a spokesperson, use the same person in every commercial to build identity from one spot to the next. You want continuity in your commercials, so produce them all in a similar manner. Use similar production methods and art techniques. If you use film to shoot a commercial, don't change to videotape for the sake of change. Build recognition in all your commercials by using your logo and other graphics—and use them for the duration of the campaign.

Advertisers use several production techniques that help them build continuity and recognition. These production tricks can also save you a good deal of money if used properly. They include:

The donut commercial. Sometimes it's called "bookends," but whatever you call it, it has a standard introduction, which is the same each time it is aired. The middle part of the commercial is left free for a change of message whenever you desire. The ending, like the beginning, is prerecorded and has the same message every time it runs. This is one of the techniques most frequently used by retailers and small advertisers seeking to build recognition.

The core commercial. In this case, a number of openings and closings are prerecorded and are kept in a library by the advertiser or station. The middle part of the commercial, or core, is always the same. The advertiser has the option of changing his opening "hook" and closing "sting" to suit the changes in the marketplace but retains the same core in each commercial.

The open-faced sandwich commercial. This commercial is divided into two sections, rather than three as in the core and donut spots. The opening is standard and never changes. It is generally longer than those used in the core or donut commercials. It can use up to half or more of the time available. The second section has information about your practice, which you can change as you desire.

8. *Use a "hook" in your commercial.* Every successful commercial has a hook at the beginning. What is a hook? It's a device that will get the listener's or viewer's attention.

No one has to listen to or look at commercials—and most people tend to pay little attention to them—so you have to use something that will capture their attention. Start off with a hook that will evoke curiosity and interest. Sometimes the hook might be music, a sound effect, or a jingle. In most cases, it's a provocative statement that draws their attention.

Here are some hooks being used by professionals on radio and TV:

○ "At one time or another, we all have to face a serious legal problem, whether it's a traffic accident, divorce, bankruptcy, or buying a new home. When it occurs, most people don't have any idea of how to find the right kind of legal help."

○ "Does the high cost of dental care have you concerned? Does it keep you and your family from receiving quality dental care?"

○ "Finding a good lawyer when you need one can be a frustrating experience. You can ask your friends, check the Yellow Pages, but when you eventually find one, how do you know the lawyer you select has the right kind of experience to handle your particular problem?"

○ "When did you last have a thorough medical examination? Years ago? Or maybe you've never had one! In either case, you owe it to yourself to get a checkup now!"

9. *Use a "sting" at the end.* No, I'm not talking about the movie with Robert Redford and Paul Newman. I mean an expression at the end of the commercial that gives it more bite.

A sting can be an outright pitch for business, a major benefit of your service, or even a surprising bit of news. It can also be a humorous restatement of the basic selling theme. The point is, it should be there. Without it, the commercial is like the salesman who makes a call and forgets to ask for the order.

10. *Decide how much time you need.* One of the most important decisions that every advertiser who is considering broadcast advertising makes is how long the commercial should be. Consider your marketing objectives, advertising strategy, message, and total budget. After a day or so, you should be able to determine exactly how much time you will really need to tell your story.

There are 10-, 20-, 30-, and 60-second announcements. By special arrangement with the station, you can also buy extra long spots (2–5 minutes) for special uses. Direct-response advertisers like to use 2-minute commercials to sell records and other items on late-night television.

However, the most popular length of time for the nonnetwork TV commercial is 30 seconds; 81 percent are 30 seconds long. On radio, the 60-second commercial is the most popular for a number of reasons. It permits the advertiser to deliver an effective message by separating the commercial from all the clutter around it, and it's just long enough to say things with impact. Also the rates charged for a 60-second commercial are the most economical buy in radio. A 30-second spot could cost 75 percent of a 60-second spot. So it's most efficient to use one-minute radio spots. The American Dental Plan (#12) and the Metropolitan Lawyer Referral Service (#13) have both used 60-second radio spots effectively. The MLRS spot uses the voice of John Rayburn, a well-known personality in the Denver area.

Equally important, you should bear in mind that commercials of different time lengths are used for different purposes. The 10-second TV announcement is used to stir a fast reaction to a single message. It is normally used when an advertiser has already established an identity and wants a quick attention getter to reinforce the ad campaign. The 30-second TV commercial is used when the advertiser wants to give specific details about the company product or service. This time length is the most frequently selected by advertisers because it allows just enough time to support a commercial's basic selling message. Finally, the 60-second TV spot is used by advertisers who want to give a lot of information to the viewer.

In any event, the length of your commercial should be finalized before you attempt to create a message. You have to know if you can deliver the message in 30 seconds as opposed to 60 seconds. If you find that no matter what you do, you cannot deliver an effective message in the time selected—and repeat it frequently—then you better sit down and rethink your marketing and advertising strategy.

TYPES OF RADIO COMMERCIALS

In 1972 the Radio Advertising Bureau (RAB) conducted a survey of the different creative approaches used in radio commercials. These announcements were chosen from the CLIO Awards Festival, an annual competition recognizing the most effective local, regional, and national spots. The spots are judged on the basis of overall excellence in creativity.

The commercials studied by the RAB were analyzed with the goal of isolating principal elements—such as humor, music, dialogue—that went into their construction. Eight elements could be clearly isolated. Six of these occurred in at least one-third of the commercials.

American Dental Plan
60-Second Radio Commercial

Does the high cost of dental care have you concerned?
Does it keep you and your family from receiving quality
dental care? Then write down this important phone number:

800—325—6400.

That's the number of the American Dental Plan. Now, for the
first time, you can receive quality dental care from a private
neighborhood dentist selected by you from the hundreds of
American Dental Plan participating dentists. Annual membership
entitles you to complete cleaning, full mouth X rays, complete oral
examination diagnosis, fluoride treatments for children,
gum treatments and more. All twice a year and all absolutely
free. And our reduced dental fees can save you up to 70 percent
on your dental bills.

What's the catch? There is no catch. American Dental Plan
acts as a source of patients for dentists. . . . It's good business
for them, and good value for you.

Join now. Save hundreds of dollars on dental care from your
own American Dental Plan private family dentist. Call 800—325—
6400 for membership information. That's 800—325—6400.
The American Dental Plan gives you lots of reasons to make you
smile.

Metropolitan Lawyer Referral Service
60-Second Radio Commercial

Hi, this is John Rayburn, and I'd like to talk with you about money and finances.

Whether you don't have enough money to meet your bills and may be considering bankruptcy or can't get people who owe you money to pay their bills, you have certain legal rights you should know about.

And if you want to protect the assets you have accumulated, estate planning can involve much more than simply filing a will. There are investment and tax shelter laws governing ways to cut taxes or give gifts to minors, for example. These laws protect your rights and your money, but first you must know what the laws are and how they work.

That's why you should know about the Metropolitan Lawyer Referral Service. MLRS is a public service, approved by the Bar Association, created to help you find professional legal help quickly and easily.
MLRS can find you a lawyer experienced in your particular problem, and make an appointment for you, generally all in the same day.

All you have to do is call . . . 831–8000. That's 831–8000. The Metropolitan Lawyer Referral Service.

Key Elements	Percentages of Use
Announcer used in primary role	47
Humor	46
Singing	45
Dialogue/interview	39
Sound effects	33
Announcer used in secondary role	32
Instrumental music only	18
Celebrity announcer	5

In no instance was a commercial built on only one of the eight elements. All the commercials were constructed from a number of different combinations. "Which of these elements is used and to what degree is determined by the creative approach used. The number of elements which may be used is limited; the number of creative approaches for a commercial is infinite and limited only by your imagination," stated the RAB report.

PRODUCING THE RADIO COMMERCIAL

Every radio commercial starts with a script. The script is generally between 130 and 150 words for one minute of air time. Sound effects, music, and situations are indicated where they fall in the script. Dialogue is presented like a play. Copy should be submitted typed double-spaced, using upper- and lower- case letters since they're easier to read.

In writing a script, every word counts. You have to figure on no more than 25 words for every 10 seconds of time. Remember that you want a commercial to be read with maximum impact, so select your words carefully. A good radio copywriter will paint a picture with words.

Many radio stations have copywriters on staff who will write scripts for your commercial. They also have recording studios and other production facilities for your use. Most stations will even supply an announcer who will record your message to your satisfaction. There is no charge for all of this, because the stations are interested in selling air time. (But if you decide to use the commercial on another stations, there will be a charge.) So consider working with your local radio stations, through your station representative.

A word of caution about using addresses and telephone numbers in your commercial. They are extremely hard to remember, even when they are repeated a number of times. If you want to refer to a telephone number—and many professionals are using telephone numbers in their spots—consider simplifying the number. For instance, the Denture Center in New York City invites inquiries on radio by asking the listener to dial D-E-N-T-U-R-E. Contact your telephone company business office and find out what can be done about simplifying your telephone number.

If you must give the location of your practice in your commercial, avoid giving the exact address. Numbers can be confusing, and no one remembers them. Instead, just give the street intersection. For example, "Located on 34th Street and Fifth Avenue." Or if you are located in a shopping center, mall, or professional building, mention the name. And if you're located near a famous landmark, use it. For example, "Just opposite Macy's in White Plains."

Remember, you're expecting too much of your audience if you think they will write down your telephone number and address. They won't.

Another thing to avoid on the radio is gimmick sound effects that will draw attention away from your message. Some attention-getting devices are great, provided they relate to your basic selling idea. They will increase recall and effectiveness. But there are temptations to use too many attention-getting devices, and in most cases, they will overpower your selling message.

CREATING THE TV COMMERCIAL

There is no phase of advertising where so little is known by advertisers as in TV commercial production. One ad manager wrote, "I can see a storyboard, choose the talent—but I never really know what's going on until the commercial is finished and its too late to make changes."

Most TV production still remains a mystery to advertisers. The advertiser places an incredible amount of trust in the hands of the agency creative director, the producer, the director, and all the other specialized people involved in making a commercial. The top producers and directors have the ability to visualize what the finished commercial will look like and to make it better than the original storyboard. They can literally take an idea and make it come alive.

The first step in producing a TV commercial is either a script or a rough storyboard. A script is usually divided into two vertical columns (#14). The left-hand column describes the video and casting instructions. In the right-hand column, the audio part of the commercial is typed.

Many professionals still prefer the copy-script approach. They think that too much emphasis is put on the visual drawing and not enough on the visual concept, and that the concept can best be expressed through words. "Storyboards are OK," wrote Hooper White in *Advertising Age*

Minnesota Dental Association

30-Second Television Commercial

"Dropping In"

VIDEO	AUDIO
MCU businessman talking on phone to business associate	ANNCR (VO): How many times have you thought about going to the dentist and then put it off?
	MAN: If I wanted it that way, Harry, I'd have asked you for it. My
Man looks into camera	teeth? I'm a busy man.
CUT to slow-motion false teeth falling in limbo	
CUT to MCU housewife sitting exhausted at kitchen table	WOMAN: I took the kids. First things first.
CUT to slow-motion false teeth falling in limbo	
CUT to MCU view through mouth of dentist examining teeth	DENTIST: Your gum disease is under control, for now.
	PATIENT: 'ood, Wha' neks?
	DENTIST: Take care of your gums... and
CUT to MCU patient's teeth in hand mirror	teeth... and they'll be even better next time.
CUT to slow-motion false teeth falling into glass of water on limbo set. SUPER: <u>Drop in on the dentist every few months, before you're dropping in every night.</u>	ANNCR (VO): Drop in on the dentist every few months, before you're dropping in every night.

MCU = medium close-up; CUT = scene changes; ANNCR (VO) = voice off camera; SUPER = type superimposed over background.

(July 23, 1979), "but written-out production plans are better. You can describe your suggestions for casting better in writing than you can in drawing."

Today, however, most agencies will go directly to the rough storyboard in creating a commercial. Like the layout of a print ad, the storyboard is a blueprint of what the commercial will look like (#15). It is a series of roughly drawn frames in sequence with video instructions and audio copy typed in a panel below. The storyboard serves a number of purposes; most importantly, it sets the direction and pace of the commercial. It is also used to obtain bids from producers on the cost of making the commercial. Photostatic copies of the storyboard are sent to several production companies for bids.

Some ad agencies like to use the one-frame storyboard. In this presentation, you use one powerful illustration or photograph, with your copy below, to indicate your central idea. This works particularly well when you have one main character in a setting that doesn't change. It might be a lawyer in his office or next to a storefront delivering a powerful message about the uniqueness of his practice.

The storyboard is not the finished commercial; it doesn't move, has no sound, and is generally drawn in a rough manner. It may not be the ideal communications tool for producing a commercial, but it's probably the most acceptable way to get approval, bids, and general understanding of what the commercial will be. The set, location, equipment and talent requirements, length of shooting, and other costs will be determined from the storyboard. The most important thing to remember when shooting a commercial is to stick to the basic concept of the storyboard.

Making a Commercial

Important as it is to have a unique concept in a TV commercial, it is equally important that the commercial be executed in a creative, fresh, and believable manner. You can waste a lot of money with an ineffective, poorly produced commercial. It's the only thing the viewer sees and hears and it's no surprise that viewers can't even remember the vast majority of commercials on the air. Most commercials are dull and unimaginative. In fact, research indicates that 90 percent of TV viewers don't understand some aspect of the commercials and programs they are watching.

One of the things that turns most potential TV advertisers off is the cost of producing a TV commercial. Today, a commercial can cost anywhere from $5,000 to $100,000; there is really no limit to how much you can spend on making a commercial. The cost of the average 30-second

TV commercial runs around $25,000. This figure can vary depending on the talent chosen and the complexity of the commercial.

Producing a commercial has both technical and creative costs. The technical include the normal elements of production, such as the costs of hiring a producer, director, cameraman, soundman, and other members of the crew; renting all equipment, props, and a stage or location; transportation; processing; editing; and final completion. They also include the cost of transferring the film to videotape for station use. The creative costs include the fees for talent, animation, visual and sound effects, and musical background.

There is one other important aspect of TV production costs that you should know: There is no correlation between the cost of a commercial and its effectiveness. You can produce a commercial for $100,000, and it can be a bomb. And there have been commercials produced for $5,000 that have been very potent.

You can keep TV production costs under control and make a commercial at a relatively low cost by taking the precautionary steps outlined below:

1. *Submit your storyboard to TV stations for approval.* This can avoid a lot of grief later on. If you are considering running your commercial on several stations in your area, submit copies of your storyboard to the continuity clearance department of each station. Don't go ahead and produce the commercial until you have clearance from all the stations. If you make any claims, the stations will probably ask you to substantiate them with documentation. Each station has different standards of acceptability. Where one might accept your commercial without reservation, another might reject it. Recently, one network reported that it rejected one-third of all storyboards. It would also be wise to work through your station representatives. They might be able to expedite clearance for your announcements. But if it is rejected, don't expect your rep to be able to help. Reps don't have the clout to fight the station's acceptability standards.

Another thing you might consider doing is submitting your storyboard to your state or county professional association to see if it falls within the guidelines set forth in the code of ethics. It's best to have the approval of your peers before venturing into a new area like TV advertising.

2. *Ask your local TV station for help.* If you don't have an advertising agency, you might consider using the services of your local television station and the station's production department. Work through your station representative, because he can help you produce a commercial at a rea-

sonable cost. He can also help take some of the mystery out of making a commercial by explaining the variety of production techniques available.

When you call your local station and ask for a sales representative, make sure that the station sends one who has experience with other professionals. Ask the rep to bring tapes of commercials that have been run by dentists, physicians, lawyers, and accountants. The rep can help you find local creative talent and schedule studio time to produce your commercial. He's sure to invite you to the station for a tour and introduce you to all the people who can help you make a commercial. These copywriters, art directors, cameramen, sound engineers, and lighting experts are all available to discuss your objectives and how to go about reaching them. They'll advise you on special effects, graphics, and where to get the right talent.

You'll be truly surprised at the variety of ways a good station production studio can help you get your message across. The studio's array of equipment, including video cameras, videotape recorders, and sets, can be of great assistance to you. Usually there is no charge for using facilities that already exist, but you'll probably have to pay for the production of any special backgrounds, sets, signs, and title cards, as well as for on-location filming or anything that requires the movement of personnel and equipment to your location. A well-stocked station can help you produce an exciting commercial that has impact.

Commercials taped at your local station can often include music as part of the total production. The station can show you how to do this. Music that is in the public domain can be obtained from station libraries at little or no cost. Music can help create a mood that becomes identified with your commercials.

In addition to the equipment mentioned, all TV stations have 16mm motion picture equipment and TV minicameras that can go on location. The minicamera is a portable videotape camera, which looks like a large movie camera. It opens up another possibility—recording effective, professional commercials in your own office. Although you will probably be charged for these on-location services, the fees tend to be low because stations want to encourage you to advertise.

In major metropolitan areas, such as New York and Los Angeles, stations are reluctant to get involved in producing commercials. However, the station rep can refer you to freelance creative and production people to produce your announcement.

3. *Create your own TV commercials.* There are times that a professional may just have to produce his own commercials, particularly if he is lo-

cated around a big city where TV stations don't make their production facilities available. It's possible for a practitioner to make an effective commercial at a reasonable cost if he knows production techniques. He can bring camera, sound, lighting, and script experts into his office. If he is articulate and experienced, he can probably do the entire commercial in one take. If he presents himself well and has something to say, he could sit at his desk and do a convincing spot. "The most important thing a practitioner should remember is to be himself . . . emphasizing the benefits of his practice and minimizing embellishments," said one TV production consultant. "This could be the ideal commercial, because you can get hurt by putting too many production details in a spot. You don't need a lot of experience in production. The best advice is to keep it simple. Tell who, what, where, and why. If you have a unique practice, tell the audience that. I've seen brilliant commercials using the camera focused on one person saying it as it is."

Some professionals are producing their own commercials using the technique described above. One such lawyer writes his own script. He rehearses, using a home video camera and video cassette recording system, until he is completely satisfied with his performance and delivery. Afterward, he brings the complete production crew to his office and records the commercial. His "advance preparation saved a lot of money," he said.

Another inexpensive way to produce a TV commercial is to use one, two, or more 35mm slides. These slides are placed on a projector in a "telecine" room at the station's studio and picked up by a "film chain" camera. As many as ten slides can be shown in a ten-second spot. A station announcer reads the script, and it's recorded on tape. The film of the slides and the recorded script are then run simultaneously and transferred to videotape with proper synchronization. It's a great way to produce many commercials because of the low cost.

4. *Work with an ad agency.* There are several things you should know about working with your ad agency in producing a commercial. Once your agency has finalized the storyboard and obtained approval from the station's continuity clearance department, it will send photostatic copies to at least three production companies for competitive bids. Each production company will be given the same exact specifications (specs) so you can get accurate estimates. Each spec should reflect the basic concept and the marketing strategy. Your agency should also tell the production company what target audience you are trying to reach. This information is important and can influence the creative output.

There are hundreds of competent production companies all over the country, but the best ones are located in New York City and Los Angeles. That's because the top talent is located in these cities. Production companies can be classified on the basis of creativity and efficiency. Also, some production firms work best in a studio, while others work better on location. The best way to judge a company's ability is to take a look at sample reels. Look at the special effects that you might want to use in your own commercial. Some techniques that you can expect to see include a slice-of-life dramatization, straight narration, and animation. You'll also see many optical and electronic techniques that you never paid attention to such as zooming in and out, close-ups, superimpositions, fade-ins and fade-outs, cuts, and split screens.

Your agency will collect and analyze the bids, clarify specifications, and discuss production details before assigning the commercial to a production house. You should discuss the bids with your agency before they award the contract.

After the selection has been made, there will be preproduction meetings between agency people, the production company, and yourself. Every aspect of the commercial will be discussed—what talent to use, what they will wear, the sets, the length of time for each scene, and the props—before the camera starts to shoot.

Another thing to discuss is production time. One of the major reasons why most commercials turn out to be very expensive is the time factor. If you have to rush a commercial and produce it in a few days, the costs can really mount. Most commercials today are pressed for time—and the bills for overtime charges start to flow in from the production house. One way to avoid this is to work with your agency and production firm in developing a time schedule. Planning in advance can save you overtime charges for film processing or rush editing.

The production house will pick the specialists involved in making the commercial. This will include a director, who will be responsible for the overall look and quality of the commercial. The cameraman will be responsible for filming the action. The soundman will be responsible for making sure that all the sound is properly recorded without interference and outside noise. The electrician (or gaffer) will make sure that everything is lit according to the director's wishes. A script person will make sure that everything is shot and nothing is left out. He or she will also time each sequence with a stopwatch so that it conforms to the storyboard. An assistant cameraman will move the camera around according to the director's instructions. There will also be set designers, prop men, make-up men, and wardrobe stylists.

Working together, all these experts will turn out a professional commercial on film (or videotape) as it was conceived in the storyboard. Normally, they will take many shots of each sequence. They will shoot and reshoot until the agency and the producer are satisfied that they have excellent results. The best of these "takes" will be processed and projected for inspection the following day. These are called "rushes"; they become the working print for making the final release film print. The pictures and sound are produced separately but are shown to you simultaneously. You can still make changes at this point without it costing you a fortune. The next step is editing. The editor will be responsible for taking the film and sound track and piecing it together into a finished commercial. Eventually the entire commercial will be duplicated on 16mm film with a sound track and will be sent to each TV station. Some stations specify videotape, so you might have to transfer the film to tape.

Using Talent to Deliver Your Message

There are many places to go to select professional talent to deliver your message. A few suggestions follow, with the advantages and disadvantages of each.

Delivering your own commercial. Many advertisers are tempted to deliver their own commercials. In fact, many national advertisers have featured their top executives in commercials, from Lee Iacocca telling you about Chrysler to Frank Perdue pushing his tender chickens with a touch of humor. However, unless you have a flair for the dramatic and a unique personality, avoid giving your own commercials. Leave it to the professionals. Nothing can destroy an effective message like a third-rate presentation.

Using the station talent. Many radio and TV stations have announcers who are available to deliver your commercial at little or no cost. If the station has a union agreement, you will have to comply with the contract. Ask your station rep to have the announcer tape a reading of your commercial, and listen to it carefully at home. Does the personality project the image that you are trying to convey? Does the tonal quality of the voice project confidence and believability? Listen carefully and decide if you want to use the station talent.

Using local personalities. Many local newscasters, sports figures, and professional actors will be only too happy to do your commercial at a set fee. You will have to negotiate the dollar figure with them or their agents. These personalities may have a strong identity with a city or geographic area, so why not use their popularity to promote your practice. In building referrals for lawyers in the Denver area, the Metropolitan Lawyer Referral Service used a well-known former newscaster as its spokesman. He had believability and recognition in the community, and the commercials produced outstanding results. Fees for talent can vary from individual to individual and from city to city.

Using a talent agent. There is another way to get talent, and that is going through a talent agent. The agents' main job is to get work for their clients, for a 10 percent commission. They are franchised by the Screen Actors Guild (SAG) and the American Federation of Television and Radio Artists (AFTRA). SAG and AFTRA set a minimum scale for performers, but most are paid over scale. The fee will be negotiated between your ad agency and the talent agent, who will try to get as much as the traffic will bear. It takes a skilled negotiator to keep these costs in line.

The minimum scale will vary depending upon the market, the duration of the campaign, and the type of commercial. A wild spot—a commercial running any time of day—bought for a particular market will have just one payment regardless of the number of times it plays in a 13-week period. The scale also varies from city to city. In 1980 the minimum scale for an on-camera spot in New York was $545, and $475 in Los Angeles and Chicago. A voice-over in New York was $385 in Los Angeles and Chicago.

On radio, the minimum scale for a 13-week wild spot in the New York area is $160. In Chicago and Los Angeles, the scale is $145. Remember this is the minimum scale and subject to inflationary increases. If the commercial is aired beyond the 13-week period, there will be an additional payment to the performer unless you have negotiated an all-inclusive agreement. This could be a flat fee for a one-year period, including use of the personality in print ads and other promotional materials. How much you pay depends on how shrewdly you negotiate with the performers.

Many professionals are now experimenting with well-known personalities in their radio commercials. The Preventive Medicine Institute/Strang Clinic uses Arthur Godfrey as its spokesman. No one has more believability and recognition than the "ol' redhead." Godfrey delivers 60-second commercials urging radio listeners to come into the clinic for a checkup (#16). These commercials are targeted to mature audiences. One commer-

PMI/Strang Clinic
60-Second Radio Commercial

This is your ol' friend—the ol' redhead—Arthur Godfrey reminding you that we all suffer from aches and pains from time to time. And often they go away by themselves. But when symptoms persist, it's time to get a physical checkup. Your problem may prove to be a minor one—the Good Lord willing. Or it may be a sign of an illness that can be cured if detected early. So if you haven't been feeling up to par ... or if you've been troubled by unexplained symptoms that hang on, get a thorough diagnostic examination at the Preventive Medicine Institute/Strang Clinic. Strang Clinic is an outstanding medical facility that specializes in such checkups. For more information, just call PMI/Strang Clinic at 212 683–1000. There's no obligation. That's S-T-R-A-N-G—Strang Clinic, conveniently located on East 34th Street.

Give yourself peace of mind. Call 683–1000 between 8:30 and 5:00 any weekday.

Tell them Arthur Godfrey told you to call.

cial is particularly memorable, because he recounts his experiences in battling cancer. In a less successful case, comedian Henny Youngman was hired to act as the spokesman for Universal Dental Centers. In one-minute radio spots, Youngman starts off with a series of jokes about how dentists are overcharging patients. Eventually, he gets into his pitch about Universal Dental Centers and its benefits. It all ends up as an unbelievable announcement, with listeners remembering Henny Youngman rather than the sponsor.

Film or Videotape?

Despite the continuing inroads made in taping TV commercials, the vast majority of commercials are produced on film. In the New York market, 60 percent of all commercials are produced on film. The reason is that most producers are more comfortable with film than with other media. Most producers cite the look of the finished product as their main concern. They refer to the texture, richness, and other qualities of film they feel are lacking in tape. Tape tends to have a flat, synthetic quality.

Many big-time advertisers like Procter & Gamble use 16mm film (instead of 35mm film) for commercials in order to save money. They have found that there is no conclusive proof that the sales message is adversely affected by the grainier texture of 16mm film. They also believe that the average TV viewer at home cannot tell the difference. Likewise, smaller-budget advertisers are also using 16mm to shoot commercials and saving money in the process.

The main advantage of videotape is its ability to deliver the commercial immediately. You have the opportunity to replay what you have just shot and make instant judgments. It is also possible to produce a finished commercial on tape in 24 hours. It is not uncommon to shoot on stage in the morning, add voice-overs in the afternoon, edit at night, and have a finished commercial the next day.

PRETESTING RADIO AND TV COMMERCIALS

With the soaring costs of radio and TV time, most large advertisers are pretesting their commercials. They want to go on the air with a message that will have the greatest chance of success. They want to know what copy appeal and creative approach is best—and will be remembered.

There are a number of companies that specialize in pretesting commercials and offer a standard testing package at a specific fee. The methods of these companies are different as are their objectives. Many are capable of custom designing a program for measuring copy appeals, recall of brand name and major message points, and the stopping and holding power of a commercial.

In many cases, the research companies will play the commercials and then conduct extensive interviews to determine what the respondents liked and disliked. These interviews may be conducted at home, on the telephone, in a central facility, in a mobile testing laboratory, or in a shopping center. The standard test sample number will vary from firm to firm and will meet the demographic specifications furnished by the client.

The cost of testing a commercial varies from company to company. A pretest can cost anywhere from $600 to $10,000 depending on what is required.

If you would like to obtain the names of research organizations, write to the Radio Advertising Bureau or TV Bureau of Advertising (see Appendix 3).

CHAPTER 12

Creating Outdoor, Transit, and Direct-Mail Advertising

MORE AND MORE ADVERTISERS are considering direct-mail, transit, and outdoor advertising to deliver their messages. The reason for this is the soaring costs of all media, as well as the efficiency of certain media (like direct mail) in delivering a specific audience. Many advertising directors have vented their frustration with the inflated time and space costs of TV, magazines, and newspapers. One said, "We spend a lot of money in television and other media and frankly I don't know if we are getting our money's worth any more."

Many professionals are now using other media to deliver their messages. A number use transit advertising; others are experimenting with outdoor advertising; and a majority are using direct mail to reach and influence their target audiences. In some cases, direct mail may be the only medium—or the major medium—used by the professionals to advertise their practices. They are testing these media and creating unique messages to sell the benefits of their practices.

OUTDOOR ADVERTISING

Outdoor advertising offers a unique opportunity for professionals. You can buy just one sign or hundreds of signs to get your message across. You can buy a poster campaign throughout a city, or you can buy just one billboard near your office. You can buy a sign on a street or along a major highway. You have unusual flexibility with outdoor advertising, at one of the lowest cost-per-thousand viewers. It allows you to reach masses of people or target specific audiences.

But what is outdoor advertising? It is the printed posters and painted signs that we see on buildings, along highways or streets, and in shopping malls. It is usually directed to people on the move—whether they are in automobiles, on mass transit, or just walking. Outdoor advertising does not include the variety of signs that you see on stores, on factories, and in fast-food restaurants. These are on-premise signs to identify the business on whose property they appear.

172

In the past, outdoor advertising took many shapes and forms. In 1965, however, the Highway Beautification Act eliminated many billboards that were eyesores along highways and in cities. In fact, since 1965 about 100,000 signs that did not conform to industry standards were removed along interstate and primary highways. All these signs are subject to local, state, and federal laws governing the placement of signs. A number of states even prohibit signs along highways. The overall result of this action was the standardizing of outdoor signs along highways and in cities.

Standardized Posters and Signs

There are several standardized poster sizes. The large billboard panel will take three different posters: the 24-sheet, 30-sheet, and bleed poster (see Figure 8). These are all in a proportion of 2½ to 1. There are also the 8-sheet poster and the bulletin. Table 10 shows the variety of outdoor sign sizes available. The printed poster is attached to the billboard with an adhesive.

The 24-sheet poster got its name many years ago when printing presses were smaller and it took 24 separate sheets of paper to make one poster. Today, there are large printing presses that make it possible to print a poster of this size with 10 sheets of paper. The old name, however, still persists. The area between the design and the frame is covered by white space that resembles a mat around a picture. It is the most popular of all billboard sizes. The 30-sheet poster provides about 25 percent more space than the 24-sheet poster in the same area, by reducing the border of white space that surrounds the poster.

In a bleed poster, the design is carried all the way to the frame. It is 40 percent larger than the 24-sheet poster, since the entire blank area is printed on. There are slight variations in the overall size of the poster panels, so it is advisable to keep all important copy—such as logos and headlines—6 inches from the edge. This will guarantee that nothing important will be cut off the panel.

According to several sources, 8-sheet posters are the fastest growing

Table 10. Outdoor sign sizes.

Type of Sign	Production Method	Poster Size	Overall Size
24-sheet poster	Printed	8'8" × 19'6"	12'3" × 24'6"
30-sheet poster	Printed	9'7" × 21'7"	12'3" × 24'6"
Bleed poster	Printed	10'5" × 22'8"	12'3" × 24'6"
8-sheet poster	Printed	5' × 11'	6' × 12'
Bulletin	Painted	14' × 48'	14' × 48'

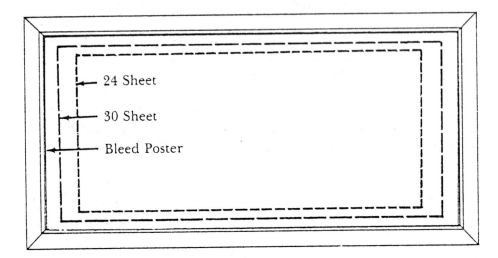

Figure 8. A large billboard panel with three different poster sizes.

segment of outdoor advertising. The reason for this is that the smaller size permits them to be located in cities and suburban areas, at almost eye level—8 feet off the ground. These mini-billboards can be used by any practioner.

Painted bulletins are prepared individually by artists either in the company shop or on location. The artists work from an accurate detailed layout that you submit in scale. The bulletin is 3½ times as long as it is high. It is nearly three times as large as the poster. The size of the bulletin can be increased through the use of extensions as big as 5 feet 6 inches at the top and 2 feet at the sides and bottom. These bulletins with extensions are called "embellished bulletins." Because of its size and flexibility in using embellishments, the bulletin can achieve many dramatic effects. One of these is the illusion of three dimensions on a two-dimensional surface. Another is multi-images produced by revolving panels.

Creating for Outdoor Advertising

Outdoor advertising is the largest physical form of advertising. It is designed to make an instantaneous and lasting impression. It is a reminder, identification, and selling medium.

Outdoor advertising requires a tremendous amount of discipline, because it must go to the heart of a selling proposition without frills or distractions. Most outdoor advertising will be viewed at a distance of 50 to 400 feet by people who are moving—whether walking or driving. The key to all outdoor advertising is "brevity, simplicity, and clarity," advises the Institute of Outdoor Advertising. The bolder the colors and the simpler the background, the better the outdoor advertisement. It has got to be powerful to attract attention. Two billboards used by the Minnesota Dental Association, one of the pioneers of outdoor professional advertising, show how powerful simplicity can be (#17).

As stated, brevity is essential to an effective message. Copy should be as short as possible; six or seven words are plenty. Each billboard should be designed to be seen 200 feet from the highway, by traffic passing at 55 miles per hour. The illustration should be simple and interesting so that it is easily recognizable.

Typefaces should also be simple, clean, and easy to read. Avoid ultra-bold or ultra-thin type. Bold typefaces become blobs when seen at long distances, while fine type tends to fade. It is generally a good idea to keep the use of capital letters to a minimum, since they are often hard to read. But they can sometimes be used effectively, as in the Minnesota Dental Association's billboard shown here. Spacing between letters should also be considered. Too little space will make the letters appear to merge when viewed from a distance.

In selecting colors for outdoor advertising, choose colors with high contrast in both hue (the identify of the color, such as red, green, blue, or yellow) and value (the lightness or darkness of the color). Contrasting colors are effective for distance viewing, whereas colors without contrast blend and make the sign less effective. Yellow and purple are dissimilar in both hue and value and are strong colors for outdoor use. Of course, white will go well with any strong dark color, and black is good with colors of light value. White also gives a poster a prestigious, professional look and should be considered by practitioners using outdoor advertising.

The same principles that apply to all outdoor advertising also apply to 8-sheet posters, because you must involve the reader and have just six or seven seconds to get your message across. This puts severe limits on your creative approach. So brevity and simplicity are the rules. The same design and artwork used in 24- and 30-sheet posters can be used for 8-sheet, since they are all in the same proportional scale. So new artwork isn't necessary if you are using the larger billboards.

Working with Your Outdoor Representative

Your outdoor representative can be invaluable in helping you prepare an effective sign. These sales reps will sit down with you and show you a portfolio of outdoor billboards. They will discuss billboard availabilities and guide you in planning your layout, copy, and illustration. They will

Ignore your
teeth and
they'll go away.

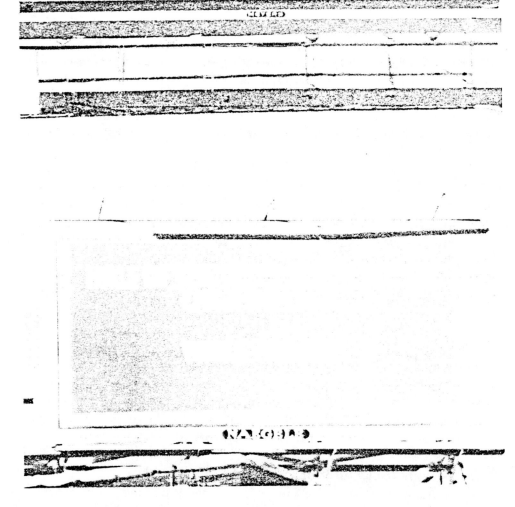

be able to advise you on what colors will be effective as well as what colors will stand up to the weather. (Certain colors will fade faster than others in harsh climates.) So ask your sales rep for his suggestions and advice.

If your rep isn't able to guide you in creating a billboard, his art department can. It has the experience for creating in this medium. The artist will first prepare a comprehensive rendering in scale, about 13½ inches by 6 inches for a poster and 21 inches by 6 inches for a painted bulletin.

Study the layout carefully. Also look at it from a distance of 50 feet, then start to walk toward it. This trick will point out the weaknesses as well as the strengths of your sign. A billboard must compete with many distractions, so your message should be absolutely clear. Make changes at this point in the design concept and avoid a lot of grief later on. The finished artwork for a poster will usually be prepared for submission to the printer in scale—27 inches by 12 inches or 36 inches by 16 inches. Artwork for a bulletin will also be submitted to the outdoor plant in scale—42 inches by 12 inches or 56 inches by 16 inches.

The outdoor advertising company will generally not charge for design services. However, you will have to pay for any photographs, illustrations, type, printing, or other additional costs incurred in producing your billboard. A bulletin will either be painted in the shop or on location. If it is painted in the shop, it will be transported in sections and assembled at the site. If the sign is painted on the site, it will be done by specialized artists and illustrators. If you would like more information on outdoor advertising, write to the Institute of Outdoor Advertising or Eight Sheet Outdoor Advertising Association (See Appendix 3).

TRANSIT ADVERTISING

Transit advertising by professionals is a reality. You see their posters and cards everywhere—on the outside of buses, inside subways, in commuter terminals, and on station platforms. Lawyers, dentists, and physicians are experimenting with this powerful medium. Transit advertising is exciting, and the potential for it is limited only by one's imagination.

Standardized Cards and Posters

The three major forms of transit advertising are interior car cards, traveling exterior posters, and terminal/station posters. Car cards are interior advertisements of standard sizes, which are placed overhead or on the ends of trains, buses, subway cars, and suburban railroad cars (see Figure 9). They also include the bigger cards found near the doors of

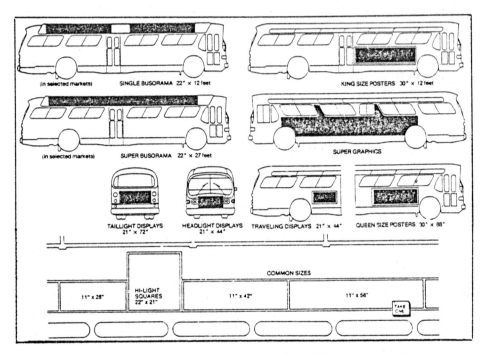

Figure 9. Types of interior and exterior car cards and bus signs.
(Reproduced by permission of TDI/Winston.)   .

trains. Interior bus cards range in size: 11 inches by 28 inches, 11 inches by 42 inches, or 11 inches by 56 inches. There are also larger cards, measuring 22 inches by 21 inches or 16 inches by 44 inches. You can also have take-one pads included on your sign, at an additional cost. This will increase the response rate if you have something to offer like a brochure. It will help you to measure the effectiveness of your advertising. However, you may be limited to just four pads per card by some transit companies.

Traveling exterior displays (also shown in Figure 9) are placed on the outside of buses. They are available in a variety of sizes and for different locations on the bus: front, rear, top, and sides. The various types of displays available include Bus-O-Ramas and posters.

A Bus-O-Rama is an illuminated panel, 22 inches by 12 feet, mounted on the roof of the bus. It is backlighted by fluorescent tubes. The advertiser's message is laminated to the face of the display area. Super Bus-O-Ramas are also used on the top of buses; these measure 22 inches by 27 feet.

There are a variety of different size posters that are mounted in frames on the side, front, and rear of buses: king-size (30″ × 144″); queen-size (30″ × 88″); headlight and traveling display (21″ × 44″); taillight display (21″ × 72″); and supergraphics. Station and terminal posters are also available in major markets where there are mass transit systems. They come in 1-sheet (30″ × 46″), 2-sheet (60″ × 46″), and 3-sheet (42″ × 84″) sizes.

Creating Transit Advertising

When you create for transit advertising, there are two types of audiences you must consider: stationary and moving. When the advertisement appears inside buses and trains, you have a longer period of time to get your message across. The people who use mass transit are really a captive audience. They are exposed to transit advertising for a longer period of time than to other forms of outdoor advertising. That is why car cards and inside posters can contain a good deal more information. It is not unreasonable to find anywhere from 20 to 50 words on car cards. However, these cards are not seen under the best lighting conditions, so this should be taken into consideration when they are designed. Also, you should note that these cards are normally placed above eye level of the passengers, whether they are standing or seated.

The principles of creating for outdoor advertising also apply to car cards. Keep your posters simple, with one basic concept. Stick to easy-to-read typefaces and strong contrasting colors. Your card is competing with dozens of others for the rider's attention, so try to produce a card that is eye-catching and still projects a professional image. Study signs in the subway or on buses, and notice the tricks used by graphic artists to attract attention and convey a message. Also ask your transit sales representative to help you create a car card. Transit advertising companies have experienced art departments that will assist you in producing a car card that has impact.

A black-and-white car card for Sieck & Zelinka (#18) appeared in the New York City Subway in February 1979. It produced close to 50 percent of the firm's clients. Sieck & Zelinka placed 700 cards in subway trains that ran in the areas where the firm had offices and client potential. Fees for divorces, bankruptcies, legal separations, adoptions, and immigration matters were shown under the telephone number. A follow-up car card by Sieck & Zelinka (#19) featured a take-one pad at the bottom.

In 1977 the Advertising Research Foundation conducted a study that

AD#18

YOU MAY THINK YOU NEED A LOAN WHEN YOU REALLY NEED A LAWYER.

Borrowing more money on top of what you already owe won't help make ends meet.

Seeing us will. Our law firm will take full advantage of a new federal law to get you out from under.

We'll end threatening phone calls, and other harrassing collection efforts, including salary garnishment.

We'll reduce or end monthly payments.

We'll eliminate student and other loans. In addition, you'll be able to keep your savings, your car, your property, your furniture, and your other valuable assets.

We'll end all lawsuits.

Our consultation is free. And our fees are extremely reasonable.

Call us for an appointment, and enjoy the same legal clout as your creditors.

SIECK & ZELINKA
581-6556
250 WEST 57TH ST., SUITE 431, NY, NY 10019

determined the components of an attention-getting car card. The percentage of effective advertisements studied that contained each component are shown below:

	Percentage
Simple layout	100
Headlines containing the product name	100
One or more illustrations	93
Fewer than 36 words	87
Picture or pictures as a dominant feature	80
Pictures of people	73

Since traveling displays are moving, the guidelines for creating billboards also apply to these displays. Brevity and simplicity are the keys to good traveling displays. Copy, color, and design should be similar to those used in outdoor posters.

Posters in terminals and stations get more viewing time than do traveling displays, but less time than car cards. For example, the average person in New York City might spend approximately 8–14 minutes waiting for a subway train. This gives the rider time to read the subway poster. These posters are seen by people standing on the station platform or by passengers getting on or off trains. In most cases, the same principles outlined earlier for creating billboards also apply here. However, there have been exceptions where more copy was included and the posters proved very effective. You have to know exactly where your poster is going to be placed before creating a message.

DIRECT MAIL

The first attempt at professional direct-mail advertising in New York State was a letter sent out by attorneys Alfred Koffler and William Harrison, Jr. (#20). The letter was mailed to 7,500 families in Suffolk County that had placed their homes on the market; it produced 200 new clients for the firm. It also resulted in a landmark court decision permitting lawyers to use direct-mail advertising in the state.

Direct mail is one of the most popular methods of communication used by professionals. At one time or another, every practitioner has employed the medium.

When you opened your first office, you no doubt sent out an announcement to a select list of friends, acquaintances, and potential C/Ps.

ALFRED S. KOFFLER
&
WILLIAM HENRY HARRISON, JR.
LAWYERS

670 Main Street
Islip, New York 11751
516-581-6000
(days)
61 Randall Road
Shoreham, New York 11786
516-744-4444
(weekends & after 9:00 pm)

REAL ESTATE

CLOSINGS
$235.

INCL. CONTRACTS
516-581-6000 days
516-744-4444 eves

William H. Harrison—Lawyer

August 23, 1977

Dear Homeowner:

The advertisement shown above is being run by our office in Newsday's real estate section.

We understand that you are selling your home and we would like to take this opportunity to inform you that because we are now allowed to advertise our services, YOU no longer need to pay $400.00 to $600.00 for legal representation when you close title.

IN FACT, BECAUSE WE ARE ABLE TO CONTACT YOU BY DIRECT MAIL, WE ARE WILLING TO TRANSACT AND REPRESENT YOU AT THE SALE OF YOUR PROPERTY FOR $195.00.

Feel free to contact us if you have any questions.

If you wish, you may make an appointment with us prior to selling your house. This will enable us to draw your contracts quickly when you and a purchaser come to terms.

Enclosed you will find our business card. We look forward to representing you.

Very truly yours,

A.S. Koffler

ALFRED S. KOFFLER

William Henry Harrison Jr.

WILLIAM HENRY HARRISON, JR.

This is direct mail. If you're a dentist, you send out regular reminders to patients about coming in for an examination and prophylaxis. This is direct mail. If you're a lawyer and you send out a periodic newsletter to clients, this is direct mail.

In general, direct mail is the sending out of a message through the mail or some other delivery system to a select group of individuals. It may be a letter, note, brochure, postcard, tape cassette, vinyl record, slides, or any combination of these. Whatever it is, it usually is in a permanent form, and the distribution is controlled by the sender.

Direct mail offers the advertiser the ultimate in selectivity and flexibility. You are not limited to any particular size to communicate your message, as in a newspaper. You can run as many colors as you desire. You can include illustrated brochures, inserts, or even two letters if you like. You're limited only by your imagination.

And you can send it to any group of people. You can be as selective in picking your target audience as you like. You can buy mailing lists on the basis of different characteristics: location, race, income, occupation, age, gender, special interest, or religion. You can pinpoint your market instead of using the shotgun approach. You can reach a defined neighborhood or an entire city. You are in complete control of what people will receive your communication.

Another advantage of direct mail is that when people receive the mailing at home, they can focus their entire attention on it. There are no competing ads or commercials. You're not fighting the editorial or programming. A person can read it immediately or save it for later.

Direct mail is the most personal and efficient way to let your C/Ps know that you care about them. A direct-mail letter can be mass-produced using the latest technology and be indistinguishable from a personalized letter.

The Cost of Direct Mail

Direct mail, in terms of per capita cost, is an expensive medium. It can cost you up to 20 times as much to reach a person with direct mail as with other media. However, in terms of return, it can be the least expensive way to advertise. There is very little wasted circulation, unlike in other media. This offsets the high individual cost of each mailing.

Before you get into direct mail, total up the costs of a program and set a budget for reaching each C/P. The costs to be considered include:

1. The postage for reaching all your prospects.

2. The cost of preparing artwork, including mechanicals, type, photographs, illustrations, etc.
3. The cost of printing brochures, letters, envelopes, and reply cards.
4. The cost of renting a mailing list.
5. The cost of labeling and inserting the mailing, and other handling costs.

You may be able to reduce or eliminate some of these costs if your staff can do the work without engaging the services of an outside organization. This includes preparing your own mailing list. They certainly can handle the inserting of the envelopes as well as the labeling.

Many factors influence the kind of response you will get from your direct mail. However, there are three major elements that you should carefully plan before getting involved in direct mail: the mailing list, the mailing package, and the timing.

Mailing Lists

The mailing list is the heart of every direct-mail program. The greatest mailing package sent out to the wrong list will produce very little in terms of a response. Each mailing list has its own unique characteristics. It can be based on demographic factors, life-styles, or geographic areas. You can create your own mailing list, or you can buy or rent one.

Compiling your own mailing list. If you want to compile your own mailing list, the best place to start is with your C/P records. Go through your file to determine when each C/P last visited your office. It may have been a year ago or four years ago, and you will have to select a cutoff date.

One out of every five Americans moves each year, so your C/P list can be outdated in just a few years. In selecting the cutoff date for your list, consider the stability of the neighborhood where your practice is located and the size of your practice. If it is an area of high household mobility, then you might set a two-year cutoff date. If your practice is very large, you might want to narrow down your mailing list to people who have used your services recently. It could be a one-year period.

One medical organization went back four years in its patient files to compile a mailing list. The further you go back, the greater the chances are for error. Your list can become outdated very quickly, and constant updating is required to keep it accurate.

There are many other sources in your community that you can draw from to increase the size of your mailing list. These include:

1. Annual trade and business directories.
2. Memberships of churches, service organizations, and clubs.
3. Telephone directories, including reverse directories that list individuals by blocks and areas.
4. Lists of new families (or firms) that move to your neighborhood.

Keeping your list up to date. Since mobility is an integral part of the American way of life, your list should be numerically coded and alphabetically arranged. You should be able to locate any name that is no longer active. You might also want to organize your list into active and inactive C/Ps. In this case, you could send one mailing to your active list and another mailing to the inactive list. Remove any name from your list when a mailing piece is returned to you by the post office. Also check your list to make sure that all duplications are eliminated. Sending a C/P two mailings gives the impression that you are not well organized.

If you have a small mailing list (under 1,000 names), consider maintaining it yourself. Xerox supplies 8½ inch by 11 inch matrix forms that have spaces for 33 names. The names can be typed on the master in any manner and system that you determine. These master lists can be duplicated on special Xerox pressure-sensitive labels at most neighborhood duplicating centers. These centers can make as many copies of your list as you desire. It would be a good idea to check with them before you start typing your master list to see that you are doing it right.

If you have a sizable mailing list, you might want to have a mailing firm maintain your list as well as handle all mailings. Names will be placed on magnetic tape for computer use or on mailing cards or plates. This makes updating extremely easy. You can notify the mailing firm any time you want a name added or deleted from the master list.

Buying a mailing list. If you want to buy a mailing list, the best place to start is with a list broker or compiler. You have to supply compilers with a complete demographic or life-style profile, of your target audience. so that they can give you as accurate a mailing list as possible.

The way that compilers produce a tailor-made list is to start with facts and not assumptions about your market. You have to know who your prospects are and where and how they live. Each professional practice has a specific target audience. You have to identify it before you do anything else. This will also determine what kind of direct-mail package you will create as well as the timing of the mailing. Without a well-defined target audience, you are wasting your money in direct mail.

Many brokers compile lists of consumers for professionals based on households in states, cities, zip code areas, or census tracts. There are even specialized brokers, who compile lists based on buying patterns, hobbies, and interests.

Today, with the sophisticated analysis provided by computers, you can really pinpoint your audience. There are thousands of consumers out there who are potential C/Ps. One way to find them is to do test mailings. You can send out a small-quantity mailing to test the response of a list before you do a mass mailing. Many brokers will help you evaluate the response to a test mailing. They will analyze the results of the respondents according to demographic factors, life-styles, and attitudes. These firms have advanced data processing facilities for analysis and list maintenance. This information can increase your response in future mailings.

Localizing your mailing list. Professionals who have neighborhood practices will be interested in renting lists of individuals residing within specific areas. List brokers can compile segmented lists broken down into different demographic units using the United States Census Bureau's socioeconomic information for each block group. census tract, or zip code:

- *Block groups.* This list will contain about 250 families and offers the highest degree of homogeneity.
- *Census tracts.* This group has about a thousand families and is second in terms of homogeneity.
- *Zip codes.* This can take in an entire county or town and may have as many as 10,000 families. It is the least homogeneous of the three mentioned.

Brokers can also identify the length of time a family has resided at their present address and other characteristics not available from census data.

Cost of mailing lists. Brokers will charge a rental fee for use of their mailing lists. The charge is based on the number of names on the list, about $30 on the average for each thousand names. Most reliable brokers will guarantee the lists to be 90 percent deliverable, and they will refund postage on any returned mail in excess of 10 percent of the list. The lists can be supplied to you in three forms:

- *On Cheshire labels.* This is the most common form of mailing lists. Four rows of labels are produced on continuous. computer-readout forms. The labels are ungummed and unperforated and can be affixed only by a Cheshire machine.

○ *On pressure-sensitive labels.* These are gummed, peel-off labels, which can be affixed by hand or by Cheshire machine. There are 44 labels to a page. This is the best type of list format for a small mailing.

○ *On magnetic computer tape.* Lists are also available on seven- or nine-track magnetic tape, for those mailing firms that have the equipment to handle it.

The Direct-Mail Package

When you create a direct-mail package, bear in mind that your mailing is competing with other pieces of mail. You must create a package that will grab and hold the reader's attention from the moment he picks up the envelope. You have to give the recipient a good reason for opening it and reading the contents.

There are some rules that you should be familiar with in order to be successful in direct mail:

1. Every successful direct-mail piece has a proposition with an offer to the receiver. What are you proposing to your future C/Ps that will make them respond to your mailing?
2. The message should stress benefits that you can offer your C/Ps.
3. Your message should be a personal one.
4. The message should reflect the unique personality of your practice.
5. Each mailing piece should be a selling piece. Include some way for the receiver to respond to your offer.

A typical direct-mail package includes a letter, brochure, response card, order form, and reply envelope—all as separate units inserted into an envelope. Each component serves a function in obtaining a response.

The letter. This is probably the most important component in the direct-mail package—particularly for professionals. It can be either a form letter or a personalized letter, depending on what you are trying to accomplish. If you have a practice in which C/P involvement is high, then you might consider personalized letters. This type of letter will outpull nonpersonalized ones.

Today, you can send a personalized letter to every C/P on your list. There are specialized firms that use some of the most advanced computer technology to print personalized letters. These advanced systems will type any name, address, and personal salutation along with the body of the letter. Further, your C/P's name can be inserted in as many places in the letter as you desire. The systems can also turn out the letters quickly. For example, an IBM Systems 6 can type a letter in one minute.

However, computer typing has limitations. It can print only one size type, one typeface, and one color for each letter. Other methods, such as ink jet imaging and laser printing, offer greater flexibility. Ink jet imaging can vary the type size and typeface within a single letter. Laser printing is the most versatile of all, because it can not only vary type sizes but even reproduce individual signatures.

One of the most common questions asked by practitioners is "How long should a letter be?" A letter should be long enough to do a convincing selling job and not a bit longer. People will read a letter that holds their interest even if it is four pages long. In fact, direct-mail pros have found that a two-page letter will outpull a one-page letter, and a three-page letter will outpull a two-pager, provided it is interesting and convincing. The American Dental Plan sent out a three-page letter as a test mailing (#21).

The form of the letter is very important, too. Try to use wide margins with lots of white space. Keep your paragraphs short, with no more than two or three sentences in each and no more than six or seven lines in overall depth. Important thoughts and paragraphs should be indented to call attention to them. Key words and phrases should be underlined. A postscript is also effective for summing up the most important points or making an offer that will move the reader to action. (In many cases, after reading the postscript, the reader will go back and reread the entire letter.) Direct-mail pros have found that two-color letters will pull a better response than one-color letters.

Bob Stone, an authority on direct-response advertising, offered these suggestions for writing an effective letter:

1. Promise a benefit in your headline or first paragraph—your most important benefit. You simply can't go wrong by leading off with the most important benefit to the reader. Some writers believe in the slow buildup. But, most experienced writers I know favor making the important point first.
2. Immediately enlarge on your most important benefit. This step is crucial. Many writers come up with a great lead, then fail to follow through. Or they catch attention with their heading, but then take two or three paragraphs to warm up to their subject. The reader's attention is gone! Try hard to elaborate on your most important benefit right away, and you'll build up interest fast.
3. Tell the reader specifically what he or she is going to get. It's amazing how many letters lack details on such basic product features. Perhaps the writer is so close to his proposition he assumes the reader knows all about it. A dangerous assumption! And when you

American Dental Plan
800 Third Avenue
New York, New York 10022

Dear Friend:

I am pleased to hear you are considering membership in the <u>American Dental Plan</u>.

This is one of the most financially shrewd decisions you can make today, with the cost of quality health care—especially <u>dental</u> care—rising at an alarming rate.

The <u>American Dental Plan</u> is a way around this problem. It's an innovative, proven concept that can provide high calibre treatment for all your family's dental needs while <u>dramatically saving you dollars</u>.

Consider all that this program offers you...

As a member of the <u>American Dental Plan</u>, you pay just one low annual membership fee, which entitles you to—

<u>Two</u> complete annual checkups—<u>at no additional cost</u>— including X-rays, cleaning, flucride treatment, oral cancer examination, diagnosis and preventative dental care.

You also enjoy a variety of other dental services at a fraction of the customary fees charged by most dental practitioners. For example...

<u>You pay as little as $3</u> for fillings, depending on which plan you select.

<u>You save 50% or more</u> on crown and bridge work, orthodontia, periodontics, dentures and other dental services.

<u>You can save</u> hundreds of dollars on all your dental bills annually.

Now, you may be thinking that sizeable reductions such as these can only be offered by a clinic. I want to assure you that the <u>American Dental Plan</u> is <u>not</u> a clinic. Nor is it a cut-rate department store operation.

Each dentist participating in the <u>American Dental Plan</u> is an established and respected member of his community in private practice, with years of experience in providing quality dental care to hundreds of patients.

What sets him apart is his concern for the skyrocketing cost of basic dental services—and his decision to do something about it.

He's joined forces with other dental professionals throughout the tri-state metropolitan area to launch an important counter-offensive against inflation. Its strategy is simple—

ADP-H

> to drastically reduce fees without sacrificing quality,
> care or individual attention... to save you up to 70% on
> your dental bills.

Your own dentist may be among the hundreds taking part in this important
cooperative effort on your behalf. If not, you'll find many who are
located conveniently near you, simply by looking in the enclosed Directory
of Dentists.

Your Assurance of Quality Dental Care.

Only dentists who meet the American Dental Plan's standards of professional practice are allowed to be listed in the Directory of Dentists.

These standards, together with the Principles of Ethics of the American
Dental Association, are the basis of the American Dental Plan. They are
enforced by the Professional Peer Group Committee of the American Dental
Plan, composed of dentists from the tri-state metropolitan area, and are
your guarantee of quality dental care.

As a member, you select the dentist you want...make an appointment to see
him at your convenience...and you are treated in his private neighborhood
office with care, concern and respect.

> If you're new in the community—or, if you're seeking a new
> dentist for any reason—the American Dental Plan is an
> intelligent way to be put in touch with a dentist known for
> his high standards.

And because it's not an insurance plan, membership in the American Dental
Plan is open to everyone—singles, couples and families, including all
your children. There are no restrictions. Joining is simplicity itself.

No Claim Forms. No Complicated Paperwork.

To enroll in the American Dental Plan just fill out the Enrollment Application enclosed. To select your dentist, consult the Directory of Dentists
we've included, and choose the office most convenient for you. Then enter
this code number on the Application.

The moment your Enrollment Application has been processed you will receive
your American Dental Plan Membership Card with the name, address and
phone number of the dentist you've selected. Call him immediately to
schedule your first checkup.

Your low membership fee is determined by the plan you select. It entitles
you to complete, twice-yearly checkups at no additional cost and the reduced fee schedule for all other dental services as described in the
brochure. You'll find a complete fee schedule and chart showing how much
you'll save in the brochure.

> The American Dental Plan also offers substantial savings on
> Orthodontic care from Board-Certified or Eligible Ortho-
> dontists. Details and costs also appear in the brochure.

Payment for the American Dental Plan services involves no red tape. You
simply pay the reduced fees directly to your participating dentist.

<u>Mail the Enrollment Form Today</u>.

After you have completed the Application for Enrollment, simply enclose
check or money order in the return envelope we've provided. Or, if you
prefer, you may charge your membership fee to your favorite credit card.
Then just drop the envelope in the mail—the postage has already been paid.

I urge you to look over the enclosed material at your earliest convenience.
This is a real opportunity to obtain dental protection for your family at
unusually low rates.

With the way costs are going up these days, can you afford to wait?

Cordially,

Robert J. Feuerzeig
President

RJF:hm
Enclosure

P.S. Because the <u>American Dental Plan</u> maintains rather high requirements,
we are confident that you will be pleased with the dental professional
you select. But if not—<u>for any reason</u>—you are free to switch to any of
the hundreds of dentists listed in the enclosed Directory. The choice is
<u>always</u> your own.

ADP-H

tell the reader what he or she's going to get, don't overlook the intangibles that go along with your product or service.

4. Back up your statements with proof and endorsements. Most prospects are somewhat skeptical about advertising. They know it sometimes gets a little overenthusiastic about a product. So they accept it only with a grain of salt. If you can back up your own statements with third-party testimonials or a list of satisfied users, everything you say becomes more believable.

5. Tell the reader what she might lose if she doesn't act. People respond affirmatively either to gain something they do not possess or to avoid losing something they already have. Here's a good spot in your letter to overcome human inertia—imply what may be lost if action is postponed. People don't like to be left out. A skillful writer can use this human trait as a powerful influence in his or her message.

6. Rephrase your prominent benefits in your closing offer. As a good salesperson does, sum up the benefits to the prospect in your closing offer. This is the proper prelude to asking for action. This is where you can intensify the prospect's desire to have the product. The stronger the benefits you can persuade the reader to recall, the easier it will be for him or her to justify an affirmative decision.

7. Incite action, NOW. This is the spot where you win or lose the battle with inertia. Experienced advertisers know once a letter is put aside or tossed into that file, you're out of luck. So wind up with a call for action and a logical reason for acting now.*

The brochure, booklet, or folder. Practically every direct-mail package contains a brochure, folder, booklet, or broadside. It may be printed in one color, or four colors. It might have beautiful color illustrations or just copy. The brochure should explain the benefits of your practice in detail. One booklet offered by a plastic surgeon showed before-and-after photographs of the most common cosmetic surgical procedures. A folder by a group of dentists explained in detail their philosophy regarding preventive dentistry and contained a listing of fees. Another booklet by a law firm explained how personal planning can help you achieve business objectives and how to make time spent with an attorney more productive. One brochure produced by a medical organization explained the history of the organization and the benefits of the different examinations available, such as stress, cancer screening, and cardiovascular tests.

---

*Bob Stone, *Successful Direct Marketing Methods*, 2nd ed.; Chicago: Crain Communications, 1979.

The reply form and envelope. Ultimately, the recipient of the direct-mail package will turn to the reply form or card. In most cases, this device is included to move the prospective C/P to schedule an appointment. The card or envelope that is enclosed should be postage paid. This will produce a greater response than cards or envelopes that require stamps. It is important that the order form repeat the original proposition spelled out in the letter and folder. It should give all the details just in case it becomes separated from the rest of the package. It is also important to note that a reply form that looks important and valuable will produce greater results than a plain-looking form or card.

The outside envelope. The outer envelope is the first thing the recipient sees when he gets your mailing. It should reflect what is inside the package. Whether it uses an illustration or copy, it should entice the reader to open the package and read it. You might use a copy "teaser," like "Are you concerned about your dental bills?" If you use a teaser on your envelope, the first line of the enclosed letter should repeat it. If the letter gets separated from the envelope, it will stand on its own.

The second letter. In many cases, direct-mail pros include a second letter in the mailing package. They have found that a letter from another person increases the response rate. One dental group sent out a mailing with a detailed letter from the president. Another shorter letter from the dentist supervising the quality-control aspects of the program was also included to give credibility to the mailing.

Timing Your Mailing

One of the most important considerations in direct mail is timing.. If you send out your mailing at the wrong time of year, it will affect your response significantly. The right time to mail will vary from professional to professional—and you will have to experiment with it. Aspects to consider will be your specialty, location of your practice, and the target audience.

Direct-mail pros have found that there are certain times of the year when the success factor is greatest. The best months for direct mail are January, February, October, and August, in that order. The worst months are June, March, April, May, and December. The best days of the week for your prospects to receive mail are Tuesday, Wednesday, and Thursday. Avoid Mondays, Fridays, and Saturdays, and the days before and after a holiday. A direct-mail program can take several forms.

The single mailing. This will usually be sent out to a select list of C/Ps or prospects. It may be an announcement of the opening of a new office, the establishment of a new partnership, or just a reminder to come in for an examination. In most cases, this mailing will not be followed up and will be the only one sent out by the practitioner.

A direct-mail campaign. The purpose of multi-mailings within a specific time period is to repeat your basic selling message. Mailings are sent to a select list of potential C/Ps. There can be four, five, or six mailings—all repeating the unique benefits of your practice.

A continuous program of regular mailings. This can be on a weekly, monthly, or bimonthly basis. One of the best creative devices for a continuous campaign is the newsletter. Newsletters are currently being sent out to C/Ps or potential C/Ps by accountants, dentists, physicians, and lawyers. In fact, a number of firms are now offering professionals newsletters that can be customized with their own messages.

All About Newsletters

The newsletter is one of the most popular ways professionals can use direct mail to communicate with their present or potential C/Ps. For example, Dr. Frederick Seltzer publishes *Smile Report,* a two-page monthly newsletter; the Preventive Medicine Institute/Strang Clinic publishes *Health Action,* a four-page quarterly newsletter; Deloitte Haskins & Sells publishes *The Week in Review,* a 16-page weekly newsletter; and Braun Advertising publishes *News About Your Teeth,* a newsletter that can be customized for dentists (#22). Many professionals used this method to communicate even before the Supreme Court decision permitted professionals to advertise.

One lawyer who sends out newsletters and also advertises said, "I estimate that my newspaper and radio advertising hits about 15 percent of my target. But my newsletter hits 100 percent." Most professionals who use newsletters recognize the value of sending information on health, dental care, changes in the laws, and new developments in the tax field to C/Ps on a regular basis. In addition, newsletters offer these advantages:

○ You can send them as often as you like—weekly, monthly, or quarterly. This repetition of facts that will benefit the reader is important in building good client relations.
○ Since you have complete control of the mailing list, there isn't the wasted circulation there is with a newspaper or radio advertisement.

the Smile Report

from the office of
Frederick A. Seltzer, D.D.S.

VOLUME 4 number 1   Copyright 1980   February 1980

DR. SELTZER TO BE HEARD ON RADIO

Our Concern — YOU!

SPECIAL NOTE

NATIONAL CHILDREN'S DENTAL HEALTH WEEK

BE AWARE

NO ONE CARES
HOW MUCH YOU KNOW
UNTIL THEY KNOW
HOW MUCH YOU CARE

HEALTH ACTION

THE NEWSLETTER OF THE PREVENTIVE MEDICINE INSTITUTE, STRANG CLINIC
55 EAST 34 STREET, NEW YORK, N.Y. 10016 · 212 683-1000

March, 1979

Dear Friend of PMI/Strang:

Deloitte Haskins-Sells

Accounting & Reporting

FASB ISSUES PROPOSAL TO REPLACE STATEMENT NO. 8

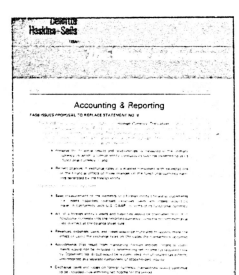

---

news about YOUR TEETH

Taking care of your teeth at home

Flossing is first

○ You can write on any subject that you desire—preventive medicine or dentistry, new developments in health care, or new tax laws. You can also include information about your practice that new or prospective C/Ps should know—your address, telephone number, hours, credit policies, and fees. Other topics that might be included in the newsletter are: your philosophy of practice, profiles of your staff (especially pointing out their backgrounds), birthdays of your C/Ps, quizzes, and book reviews. You also want to develop a rapport with your audience by inviting questions about your practice. The answers should be included in your newsletter.

○ A newsletter also keeps your name in front of your C/Ps. It is a means of telling your clients that they are very important to you and you are concerned about them. It also provides a real service to the reader in terms of education.

○ A newsletter can be a means for building a practice if it is sent to present, former, and potential C/Ps. It can be sent to everyone in your zip code area. Since you control the mailing list, you can reach precisely the people you want.

What form should a newsletter take? There is no standard answer since it can be any size. In some cases, newsletters are one-page affairs—8½ by 11 inches—and designed as self-mailers. In other instances, they are four to eight pages and inserted in envelopes for addressing and mailing.

The first step in creating a newsletter is designing a format with a striking masthead. This could be designed by a commercial artist. All subsequent newsletters should use the same format established at the beginning. All you have to do is drop in the new type.

Newsletters are a way to project your image in a positive and professional manner. It's a proven communications technique that is being updated to build practices.

Check Your Printer

Before you get involved in producing a direct-mail package, contact your printer and get his advice. Today, thanks to advanced technology, there are printing presses that are capable of combining a letter, brochure, order form, reply form, and envelope as one unit. This could cut costs considerably. Your printer will also advise you on the paper stock and even the size of the mailer. Sometimes, just by reducing the overall size of a mailer by ⅛ inch, you can save 15 or 20 percent on your printing bill. Using a printing press to its maximum size is an excellent way to reduce costs.

First Class or Third Class Mail?

The amount of postage you will need depends on the size of your mailing. If it is small and personalized, you will want to send it first class. But if you are doing a mailing to a zip code area, you should consider third class mail. In fact, third class mail pulls as well as first class mail, and postage metered envelopes attract a greater response than envelopes that have stamps attached to them.

Testing the Response

The most important element in direct mail is testing the response. Because all costs are soaring, direct-mail pros have an increased desire to know what approach will work. So marketers always test their creative approaches as well as their mailing lists.

For the practitioner, the reason for testing is to determine the best and most efficient way to attract new C/Ps. You will learn from your tests how to improve your overall response. Test your approach constantly, always bearing in mind that you want to upgrade your direct-mail program. You can test your mailing by changing the letter, putting in a new response card, or just changing the graphics. You might also want to change the paper and envelope that it is printed on. You could change your appeal—stress your specialty or highlight fees, experience, or convenience. Changing some of these elements can increase the response significantly.

CHAPTER 13

Eight Successful Case Histories of Ad Campaigns

In interviewing many professionals who have advertised, I found certain basics that were common to every successful ad campaign.

- Without exception, every professional—whether an individual or a firm—committed to a total advertising campaign. They set a budget for a specific period of time and recognized the importance of continuity.
- These professionals also set specific objectives that they expected to achieve from their advertising campaign. In most cases, professionals bettered their goals and attained additional fringe benefits that they never expected.
- Many of these pioneers also recognized that the public has a right to know all about professional services and where they can get them. They realized that the public has very little information available: this includes facts about fees, services, and specialties.
- It's not surprising that most professionals listed "awareness" as their major reason for advertising. Whatever their target audience, advertising professionals wanted to make their names or firms known in the community. Of course, the ultimate objective is attracting new clients/patients (C/Ps).
- The vast majority of professionals were interested in producing advertising that would be informative and on a "high level." They wanted to set a dignified tone and were not interested in denigrating the profession with shoddy and misleading advertising. They recognized that tasteful advertising will enhance the practitioner's reputation and the image of the profession in general.
- Firms that have an ongoing ad campaign have changed their creative approach as market conditions changed. In most cases, this repositioning has occurred as competition has increased. Low fees, once a unique benefit, have become less important as more and more practitioners feature this advantage in their advertising.

The following case histories may serve as a guide to professionals for their advertising and public relations efforts. Additional case studies for groups of advertising professionals are included in the next chapter.

Case History Number 1
PROFESSIONAL: Dr. Frederick A. Seltzer
North Woodmere, N.Y.

PROBLEM: Dr. Seltzer graduated from New York University Dental School in 1977 and opened his practice on Long Island, in an established suburban area that had a heavy concentration of dentists. His practice was located in his residence, well away from the mainstream of traffic. At the same time he opened his office, dental clinics with big advertising budgets opened in chain discount stores throughout Long Island, intensifying the competition. Dr. Seltzer said, "I had to let people know I existed. I had to teach them to want good preventive and restorative dentistry, and that I could supply it. In other words, I had to market myself—and not once, but continuously."

SOLUTION: At first, Dr. Seltzer launched a one-man public relations campaign. He gave speeches at local schools, religious organizations, and charitable groups. Whenever he spoke, his name appeared in the local newspaper. He then decided to write a weekly column in his local newspaper titled, "You Don't Treat Teeth, You Treat People" (#23). At first, he contributed the column to the newspaper without charge, but once the initial period ran out, he decided to run it as an advertisement. The column has been appearing ever since—52 times a year—in the *South Shore Record.* The message stressed in Dr. Seltzer's paid-for column is good dentistry. He budgets approximately $2,500 for buying the newspaper space, and he writes all his own copy. His basic concept is "keeping my name in the public's eye, so when they think of teeth they think of me." Dr. Seltzer's columns reflect his own unique personality and his attitude about the practice of dentistry. Each column is devoted to one subject and highlights patient benefits. Dr. Seltzer emphasized, "Whether you're a busy dentist or a starting practitioner, there are no limits to how large your practice can grow if you never lose sight of the individual components that make your practice, and those components are people." In addition to the column, Dr. Seltzer intensified his lectures, arranged school field trips to his office, and appeared as a guest on various local TV and radio programs. He also started a monthly newsletter that was sent to 800 families that were his patients.

"YOU DON'T TREAT TEETH, YOU TREAT PEOPLE"

Frederick A. Seltzer, D.D.S.

© 1979 South Shore Publishers, Inc

This week's column is devoted to a woman who telephoned my office Thursday, September 6, 1979.

Dear Phone Caller,

I feel it is necessary to reiterate the concept of this column and the message that it delivers. Unless you are a dentist, dental auxiliary or family member related to a dentist, it is unlikely that many of the technical terms used would be familiar to you. Further more, as the title of the column so aptly states, you do not treat teeth, you treat PEOPLE! The column is intended to explain not only technical intricacies of the profession, but to give the patient a new understanding of how he or she should be treated as a patient. Simply stated, it is a privilege for the doctor to treat the patient, not a privilege for the patient to be treated by the doctor.

There are topics in this column from time to time that are designed for children. Last week's column, "Tell, Show and Do," was just that type of column. It is important for every patient to be treated as a human being, not as a tooth! A tooth has never walked into my office by itself and a tooth has never called me in the middle of the night saying that it was in pain. People do! People are whom the doctors are treating!

People must be made aware that they have rights and those rights should not be abdicated. Strangely enough most professionals treat the patient and not just the tooth. Most professionals respect the patients' time and do not keep them waiting. Most professionals make post operative calls to see how well their patient is feeling as mentioned in previous columns. Simply Ms. Phone Caller, this column wants to make the general public aware of their inalienable human rights which create a happier patient. And happier patients do seem to have HEALTHIER mouths!

© 1979 South Shore Publishers, Inc

Please forward all questions to: Dr. Frederick A. Seltzer, 856 Fairview Avenue, North Woodmere, N.Y. 11581. 791-3555.

RESULTS: Dr. Seltzer doubled the dollar volume objective he had set for the first year of his program. Since then his practice has grown rapidly, and he attributes his success to his weekly column and his other public relations activities.

Case History Number 2

PROFESSIONAL: The Legal Clinic of Jacoby & Meyers
California and New York

PROBLEM: Jacoby & Meyers began in a Los Angeles storefront in 1972. In 1977, it was still a small, struggling law firm with a controversial idea: delivering low-cost legal services to the middle class. It was operating in four storefront offices in Los Angeles and seeing an average of 80 new clients per month. Then came the Supreme Court decision permitting lawyers to advertise. Jacoby & Meyers hired Horlick Levin & Hodges as its advertising agency. And the rest is history. "Advertising," said Stephen Meyers, a founding partner, "is what makes it possible to generate a clientele large enough for us to deliver services efficiently." The firm has set an objective of 50,000 clients a year and expects to expand its operation into other states in the near future.

SOLUTION: Jacoby & Meyers became the law firm that pioneered TV advertising by lawyers. Initially, the ad agency had no market research except the study conducted by the American Bar Association that indicated that the middle 70 percent of the U.S. population was not being served adequately by the legal profession.

   The advertising has gone through four distinct stages of development. In the first stage, the ad agency decided to use TV because Los Angeles was a weak newspaper market and a highly fractionalized radio market. In the first TV spot, Jacoby & Meyers was positioned as a respectable law firm serving the middle class at a reasonable cost. The commercial showed a casually dressed spokesman in front of one of Jacoby & Meyers's modest-looking offices (#24). He said, "If you are rich, you can afford any attorney. If you're poor, you can get legal aid. But if you're in the middle, you should know about a law firm called The Legal Clinic of Jacoby & Meyers. Your consultation with an attorney, $15. Your fee, very reasonable, with an estimate in writing. The Legal Clinic of Jacoby & Meyers. It's about time. For the neighborhood office near you call 678-7111." This commercial went on the air in August 1977 and ran for 14 months.

   The ad agency helped Jacoby & Meyers institute a "sourcing" system.

Photo Credit: Horlick, Levin and Hodges.

That is, for each caller, the time of day, the caller's name and address, and the type of case were recorded. This information was collected a second time, when the caller came for an appointment.

For the first ten weeks, TV spots were purchased one week at a time. Each week, the agency met with the client to review the results of the preceding week. Each Wednesday, the agency placed a spot TV schedule for the following week. Each week, the number of spots and time schedules were changed until the agency determined what schedule would attract enough business to make the advertising pay, but not more business than the offices could handle. The agency learned from experience that the earlier in the week the commercial was aired the more effective it was. The agency bought TV spots on Monday, Tuesday, Wednesday, and Thursday; it did not buy on Friday, Saturday, or Sunday under any circumstances. It ran day and late-night spots. Although it was mainly the daytime TV spots that made the phones ring with people calling for appointments, the firm recognized that there were people viewing at night who had legal problems who didn't see the daytime spots. They found that certain programs, such as soap operas and late-night programs, produced a large number of calls about divorce cases, while leads for criminal cases were produced from action and adventure programs. One of the best programs for pulling such leads was a rerun of the FBI series.

In the second stage, the ad agency used Leonard Jacoby and Steven Meyers in the commercial. They said, "How do people feel about their lawyer? One of our big universities did a consumer attitude survey of people who have used two types of law firms: Traditional . . . and The Legal Clinic of Jacoby & Meyers. The result of this survey shows that our concept of neighborhood law offices and reasonable fees is working. You know we really feel good about that. The Legal Clinic of Jacoby & Meyers. It's about time." The spot went on the air in November 1978. The firm repositioned itself, and its approach now became: Jacoby & Meyers is a respectable law firm that delivers services in a way that is efficient, more convenient, and as good as, if not better than, traditional law firms—with reasonable fees. This spot ran for eight months, and the agency and firm continued to balance the flow of new clients with the availability of attorney hours.

In April 1979, the firm entered stage three, abandoning its broad positioning approach and concentrating directly on specific cases. Jacoby & Meyers was equipped to handle cases dealing with divorce, criminal defense, wills, drunk driving, personal injury, and Social Security/disability. The first two—divorce and criminal defense—constituted nearly 50 percent of the firm's case load, so it chose to concentrate on these in its advertising message. The agency recognized that it could not use testimonials because of certain moral and legal constraints. It also recognized that Jacoby & Meyers's fees were not the lowest. So it decided to emphasize the nonlegal aspects of people who face criminal prosecution and divorce—the feelings of isolation, fear, tension, and helplessness and the need for affordable help from a sympathetic and trustworthy professional. The strategy was to get people with these problems to relate to a dramatization and respond to the call to action. Two commercials were created. In the first, an attractive woman in her thirties sits down in a living room. She says, "I just got divorced. You know, after ten years of marriage, it's hard to start over. I didn't know where to turn, let alone if I could afford a lawyer. [Her son enters and sits next to her.] Well, we got through the divorce, and now we have a whole new life." To this low-key scene was added a voice-over: "If you're getting divorced, you should know about a law firm called The Legal Clinic of Jacoby & Meyers. At Jacoby & Meyers you'll receive personal attention from an attorney experienced in divorce law. And our fee? Very reasonable. Jacoby & Meyers. Call 678-7111. It's about time." This commercial, and a similar one featuring a person who has been arrested, went on the air in July 1979.

In the fourth phase of its advertising, Jacoby & Meyers used the research of the *American Bar Association Journal* that compared Jacoby & Meyers's services with those of traditional law firms. The commercial shows the actual research report; the actual findings of the study are superimposed over the visual as a voice-over reads them aloud. These commercials were aired in the early part of 1980 in New York and California.

RESULTS: The firm has grown to over 35 offices in Los Angeles, San Diego, Sacramento, Stockton, and the New York metropolitan area. Today the firm is regarded as the General Motors of legal clinics. Case loads for other types of cases have held relatively constant, while divorce and criminal cases have increased significantly. Overall case loads are up about 15 percent. In 1980 Jacoby & Meyers clinics saw upward of 4,500 new cases per month and forecast breaking 5,000 in the near future.

Case History Number 3

PROFESSIONAL: Siegel, Sugarman & Seput
San Francisco, California

PROBLEM: Siegel, Sugarman & Seput is a middle-size accounting firm, with one office, three partners, and 22 employees. Like most professional firms its size, it was seeking new ways to attract clients within its areas of specialization and whose demands did not exceed the service capabilities of the firm. These clients included small to middle-size companies and relatively sophisticated taxpayers in the middle- to upper-level income brackets. The firm also recognized that there was a large number of people who needed the services of a CPA but didn't realize how a CPA could help them. These included people who had never used a CPA and didn't know where to find one. "Advertising might be the ideal vehicle for delivering a specific message about our firm's services to the very specific markets we had identified," said partner Arnold Siegel. In addition, the firm was seeking recognition and approval from the accounting profession for its pioneering venture. The partners thought that this posed the greatest risk as well as the greatest potential benefit. The firm was also seeking ways of attracting young, entry-level accountants, the lifeblood of any professional practice.

SOLUTION: The firm decided to launch an advertising campaign in July 1978. It set up a total budget of $25,000. Of this amount, $16,000 was for media and $9,000 was spent on creative and production costs. The ads began to appear in October and ran for seven weeks. The firm decided to use print advertising in local newspapers and magazines, because it was a medium that the target audience was familiar with and most likely to see. It advertised in the financial and real estate sections of major local metropolitan newspapers and in the regional edition of *The Wall Street Journal.* The magazines chosen were city-oriented publications and two financial trade journals.

In creating the message, the firm carefully studied every word of the copy, analyzed the layout, and selected typefaces. The partners decided to use an illustration of themselves, because they thought it personalized the ad and conveyed a feeling of individual attention and service that is the major benefit of their firm.

The firm found certain markets were tailor-made for its skills and background. It had substantial experience with real estate, retail, and service businesses as well as with entrepreneurs. The partners believed their most unique attribute was their ability to speak their clients' language. This message is expressed in the headlines of many of their ads (#25). One partner, Arnold Siegel, assumed responsibility for the entire ad campaign, working with an advertising agency. He wrote in the *California CPA Quarterly* (March 1979), "The agency people helped us move the ads from our minds onto paper and to decide among the technical possibilities. Our experience supports the contention that CPAs using advertising

agencies must still take complete responsibility for every decision in the advertising campaign." Subsequent ads presented the firm as perceptive and informed and adopted the slogan "we know how"(#26).

RESULTS: Did the advertising campaign work? Yes. When the firm ran the ads it received a number of inquiries. The ads attracted people in the specific markets mentioned. In fact, the ads that were directed to specific markets attracted the most responses. Of those who inquired, a large number engaged the firm at full billing rates. Mr. Siegel estimated that these new clients would generate billings that would cover the cost of the ad campaign. He speculated that if the clients remained with the firm for a year and the billings materialized as projected, the new clients would have billings of approximately $50,000. This would be twice the ad budget of $25,000 (and three times the media costs).

Another important benefit of the advertising was the reaction of colleagues. The firm received the highest praise from peers, clients, and business people in the community. One of the unexpected benefits was the inquiries from young accountants and college students who saw the ads and were interested in setting up interviews for possible employment. However, the most important collateral benefit of the campaign was the effect it had on the firm's staff. It gave the employees a feeling that they were with a progressive, forward-thinking organization that had growth potential.

Case History Number 4

PROFESSIONAL: Creative Surgery Center
New York, N.Y.

PROBLEM: The Creative Surgery Center was conceived of as a referral service for experienced plastic surgeons for both the medical community and the community in general. The staff is composed of board-certified plastic surgeons who are on call for consultations with the public. The center could expand its facilities as the demand for surgery increased, so handling a large volume of new patients was not a problem. The center believed that the key problem was that the public did not know where to go for cosmetic surgery. People just did not have access to referrals. In many cases, individuals were apprehensive about asking their friends about cosmetic surgery because they felt embarrassed. The Creative Surgery Center knew that by informing people through advertising it could perform a public service as well as increase its patient flow and dollar vol-

ume. The center found the market for cosmetic surgery to be an "up-scale" market composed of 60 percent female and 40 percent male. It attributed the large number of men to the new interest of men in their physical appearance and to the era of self-improvement. The ages of patients ranged from 17 to people well into their sixties.

SOLUTION:　The firm launched a print advertising campaign in June 1979. The main purpose of the advertising was to get the public to inquire about the benefits of cosmetic surgery. The ad (#27) was designed in a highly dignified manner, with an interesting line illustration and provocative headline.

　The approach is typical of two-step, direct-response advertising. The inquirer fills out the coupon in the ad to get more information. When the Creative Surgery Center receives the coupon, it sends an attractive booklet that contains detailed photographs and information on what cosmetic surgery can do. The coupons have a key number or letter that identifies the publication in which the ad appeared. The advertiser can then determine how many inquiries each publication pulled. In selecting print media, the Creative Surgery Center chose *The New York Times, Gentlemen's Quarterly,* and various other magazines. The center found it was important that ads be placed in the proper editorial environment. It placed its ad in the Living Section of the *Times,* because this section contained self-improvement articles. The center has an annual media budget of $100,000 and carefully monitors all responses to advertising to determine media and message effectiveness.

RESULTS:　The advertising created greater awareness about the role of the Creative Surgery Center and plastic surgeons. It produced a large number of inquiries and new patients. Since the center started advertising, there have been close to a thousand requests for information every week, and the number of surgical procedures has gone up over 30 percent. In addition, many surgeons were so impressed with the quality of the advertising that they sought information on how to join the center.

Case History Number 5

PROFESSIONAL:　F. Lee Bailey & Aaron J. Broder
　　　　　　　New York, N.Y.

PROBLEM:　F. Lee Bailey is probably one of the most famous criminal lawyers in the United States, and normally, he does not have to pay for publicity. However, Mr. Bailey and his partner Aaron Broder have been

specializing in aircraft disasters for many years, and no one but a handful of lawyers knew about it. The firm was getting referrals from other attorneys but not from the public. The vast majority of people were totally unaware of the firm and its area of specialization. Mr. Broder said, "We'd been practicing for eight years, and the public wasn't aware that our firm was in aviation accidents. The only way to inform them was to advertise."

SOLUTION: Bailey & Broder launched a national advertising campaign in the classified sections of papers in Los Angeles, San Francisco, and Chicago and on the front page of *The New York Times*. The firm budgeted approximately $10,000 for this ad campaign. The classified advertisement read as follows:

> F. LEE BAILEY & AARON J. BRODER
> F. Lee Bailey (Mass. Bar)
> Aaron J. Broder (N.Y. Bar)
> Practicing in the representation
> of wrongful death and personal injury
> cases arising out of aircraft disasters
> (212) 244-2000—ADVT.

Bailey & Broder's first ad, a seven-line announcement, appeared on the first page of *The New York Times* one Sunday in January 1979. The firm ran the same ad in the Sunday *Oregonian* following a crash of a United Airlines DC-8 in Portland, which killed 10 persons and critically injured about 20 more. The ad angered many local lawyers, who complained to the Oregon state bar. According to the rules of the Oregon state board, only active members of the board can practice law in Oregon. However, it is not uncommon for an out-of-state lawyer to work with a local lawyer.

RESULTS: The ads were extremely successful in creating greater awareness about Bailey & Broder's aircraft disaster specialty. "Overnight, we suddenly developed a public image as aviation specialists. People started to call us who had been involved in airline accidents," said Mr. Broder. One of the interesting side effects of the advertising was the tremendous number of news stories generated in the press about F. Lee Bailey's advertising. Articles appeared in major newspapers, professional journals, and magazines. Some were critical, others were not; but the overall effect was to make the public aware that Bailey & Broder was now handling aviation accidents. After the tremendous amount of publicity, Bailey & Broder decided to cease advertising.

In the spring of 1981, Bailey and Broder resumed their newspaper advertising. They broadened their original position with this message: "Lawyers practicing in the wrongful death and personal injury cases arising out of aviation and *mass* disasters."

Case History Number 6

PROFESSIONAL: Universal Dental Centers
New York Metropolitan Area

PROBLEM: Dr. Allen Gutstein, the founder of Universal Dental Centers, recognized many years ago that the majority of the people in this country were not receiving any dental care. Each year about 50 percent of the United States population visit a dentist, while only 25 percent practice preventive dentistry. He recognized that if you could attract a good percentage of Americans who do not visit dentists, you would have close to a $10 billion new industry. At this point, he started to write to department stores and other retail establishments. "The reason I chose department stores," he said, "was I wanted to go where the people go, rather than wait for them to come to me." The firm has fees that are 30–50 percent lower than those charged by private practitioners. It also offers dentures and bridgework in three days or less and has office hours seven days a week and in the evenings. In the fall of 1977, Dr. Gutstein leased space in a Times Square Discount Store in Hempstead, New York, and opened his center in November. It was an immediate success thanks to a barrage of publicity in major newspapers and national magazines. In the spring of 1978, the firm expanded to 11 centers in Times Square Stores in the New York metropolitan area. The problem was now to inform the public of the availability of dentistry in their local Times Square Store. In addition, as more and more moderately priced dentists started to advertise, fees became somewhat comparable. So Universal Dental Centers had to reposition itself in the market. "We had to describe our uniqueness and why people should come to us," said Dr. Gutstein.

SOLUTION: The initial ads run by Universal Dental Centers were price-oriented. They featured a list of fees for various services, including examinations, X-rays, dentures, and fillings. The fees were important in the first phase since many consumers were afraid to go to the dentist because they expected a bill for hundreds of dollars. "We put the fees in our ads at the start to tell people in advance that it was not expensive to have their teeth fixed," said Dr. Gutstein. However, Dr. Gutstein recognized the drawbacks of price advertising, "I don't think the idea of advertising price is a positive one. . . . The long term is to build up a group of people who like the convenience of coming to you because you're open seven days a week, accept credit cards, and stand behind the work you do."

In 1978 and the early part of 1979, Universal Dental Centers set a high six-month budget to support the opening of new dental centers. Universal Dental Centers was reported as spending $25,000 per month and $300,000 per year.

The second phase of the campaign featured ads in daily newspapers, such as *Newsday,* and weekly town papers. Universal Dental Centers concentrated its ads in one-and-a-half-month periods, then slacked off for a similar period and resumed the campaign for another month and a half. Bus cards and store circulars were also used to promote the centers' services. Universal Dental Centers hired an advertising agency to design its ads. It sought educational and informative ads to create awareness and believability. The ads used a strong visual; the caption of one (#28) read, "Take this 60 second dental test."

About a year later, Universal Dental Centers launched the third phase of its campaign. It dropped the list of fees and featured cartoons that stressed patient benefits with such headlines as "Good dental care shouldn't cost a fortune" (#29) and "Where's the dentist when you really need him?" This phase of the advertising was run in the New York *Daily News, Newsday, The Amsterdam News, El Diario, Il Progresso, Civil Service Leader,* and selected Long Island weekly newspapers.

In determining the market, Dr. Gutstein surveyed patients in each store. He found that 40 percent had not gone to a dentist in the past five years. The other 60 percent were composed of people who were dissatisfied with their current dentist or had just moved to the area. The vast majority of the patients were in the $20,000–$28,000 income bracket. Dr. Gutstein pointed out, "Anybody earning from $8,000–$30,000 per year is a person we are most attracted to. And with inflation soaring, the larger dollar figure is going to increase."

RESULTS: Universal Dental Centers has become one of the largest chains of in-store dental facilities in the United States. Dr. Gutstein attributes this rapid growth to its extensive advertising efforts. The firm is now moving to expand its facilities into other states. This will be done through licensing programs wherein dentists will operate the facilities on a franchise basis. More and more patients are flocking to the Universal Dental Centers located in Times Square Stores. By 1980, the patient visit load had soared to 5,000 per dentist. Universal Dental Centers found that 20 percent of new patients came because of the advertising, 30 percent be-

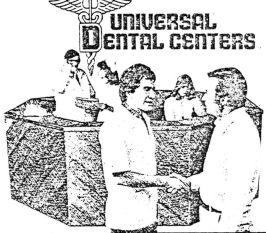

cause of recommendations of friends, and 25 percent as a result of in-store traffic and promotion. The balance came from miscellaneous sources.

Case History Number 7

PROFESSIONAL: Preventive Medicine Institute/Strang Clinic
New York, N.Y.

PROBLEM: The Strang Clinic was founded in 1940 as a component of the Sloan Kettering Memorial Hospital for the purpose of early detection and prevention of cancer. In 1963, this nonprofit organization became independent of the hospital and changed its name to the Preventive Medicine Institute/Strang Clinic. It then sought to broaden its scope by providing individualized diagnostic examinations and promoting preventive health care. The Preventive Medicine Institute derives 85 percent of its revenues from these services. Because it has a large staff of full-time as well as part-time physicians, its operating budget is extremely high. The clinic has a capacity for up to 80 examinations a day, or close to 20,000 per year. The cost of an examination is high, so lower income groups are almost prohibited from seeking such medical care. In 1975, the patient examination flow had dropped to 40 patients a day, and the decline was continuing. The Preventive Medicine Institute was facing a major operating deficit for the first time. It had to take immediate action to halt the slide and turn it around.

SOLUTION: The Preventive Medicine Institute hired a public relations firm, but the situation barely changed. It then hired a communications and public relations specialist named Ira Neiger. Neiger recommended that the Preventive Medicine Institute immediately begin an advertising program to turn the situation around. Using data obtained from patient information forms, a demographic picture of the typical patient was put together: median age of 51 years, white, with income of $25,000–$35,000 per year. The people coming to the clinics were of two types: those who were health minded and came for an annual checkup and those who had something bothering them. It was toward the second group that the advertising was directed.

Using past experience in the health care field, Neiger knew that a nonprofit organization could obtain poster space in subways and buses for free. In addition, many radio stations will run commercials at no cost. All the Preventive Medicine Institute had to do was supply the posters and pay for the posting and produce the tapes for the radio commercials.

Also, many newspapers offer reduced line rates to nonprofit organizations. The restrictions and limitations vary from paper to paper.

In the early part of 1976 (about a year and a half before the Supreme Court decision), the campaign went into action: 5,000 two-color car cards were put up in subway cars, with the headline "Stop worrying" (#30). In addition, tapes were supplied to radio stations for 10-, 20-, 30-, and 60-second spots (#31).

The campaign used two-step advertising, inviting inquiries so that the Preventive Medicine Institute could send a detailed booklet with a price schedule and other relevant information. It also allowed the institute to do follow-up mailings.

In addition, the Preventive Medicine Institute ran small newspaper ads in *The New York Times, The New York Post,* and the *Daily News.* When possible, these ads were placed in health-related sections of these papers. One ad in the *Post* Shape Up section pulled 60 patients, showing the impact of placing an ad in the proper editorial environment. This ad (#32) carried the key "Dept. N" to identify the newspaper that pulled the response.

The institute is located on 34th Street in a high-traffic area near the Empire State Building. Recognizing the central location of the institute, Neiger had a flag designed and hung in front of the building to attract passersby. Eventually, the flag became so popular that it was made into a logo and incorporated in all advertising, brochures, letterheads, and other printed matter.

Also, to encourage former and current patients to schedule new examinations, the institute launched a quarterly newsletter, *Health Action,* which gives information and tips on maintaining good health. It was initially mailed out to patients who had visited the institute over the last four years and was an immediate success. It has become one of the most effective communications devices used by the institute. Hundreds of non-patients have written the Preventive Medicine Institute to have their names included on the mailing list.

In the second phase of the program (introduced a year later), the institute decided to buy radio time. The disadvantage of free air time is that the station will run the spots only when time is available, and that could be at 3:30 A.M. or some other undesirable hour. In addition, the announcements might be grouped with other commercials, decreasing their effectiveness. Seeking mature audiences, the institute purchased radio time for an eight-week flight on specific music (soft and classical), personality, and talk shows.

Stop worrying. We all read and hear of cancer, heart attacks and other serious diseases, and lots of us worry. Well, stop worrying and be good to yourself instead. Protect your health by getting a thorough checkup.

FOR MORE INFORMATION CALL
OR WRITE THE NON-PROFIT

**PREVENTIVE
MEDICINE
INSTITUTE**

**STRANG
CLINIC**

(212) 683-1000
55 EAST 34 STREET
NEW YORK CITY 10016

PMI/Strang Clinic
10-Second Public Service Announcement

Protect your health by getting a complete
checkup. For more information, call the
PMI/Strang Clinic on 34th Street at 683-1000.

30-Second Public Service Announcement

If you haven't been up to par for a while,
or if you've been troubled by unexplained
symptoms that hang on, protect your health
by getting a thorough checkup. For 40 years
the Preventive Medicine Institute/Strang
Clinic has been providing such examinations.
For more information call PMI/Strang at
683-1000. That's S-T-R-A-N-G—the Strang
Clinic on 34th Street, 683-1000.

60-Second Public Service Announcement

We all suffer from aches and pains from
time to time, and often they go away by
themselves. But when symptoms persist and
there's no obvious reason, it's time for a
checkup. Your problem may prove to be a
minor one. Or it may be a sign of an
illness that can be cured if it is detected
early. So if you haven't been up to par
for a while, or if you've been troubled
by unexplained symptoms that hang on, your
best course of action is to arrange for a
thorough diagnostic examination. An outstanding
facility that provides such checkups is the
long-established Preventive Medicine Institute/
Strang Clinic. Just call them at 212/638—1000
for a free booklet describing their services.
That's S-T-R-A-N-G—the Strang Clinic,
and it's conveniently located on 34th Street.
The number again is 212/683—1000.

The institute also continues its nonpaid advertising in subways and commuter trains. It found that subway and commuter train advertising pulled better than advertising on buses and speculated that the average ride on a subway is longer than on a bus, giving the passenger more time to read the advertisements.

RESULTS: The immediate result of all the advertising was an increase in the number of patients scheduling examinations. There were 15,000 examinations a year before advertising, and the number was on the decline. After advertising, examinations increased to 18,000 on a yearly basis.

The Preventive Medicine Institute also found that there was a cyclical pattern to the scheduling of examinations. It noticed that November and December were low months while April, May, and June were the best months. The dip in December was attributable to the Christmas season, which is traditionally a slow period for most professionals. This information was helpful to the institute in scheduling ads.

The advertising also caused a change in the demographics of the typical patient. The median age dropped from 51 to 41. And 20 percent were now blacks. It was still a middle income group, with 90 percent having attended high school. This demographic shift was summed up by Mr. Neiger, who said, "Advertising can broaden your market."

Case History Number 8

PROFESSIONAL: Deloitte Haskins & Sells
United States

PROBLEM: In 1978, Haskins & Sells, one of the largest accounting firms in the United States, changed its name to Deloitte Haskins & Sells. This was done to give the firm a single identity worldwide; the name Deloitte Haskins & Sells had been used in most overseas countries for many years. A new logo and firm-identity system were designed to give a uniform modern look. A survey was conducted of the business community in the United States to determine attitudes toward the profession and the firm. It found that clients thought very highly of the firm, but the level of awareness among others in the business community needed improvement. One Deloitte Haskins & Sells partner said, "Our first objective is awareness. We want our name to be better known. And we want people to think of us when they select an accounting firm for the first time or when they're considering a change in accountants."

Deloitte Haskins & Sells was aware that the accounting profession was undergoing rapid change. The practices of the past were being questioned by government officials, stockholders, corporate officers, and boards of directors, including their audit committees. This increased interest in the accounting profession was causing clients to look very closely at their accounting firms and their services. The changes were bringing about greater competition among accounting firms.

"Competition has always been there, but now it is more intense. All firms have responded to these changed conditions and have become more aggressive. Operating in an environment of open competition is now a fact of professional life," wrote Charles G. Steele, Deloitte Haskins & Sells's managing partner, in the firm's 1979 report.

SOLUTION: Deloitte Haskins & Sells believed it had an important story to tell the business community and that advertising was an effective way to do this. The firm recognized that it performs important services and makes valuable recommendations beyond the minimum expected. It suggests ways of improving accounting systems and controls, keeps clients informed of new developments, develops computer programs for client use, and uses its business acumen to advise clients on improving their operations. These services are all summed up in the firm's advertising theme, "Beyond the bottom line."

This extra effort in behalf of its clients was the way Deloitte Haskins & Sells had been doing business for many years. Now it was time to convey this attitude to the financial community. The firm engaged Needham, Harper & Steers, a large international advertising agency, and launched a campaign in April 1979 in national print magazines and newspapers that reach top management in the business community. Publications selected included *Forbes, Fortune, Time* (executive edition), *Business Week, Dun's Review, Harvard Business Review,* and *The Wall Street Journal.* The first ad in the campaign (#33) asked "What kind of accounting firm doesn't stop at the bottom line?" and set the theme for the entire campaign. Another read, "Small business and big business share the same tax laws. Why shouldn't they share the same accounting firm?" The campaign also sought the high-income taxpayer with an advertisement headed "You're probably going to pay too much in personal income taxes this year" (#34). In addition, the firm ran ads promoting its Washington newsletter (#35).

RESULTS: After the advertising campaign ran for one year, external and internal studies were conducted on its effectiveness. These studies, conducted in 1980, indicated that progress was being made toward the firm's objectives. The advertising campaign is being continued.

CHAPTER 14

Association and Group Advertising—Two Case Histories

In 1776, Thomas Paine wrote in his influential pamphlet *Common Sense:* "'Tis not in numbers but in unity that our great strength lies." Paine, of course, was referring to a small group of patriots who were about to stage a revolution. But the same advice holds true today for professionals: It doesn't matter if there are a handful of practitioners or an entire association, the main point is that there is strength in unity.

One of the reasons professionals have approved of association and group advertising is because it allows them to say things that might have appeared self-serving if they had said them themselves. The American College of Surgeons recently sponsored a public information campaign in national magazines promoting "surgery by surgeons." Dr. Glen R. Leymaster, executive director of the American Board of Medical Specialties, commented on the campaign: "If an individual had done this, it would be looked upon as being sort of distasteful. Organizations can do things that individuals cannot do, so I guess it's all right" (*Medical Tribune*, May 28, 1980).

Many dentists have joined referral groups, such as the American Dental Plan, because their names are never mentioned in the ads. The umbrella organization carries the signature at the bottom of the ad, and the participating professionals remain anonymous to the public at large. Once a client/patient (C/P) is referred to a dentist, the anonymity disappears.

Another reason professionals like group advertising is because it allows them to pool their resources and engage in an extensive advertising campaign. For instance, if 20 practitioners get together and each one puts in $2,500, they have an advertising budget of $50,000. This financial clout allows professionals to hire an advertising agency to advise them on creating the ads, buying the media, and evaluating the campaign. In many cases, associations and groups will hire business managers and administrators to run the campaign and handle all inquiries.

Recent surveys by the American Bar Association indicate that, while most attorneys had reservations about individual advertising, 79 percent favored institutional ad campaigns by units of the bar association. The study also pointed out that lawyers would rather see campaigns that make people more aware of their legal rights than advertising that enhances the lawyer's own image or acts as a referral service, and 82 percent were in favor of using bar association dues to finance such an ad campaign.

COMMON OBJECTIVES

The most important part of any group advertising is to have common objectives. If your objectives are different at the outset, you will find that it will affect every aspect of your advertising plan. One bar association started planning an advertising campaign and midway through the creative effort abandoned the entire project because the objectives were vague. Putting the objectives in writing will not only guide your advertising people in creating a powerful message but also permit you to evaluate the program when it is completed. Two objectives being used by professional groups are to act as a referral service and to educate the public.

Acting as a Referral Service

Many local and regional bar associations have launched advertising campaigns to bring clients and lawyers together. These campaigns are targeted to individuals who have never used an attorney and do not know where to go when they have a specific legal problem. One of the most successful ad campaigns was launched by the Metropolitan Lawyer Referral Service of Denver, Colorado (see Case History Number 1).

In addition to professional associations, many private organizations have been organized to act as referral services for participating professionals. These profit-making organizations are run by entrepreneurs who market professional services to the consumer. They advertise consistently and use the latest marketing techniques to attract C/Ps.

One such organization is the Nationwide Law Firm. It is composed of 400 attorneys in 15 states, who have private practices. The firm advertises that for a $25 retainer a client gets six initial consultations in several legal areas and is put in touch with an attorney specializing in the type of case at hand.

Educating the Public

One of the most popular forms of professional advertising is an educational campaign designed to inform the public about some aspect of a profession or a specialty. The American College of Surgeons (ACS) ran a series of magazine ads promoting surgery by board-certified surgeons. Full-page ads in national magazines carried the theme: "You trust him with your life . . . shouldn't he be a surgeon?" The campaign was aimed at people who use family physicians who do surgery but are not board certified. The ad invited readers to write for a set of brochures on the selection of a surgeon, informed consent fees, and second opinions (#36). Smaller groups of professionals are running newspaper ads in local communities to educate the public as well as to build their practices. These ads list the professionals, their addresses, and their telephone numbers. The participating practitioners share the space costs of the campaign, making it extremely economical.

The Minnesota Dental Association has been one of the pioneers in public-information advertising. Its campaign is discussed in detail in Case History No. 2.

Case History Number 1

PROFESSIONAL: The Metropolitan Lawyer Referral Service, Inc. (MLRS) Denver, Colorado

PROBLEM: The MLRS was founded in July 1972 under the sponsorship of the bar associations of Denver, Aurora, Adams, Arapahoe County, the First Judicial District, and Boulder County. More than 750 lawyers belong to the MLRS, and each is listed by type of practice and location.

The MLRS is a nonprofit organization that puts people with legal problems in touch with lawyers who specialize in those specific problem areas. The MLRS sets up appointments with lawyers in the lawyers' offices. The only charge for the half-hour consultation is $15, which is paid to the lawyer at the time of the appointment. The $15 is returned to the MLRS for administrative and promotional costs.

Before October 1977, the only advertisement for the MLRS was in the Yellow Pages In addition, information cards were given away at courthouses, legal aid societies, and social agencies throughout the area. In May 1978, the MLRS's paid referrals hit a plateau, and when considered in terms of the growth of the area, the service was actually experiencing a downward trend.

SOLUTION: In order to increase public awareness and the number of referrals, the MLRS set an advertising budget of $50,000 for the fiscal year 1978–1979. This was to cover the cost of all media, including the Yellow Pages.

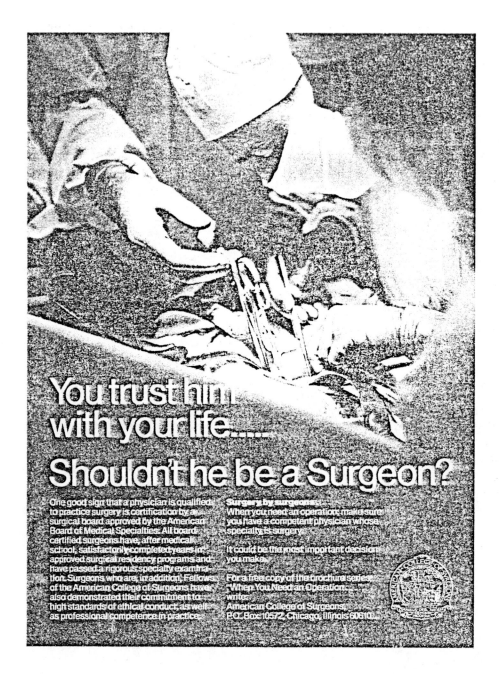

You trust him
with your life.....

Shouldn't he be a Surgeon?

One good sign that a physician is qualified to practice surgery is certification by a surgical board approved by the American Board of Medical Specialties. All board-certified surgeons have, after medical school, satisfactorily completed years in approved surgical residency programs and have passed a rigorous specialty examination. Surgeons who are, in addition, Fellows of the American College of Surgeons have also demonstrated their commitment to high standards of ethical conduct, as well as professional competence in practice.

Surgery by surgeons.
When you need an operation, make sure you have a competent physician whose specialty is surgery.

It could be the most important decision you make.

For a free copy of the brochure series "When You Need an Operation," write:
American College of Surgeons
P.O. Box 10572, Chicago, Illinois 60610.

The first step in planning an ad campaign was selecting an advertising agency to act as adviser, media buyer, and creative consultant. Acting on recommendations from advertising managers at local television stations and independent film production companies, the directors of MLRS interviewed several advertising firms and selected Marcom as its agency.

Working from information obtained from a client questionnaire, Marcom determined the target audience. This audience was defined as individuals who do not have ready access to lawyers primarily because they do not have any contact with professionals individually or through friends. Those segments were further defined as the black and Chicano ethnic groups, the blue-collar workers (often transient and thus unfamiliar with the area's legal resources), and the low- to middle-income first-time legal users.

In order to reach these groups on a regular basis to establish a broad base of public awareness, Marcom recommended that MLRS use a media mix of radio and newspaper advertising. In the radio commercials, MLRS adopted Marcom's suggestion and used a spokesman approach. John Rayburn, a former Denver newscaster, recorded three different 60-second commercials. Each uses the same sting at the end, in which a telephone rings and the MLRS appointment secretary answers "The Metropolitan Lawyer Referral Service. May I help you?" (#37).

These commercials were placed on four different radio stations to run during morning and afternoon drive times, a total of 116 times per week, with an average cost of $11.97 per spot. In addition, all the radio stations were given 30-second versions of the spots. These were placed into their public service announcements schedules and read live on the air. The four stations catered to four specific audiences: Spanish speaking, black, "country-western," and "middle of the road."

In addition to the radio commercials, a newspaper advertising campaign featuring cartoon situations was created (#38 and #39). These small ads appeared in the area's two major daily newspapers. Each cartoon ad featured one particular legal problem. By presenting the problem in a simple and entertaining manner, MLRS was attempting to humanize the legal profession and eliminate some of the fear and apprehension many people feel when approaching a lawyer for the first time.

RESULTS: By recording the source of referral on the appointment information sheets, the MLRS staff was able to keep an accurate tally of those clients who called the service as a direct result of advertising. From October 1977 through June 1978, the total percentage of clients who called because of advertising averaged less than 3 percent. In July, the first

Metropolitan Lawyer Referral Service
60-Second Radio Commercial

At one time or another, we all have to face a serious legal problem—whether it's a traffic accident, divorce, bankruptcy, or buying a new home. When it occurs, most people don't have any idea of how to find the right kind of legal help.

This is John Rayburn, to tell you about the Metropolitan Lawyer Referral Service, approved by the Colorado Bar Association. MLRS is a public service to help you find an attorney experienced in your particular legal problem, right in your own community.

They'll make an appointment for you, usually the same day, and your first half-hour with the lawyer costs only a flat $15.00 fee. After that, he'll tell you in advance what the costs may be, and you decide whether to proceed.

So when you have an important legal problem and need a lawyer, call the Metropolitan Lawyer Referral Service at 573–8871. That's 573–8871....they'll help you find professional legal help easily.

(STING—:05) RING! The Metropolitan Lawyer Referral Service. May I help you?

Table 11. Percentage of MLRS clients by source of referral.

Month	Radio	Newspaper	TV*	Other	Total
July 1978	9.5	1	1.6	1.4	13.5
August	10.4	1.7	1.8	.9	14.8
September	16.5	1.3	3.7	0	21.5
October	11	1.6	2.8	0	15.4
November	12	2.6	2.7	0	17.3

*Public service announcements.

month of the radio and newspaper campaign, this percentage rose to 13.5 and rose even further during the course of the campaign (see Table 11).

The radio schedule terminated on November 11, and the newspaper schedule terminated on November 30. November and December are traditionally "slow legal months." Because of this and because of the barrage of advertisements let loose on the public after Thanksgiving, MLRS decided to take a break in advertising and resume sometime in January.

One of the most important side effects of the surge in referrals was the interest from the board of directors and the staff in expanding the public service role of the MLRS. The board approved funding for the first year of a telephone information service, the Tel-Law Program, which was incorporated as a separate nonprofit corporation in December 1978.

Board members are also beginning to view MLRS as an organization that will soon be capable of sponsoring several public service legal projects, such as an emergency in-court counseling program, seminars for both panel members and the public, and closer ties with other legal and social service agencies. In effect, MLRS has the potential to become a legal clearinghouse for all types of people.

Case History Number 2

PROFESSIONAL: Minnesota Dental Association
Minneapolis, Minnesota

PROBLEM: In 1978, the Minnesota Dental Association (MDA) formed a special committee to investigate the feasibility of mounting a paid-for educational advertising campaign. Previously, the organization had used public service advertising to inform the public about dental health. The association retained Razidlo Advertising to develop a marketing plan.

The agency conducted primary research and analyzed research available from secondary sources. The data indicated that nearly half of the adult population does not seek regular dental care. The American Dental Association's 1978 survey results showed that among adults who do not visit the dentist regularly, the majority (63 percent) do not go because "they have no problems," "their teeth are all right," "they don't have pain," and so on. In other words, a large number of people did not perceive any reason to seek regular care.

SOLUTION: The Minnesota Dental Association decided to implement a statewide advertising campaign to persuade irregular users to seek regular dental care. The long-term goal of the campaign was to increase the total demand for professional dental services among adults. The marketing strategy was to affect demand by converting irregular users—people who have not sought care in two years or more—to regular users of professional dental services. The campaign was directed at adults, 18–49 years old, who do not perceive a need for regular dental care; and the message talked about gum disease. It presented gum disease as an often overlooked but compelling reason to seek regular dental care. As the leading cause of tooth loss among adults, gum disease is the heart of adult dental health problems. Because gum disease does not initially produce painful or easily recognizable symptoms, regular examinations are vital as a preventive or early detection measure.

The campaign objective was to change attitudes first and behavior second. Because people are creatures of habit, it would be unrealistic to expect irregular users to flock to dental offices at the urging of an advertising campaign. Rather, the MDA viewed its mission as one that must focus on changing attitudes and breaking down the resistance of people who, for a variety of complex reasons, are not seeking regular dental health care. It is only after you succeed in changing attitudes that you can expect a significant change in behavior.

The campaign's creative strategy was based on a study of the use of preventive dental services.* According to this study, preventive dental health behavior is determined by the interaction of three variables: (1) people must feel susceptible to a disease; (2) people must believe that the effects of the disease are potentially serious for them; and (3) people must believe that some preventive course of action is available to them.

A television commercial (#40) was created on the basis of the above findings. The 30-second commercial (1) suggested that the viewer may have gum disease and not know it; (2) dramatized the loss of one's teeth if the disease goes untreated; and (3) dramatized that regular dental visits can prevent gum disease or detect it in its early, treatable stages.

---

*Chester W. Douglas and Katherine O. Cole, "Utilization of Dental Services in the United States," *Journal of Dental Education*, Vol. 3, No. 4 (1979).

Minnesota Dental Association

30-Second Television Commercial

"Keep Your Teeth"

VIDEO	AUDIO
CU view through mouth of dentist examining patient's teeth	ANNCR (VO): If you haven't been to the dentist lately, look at it from your mouth's point of view.
	DENTIST: You're right, no cavities.
	PATIENT: I ho you ho.
	DENTIST: You have pyorrhea.
	PATIENT: I ha wha?
	DENTIST: Gum disease. Most people don't even know they have it.
Dentist applies topical with cotton swab	PATIENT: Whass ah?
	DENTIST: For your comfort. Dentistry has changed since you went last.
CUT to same scene later in visit	PATIENT: Bedder ow?
	DENTIST: Yep. But now it's up to you to keep them that way.
CUT to false teeth falling into glass of water on limbo set. SUPER: See your dentist and keep your teeth. Before gum disease has you looking for a place to keep them.	ANNCR (VO): See your dentist and keep your teeth. Before gum disease has you looking for a place to keep them.

CU = close-up; CUT = scene changes; ANNCR (VO) = voice off camera; SUPER = type superimposed over background.

The television campaign ran for two six-week flights during the summer of 1979 and the winter of 1980. An average of 165 gross rating points were purchased each week. Thirty-second and 10-second spots were purchased on local news programs and during early and late fringe programming. A total of $150,000 was spent on television time over the campaign period.

The summer television campaign was also supported by a newspaper ad, which ran in 19 Minnesota daily newspapers. The ad (#41) featured a coupon and invited the reader to send for a free booklet, "How to Become a Wise Dental Consumer."

RESULTS: Prior to the TV campaign, approximately a thousand residents throughout the state were polled in personal interviews. Following the campaign, another thousand Minnesotans were interviewed. Those who recalled seeing or hearing advertising about gum disease increased from 36 percent in the precampaign survey to 79 percent in the postcampaign survey. The awareness of the advertising in the 30–49 age group rose from 42 percent to 84 percent. About 71 percent of all those who remembered the ads correctly articulated their content.

The respondents who were able to identify gum disease as the major cause of adult tooth loss rose from 53 percent to 59 percent overall and 63 percent to 72 percent in the target group. Among the nonregular users of dental care, 9 percent said they planned to see the dentist more often.

CHAPTER 15

How to Find and Work with an Advertising Agency

CHOOSING AN ADVERTISING AGENCY is a bit like getting married. You are entering into a relationship that involves mutual trust, respect, honesty, commitment, and hard work. It is also one of the most important decisions you can make if you want to advertise.

Selecting an advertising agency is not easy. In fact, at times it can seem overwhelming. But if you give it the proper time and organize your efforts, it can prove to be a learning experience about the advertising business and the people in it.

How do you go about selecting an advertising agency? There is no right or wrong way. However, there are several steps you can take that will help you in screening agencies, narrowing the field, and making the final selection.

DO YOU NEED AN ADVERTISING AGENCY?

If you are considering advertising, one of the questions that you will ultimately ask yourself is "Do I need an advertising agency?" This question can be answered if you analyze the complexity of your advertising plan, the size of your budget, and the amount of time you have available to devote to learning the advertising business.

Roger Brosnahan, chairman of the American Bar Association's Commission on Advertising, believes that lawyers are hurting themselves when they create their own ads. He commented in *Advertising Age* (February 19, 1979), "We've found that the most efficient ads were done by [advertising] professionals. Advertising is a specialized field that calls for specialists."

Arnold Siegel of the accounting firm of Siegel, Sugarman & Seput wrote in the *California CPA Quarterly* (March 1979): "It takes professionals working with professionals to produce responsible advertising. We chose an agency after interviewing several, and after we had decided what we wanted our ads to do and had the basic appearance of the ads in mind."

Here are four factors to consider.

Your advertising plan. If you are considering placing small ads in the classified section of one or two local newspapers, you certainly don't need an advertising agency. It would be overqualified for this type of campaign. You can create the ads and place them with the media yourself. On the other hand, if you are planning a campaign that will employ a wide array of services—such as market research, media analysis and scheduling, copywriting, and art direction—you should consider hiring an advertising agency.

Your budget. The first thing that you will have to decide before getting involved in any advertising is how much you are prepared to spend on a campaign. If your budget is small (under $10,000), you are better off trying to do it yourself. Very few advertising agencies will take on an account that has such a limited budget. In this case, you should contact local media sales representatives and ask for the names of freelance art directors and copywriters. There are also art and design studios in most cities and towns that can assist you in creating powerful advertising; these are generally listed in the Yellow Pages. Another place to find creative sources is in the trade publication *AdWeek*.* It has Midwest, East, Southeast, Southwest, and West regional editions that carry classified ads for a wide variety of freelance talent.

If you have a sizable budget, it would be advisable for you to work with an advertising agency. There are many small, medium-size, and large agencies that can fill your needs and help you create a successful advertising campaign. Generally, the larger the budget, the more complex your advertising plan will be and the larger the agency you will need. There is a significant amount of coordination between the creative, production, media, traffic, and market research departments, and only a large agency can offer you all these services.

Your time. "There is no mystery about advertising," said one practitioner. "All it takes is a lot of hard work and a great deal of time." There is no doubt in my mind that any practitioner can learn advertising procedures

---

*Published by ASM Communications, 230 Park Ave., New York, N.Y. 10017.

quickly. You may have a flair for writing and think that you can produce your own ads. However, it will take a great deal of your time, and you are apt to make costly mistakes as you learn. And if you become inundated with work, you may have to shelve your ad program to concentrate on your practice—unless you bring in freelance talent to help you.

Your needs. Determine what functions you want an advertising agency to perform for you. Exactly what services will you need? Will they include copy, art, media, market research, production, promotion, and public relations. If you hire an agency that offers a wide array of services, you will pay for this one way or another. So make sure that the agency's capabilities match your needs.

WHAT SERVICES DOES AN AGENCY OFFER?

Though the variety of services that advertising agencies offer may differ considerably, the larger ones offer similar services. Most of these agencies belong to the American Association of Advertising Agencies (known as the "4As"), which has set up a standard of service for its members. When an agency offers all these services, it is generally referred to as a full-service advertising agency.

Listed below are a variety of services offered to professionals by 4A agencies:

1. *Study of the project.* From the beginning, the agency will study your practice (or service) to find out the advantages and disadvantages and how it compares with the competition.

2. *Market Analysis.* The agency will analyze the present and potential market for your service. It will recommend new ways to increase the C/P flow as well as to broaden your practice.

3. *Knowledge of media.* Advertising agencies will have a knowledge of all media; they will be able to identify target audiences and then propose media that deliver your message to them at the lowest cost per thousand.

4. *Factors of professional use.* Advertising agencies will study all the aspects of your practice. They will visit your office, meet your staff, and talk to C/Ps to gain first-hand knowledge of what makes your practice tick. They will study the seasonal patterns of your practice and recommend systems for using the time of your staff productively.

5. *Developing an advertising plan.* Advertising agencies will develop an advertising plan. The agency will make recommendations on marketing, media, the creative appeal, the message, and the budget.

6. *Putting the plan into action.* Once the advertising plan has been approved, the agency will move quickly to produce the print ads and commercials. This will involve the talents of copywriters, art directors, production staff, producers, etc. The media department will issue contracts for space and time. The finished ads and tapes of commercials will be distributed to the media. After the advertisement has run, the agency will check to verify it by seeking proof of implementation. Lastly, they will bill the advertiser for the space and time and pay the media.

BEFORE YOU START TALKING TO AGENCIES

Before you meet with any prospective advertising agency, you should be able to provide it with certain information. It is sure to ask you for this, so you better be prepared with answers.

1. *Your budget.* Be prepared to tell an agency what your total advertising budget will be for a specific period of time. It might be six months or one year.
2. *Your objectives.* The agency will want to know what you want to accomplish with your advertising and whether these objectives are realistic and achievable with your proposed budget.
3. *Association or society guidelines.* Find out in advance any constraints put on professional advertising by your state society or association. It will be easier for you than for your prospective agency to get this information.
4. *Your competition.* It would pay for you to clip out your competitors' ads. These will make it easier for an agency to make a meaningful proposal on how to position your practice.
5. *Other information.* This includes a situation analysis of your practice, C/P demographics, facts about your specialty, and any other data that you can supply.

ABOUT ADVERTISING AGENCIES

There are over 8,000 advertising agencies in the United States. They vary from international giants, with offices scattered throughout the world, to the tiny one-person agencies operating out of an office that resembles a closet. The vast majority of agencies in the United States are small. Close to one-third of all agencies are essentially one-person operations; another third average only five employees; but the remaining third have hundreds of employees and many offices.

The size of an agency has nothing to do with its competence. There are some very good small agencies that are turning out outstanding work. Many have principals who were formerly with big agencies and are eager to create a name for themselves and will therefore take on a small client that has potential. The larger agencies offer you a broad range of services, but most of them will not take on a small account because it will not be profitable for them. In most cases, they will set a minimum billing amount or fee for new accounts that may be prohibitive for the small firm.

One thing a small advertiser does not want is to hire an advertising agency that will neglect his account. This happens more often than you might imagine. A small advertiser stands a better chance of getting top-notch service from an agency when the account represents a substantial portion of the overall billings. According to one advertising expert, Kenneth Groesbeck, budgets of $100,000 can best be taken care of in agencies whose total billings are from 10 to 20 times that amount.

Many smaller advertisers make the mistake of hiring well-known agencies to impress their colleagues. This can be a costly mistake. A study by the consulting firm of Booz, Allen and Hamilton concluded, "Agencies, regardless of size, must gear their operation to the needs of their most significant clients . . . small advertisers will find that, if they are not attractive in profitability or growth potential, they will not be getting the best service otherwise available to them."

HOW TO FIND AN AGENCY

Finding an advertising agency can be easy if you go about it the right way. The first thing to do is to put together a list of potential agencies. Here is how:

Your C/Ps. The place to start is with your own files. You may have a C/P who is in the advertising business and who can recommend an agency that would suit your practice.

Media sales representatives. Another method to find agencies—and certainly one of the most popular—is to contact media sales representatives in your community. Tell them what your budget will be and what kind of agency you are looking for. The problem with this method is that, once the word gets out that you are looking for an agency, you will be inundated with telephone calls from aggressive agencies that want your business. So it's best to tell the rep to keep your discussion confidential and to recommend just four or five agencies.

Directories and advertising publications. The *Standard Directory of Advertising Agencies** (or Agency "Red Book" as it is called) lists practically all advertising agencies in the United States. It also lists the accounts, the latest billings, the management, and a percentage breakdown of billings according to each medium. The book is available in most libraries, or you can write to the publisher. *Advertising Age,†* the major publication in the industry, also does an annual agency roundup every February and lists agencies according to the size of billings, new accounts added, and any major campaigns launched in the preceding year.

Local advertising. Another way to find an agency is to watch local media. If you see an ad for a local business (or professional) that you think is particularly effective, call the newspaper (or station) and find out the agency that created it. It will be glad to give you the information. Another possibility is to call the firm that ran the advertisement and ask for the name of the agency and a recommendation.

Using a Questionnaire

Once you have completed a list of potential agencies, attempt to narrow down the number so that it is manageable. One way to do this is to develop a questionnaire.

Many advertisers like to use a questionnaire because they believe it is a good way to get basic information in a form that lets them compare agencies. They use the questionnaire as a method of screening agencies, not as a means of making a final selection. It also permits you to review the answers at your leisure, to check out sources, and to make any notes that might be used in future meetings.

Most agencies do not like questionnaires because they can be time consuming to fill out. So if you use one, keep it brief—not more than one or two pages.

Here are some typical questions that you might ask in a questionnaire:

1. When was the agency established?
2. What are the names and titles of its principal officers?
3. What is the total agency billing?
4. What are the billings of the smallest and largest accounts? What is the average billing for all accounts?

---

*Published by National Register Publishing Company, 147 W. 42nd St., New York, N.Y. 10036.

†Published by Crain Communications, Inc., 740 North Rush St., Chicago. Ill. 60611.

5. What is the number of full-time employees?
6. What is the agency's credit rating?
7. Where is the agency located? (Can it service your account effectively?)
8. How is the agency organized?
9. Who are the people who will work on your account? (This includes the account executive, art director, copywriter, media buyer, and research people.)
10. What are the backgrounds and accomplishments of these people?
11. Exactly who in agency management will work on your problems, and how much time will be devoted to them?
12. Does the agency have a creative process? Describe it.
13. Who are the agency's current clients, by industry?
14. What services does the agency offer?
15. How does the agency charge for services? •
16. What services will be covered by the agency commission? What services will be billed as extras?
17. Will additional fees be required?
18. How does the agency want to be compensated?

From this checklist, select the questions that apply to your own situation. Add any questions that you think will help you make a decision. However, remember to keep the questionnaire short so that it does not discourage any agency from answering it.

Narrowing Down Your Choices

On the basis of the answers obtained from your questionnaires, select the agencies that offer the greatest potential. Visit each agency personally and meet the management. Review some past and current campaigns for other clients, and discuss the agency's philosophy for creating an ad campaign.

This meeting will give you a better understanding of the agency and its people. And it is the people—researchers, market analysts, copywriters, art directors, and media buyers—who make an agency. You should feel comfortable with the agency staff and its management, because this will be important in a client–agency relationship. You want to know that the agency is concerned about your practice and will do everything to see that you are successful.

Making the Final Selection

When you have narrowed the field down to three or four agencies, invite them to your office. You can tell a lot from discussions with an agency's top management and principals. They will make suggestions and recommendations; ask them to put these, as well as what services they offer and the method of compensation, in writing.

Do not expect advertising agencies to make speculative presentations for your account if it is small. They won't do it. It requires a good deal of time, money, and effort to create an advertising campaign. You cannot expect an agency to come up with effective advertising until it is more familiar with your practice. It takes many months for an agency to develop an understanding of your practice, and this knowledge is what makes a great ad campaign.

Drawing Up an Agreement

In any new relationship between an agency and client, a letter of agreement or contract should be drawn up. Insist on it as a matter of protection. You do not want any misunderstanding to occur later that cannot be ironed out by referring to the initial agreement. The agreement should spell out in detail which services the agency will perform for you and how and what it will charge for these services. It should cover planning, research, copy, art, production costs, media, and public relations. The agreement should also have a termination clause in case either party wants to end the relationship. The clause will call for a termination period of up to 90 days from the receipt of a written notice.

It is not uncommon for many agencies to bill space and time costs in advance, before the advertising appears. It enables them to pay the media when the bills become due and to take advantage of discounts if they are offered. The vast majority of agencies cannot afford to act as a banker for their accounts.

HOW AGENCIES ARE COMPENSATED

There are a variety of agency compensation agreements, and you will find that even within the same agency clients are billed differently. The compensation arrangement between you and the agency is an individual one, based on the commissions generated from the media and the services you will require.

The 4As, after surveying its members, found the eight most common compensation arrangements between agencies and clients were:

1. Media commissions plus charges for materials and services purchased for clients plus charges for some specific inside services.
2. Media commissions plus charges for materials and services purchased, with no charges for any inside services.

3. Media commissions only.
4. Arrangement 1, 2, or 3 above, plus an overall additional fee.
5. Arrangement 1, 2, or 3 above, with a profit floor and profit ceiling.
6. A minimum fee, against which media commissions are credited.
7. An overall fee agreed upon in advance.
8. The overall cost of handling the entire account, or cost plus, calculated after the work is done.

The Media Commission System

The media commission system is still the most popular method of agency compensation. Its popularity has been declining, however, as more and more agencies switch to other methods. In 1979, about 57 percent of all agencies derived their income solely from this system. Just four years earlier, 66 percent of all agencies were on media commissions only.

Almost all media pay a 15 percent commission to recognized advertising agencies. Outdoor advertising firms pay a 16⅔ percent commission. They recognize the value of ad agencies in performing a number of functions and in representing a number of different clients. In fact, the media would prefer to deal with agencies than with local small businesses, because agencies understand the complexities of producing good advertising, and they have established credit ratings with the media. Ad agencies will be responsible for payment to the media if a client defaults. Also billing and collection procedures are simplified for media when they deal with a few agencies rather than with hundreds of small businesses.

Ethics do not permit the media to give commissions directly to advertisers. However, it is not uncommon for large companies to set up "house" agencies so that they can keep the commissions. Even smaller advertisers have done it to save the 15 percent. But this practice is not widespread and should not be attempted unless you are extremely knowledgeable in advertising procedures and have the staff to handle your own advertising.

Here is how the media commission system works. If you run an advertisement in a local newspaper or a commercial on radio or TV, your agency will be sent an invoice for the total cost; 15 percent will be deducted from the invoice. The agency keeps this amount for the service it renders. For example, if a radio commercial costs $1,000, the agency will bill you $1,000, the radio station will bill the agency $1,000 less $150, and the amount due from the agency to the station will be $850. Some media still offer a 2 percent discount if the invoice is paid promptly (within ten days). If you pay your bills on time, this 2 percent saving should be passed on to you.

If your total media budget is $50,000, the agency will receive $7,500 in commissions. In most cases, this will not be enough to cover the agency's time and overhead for handling your account, and the agency may ask you for a supplementary fee.

The Fee Arrangement

There has been a steady trend away from the media commission system in favor of fees. The Association of National Advertisers revealed that the use of a combination of fees and commissions increased from 3 to 18 percent between 1976 and 1979. The straight fee arrangement increased from 8 to 25 percent. Many big national advertisers, such as American Telephone and Telegraph, Shell Oil, and Kraft, are on a fee arrangement with advertising agencies, as are many small companies. For advertisers with small budgets, the fee arrangement recognizes the fact that agencies will have to put in a good deal of time servicing an account, and the 15 percent commissions received from the media will not cover this. An agency should be compensated adequately to insure that you will get the kind of service you need. If an agency does not make a reasonable profit on your account, the quality of the advertising and the commitment to your account will suffer.

Most agencies base a fee arrangement on the estimated amount of work to be done in behalf of an account. After six months or the first year, this fee should be renegotiated on the basis of the actual time records submitted by the agency. These time records should be kept on an hourly/daily basis for the different projects initiated and completed.

About Production Charges

In addition to income derived from commissions and fees, agencies will also realize income from the production of print advertising and commercials. Advertising agencies will add a 17.65 percent markup on all the production costs paid in behalf of a client. This includes the costs of type, printing, photography, illustrations, photostats, veloxes, offset negatives, and the production of TV and radio commercials.

Furthermore, all agencies will charge for the time of their creative people. This includes charges for layout, copywriting, pasteup, and type specification. These creative services are billed to the advertiser on an hourly rate, which can range from $35 to $100 per hour depending on the individuals involved and the agreement between the agency and client.

Many agencies submit estimates in advance to inform clients of what a particular ad or project will cost. It would be wise to ask your agency for an estimate before it launches an advertising program. Don't be afraid to discuss these estimated charges before the project is started. You might find that by using different sources (e.g., photographers, typographers) you can save hundreds of dollars.

HOW TO WORK WITH AN ADVERTISING AGENCY

If you want to get the best thinking and maximum creative effort out of your advertising agency, you better establish a line of communication. An agency has a right to know everything about your practice, from the marketing plan and C/P flow to the profitability. If you keep this a secret, don't expect the agency to recommend solutions to any of your problems. Agencies aren't clairvoyant, and unless you tell them what is on your mind, they will never know.

Here are suggestions on how to get the most out of your advertising agency:

1. *Be completely honest.* Tell the agency anything that you feel it should know for improving the advertising effort. It needs guidance, and only you can give it.

2. *Return all telephone calls and letters.* Many times letters and telephone calls to clients will go unanswered. Most agencies will accept this as typical of the client–agency relationship. However, it is not the best way to produce outstanding advertising.

3. *Make sure the agency knows your profession and practice.* It is not uncommon for advertising agencies to create a campaign with little knowledge of a practice or profession. It is your responsibility to explain in detail everything you can about your practice. Introduce the agency people to your staff and invite them to ask any questions that might be helpful in positioning your practice. Your staff can give agency personnel valuable insight into what makes your practice unique.

4. *Be constructive about the creative effort.* When an agency arranges a meeting to present creative ideas, be constructive with your criticism. Look at the basic selling proposition, the consumer benefits, and the positioning first. Then check out things like the layout and copy.

5. *Compliment your agency.* In all the years I have been in this business, I have found that it is the rare client who will tell an agency it is doing a good job. A little praise can go a long way in firing up the creative people back at the agency. And this enthusiasm can be reflected in even better advertising in the future.

GLOSSARY

How to Talk to Advertising People

adjacencies   Programs or commercial announcements that are next to, or adjacent to, each other on the same station and appear immediately before and after any specific TV program.

AFTRA   American Federation of Television and Radio Artists; a talent union.

agate line   A standard measurement of the depth of newspaper ad space. There are 14 agate lines to the inch. This refers to running column inches—for example, a one-column ad 4 inches deep measures 56 agate lines.

airbrush   A compressed air sprayer that applies fine amounts of watercolor pigment for delicate tonal and shading effects. Used in retouching photographs.

alterations   Changes made in copy matter after it has been set in type.

animation   A motion picture made by photographing a series of art pieces, each with a part of the subject slightly altered, creating an illusion of movement.

announcement   Any television commercial, regardless of length, within or between programs that presents an advertiser's message or a public service message.

ARB   American Research Bureau; one of several national firms engaged in radio and TV research. Survey reports are issued for individual markets.

area of dominant influence (ADI)   The geographic area of counties in which an advertiser's home market television stations hold a dominance of total hours viewed. It tells the advertiser the size of the market reached by local stations. ADI is the term used by Arbitron and is similar to DMA (designated market area), used by the A. C. Nielsen Company.

artwork   Any drawing, illustration, mechanical, or photograph used in advertisements.

aspect ratio   The width-height ratio of a TV picture—4 units × 3 units.

audience composition   The statistical breakdown, in terms of specific characteristics, of radio or television audiences for a particular program, time period, or advertiser's schedule. It is used most frequently to designate the number or percentage of men, women, teenagers, and children in the audience. The term can also be applied to audiences of other media.

audience duplication   The number of households or people reached by one program (or station) that is also reached by another program (or station). Also applies to print media.

audio   The sound portion of a television broadcast.

author's alterations (AAs) Changes in proofs of printed matter made at the request and expense of the author or person paying for the composition and not resulting from errors made by the printer.

availability A period of commercial announcement time that is available for purchase from a station by an advertiser.

benday A method of producing a variety of shaded tints and texture patterns on line art or film, used by engravers and artists to make tones and shadings.

billboard A short commercial announcement, usually eight or ten seconds, at the start and close of a program announcing the name of the sponsor. Also, a term used by the layman to designate a 24-sheet poster panel.

black-and-white (B&W) Prints or printing in one color, black, on white paper.

bleed (page) Any printed illustration or color in a magazine that extends to the edge of the page, eliminating the margin.

blowup A photographic enlargement of artwork or copy.

blueprint A proof from negative or positive film on special blueprint paper.

body copy The main reading material of an ad, exclusive of headline or logo.

boldface A heavier, weightier version of any typeface.

bond Letterhead or writing paper that has good strength and permanence, usually with some rag content. .

book To schedule a show, talent, meeting, or event.

booklet A small book or multipage mailing, often with self-cover, used in direct-mail advertising.

boom (up, down) To raise, lower a microphone or camera on a boom.

break The time available for purchase between two programs or between segments of a show.

broadsheet A full-size newspaper—approximately 15 inches wide by 24 inches deep, usually 2,400–2,900 lines.

broadside A large folder used in direct-mail advertising.

bronzing Applying bronze powder to still-wet printing ink, for a metallic finish.

brown paper A proof from negative or positive film on special proofing paper. Also called a "Van Dyke."

buying service A company primarily engaged in the purchase of media.

cable TV Any facility that receives and distributes via cable to individual TV sets of members who pay a monthly subscriber's fee.

campaign A specific advertising effort that extends for a specified period of time on behalf of a particular product or service.

cancellation Termination of a contract calling for a broadcast of less than five minutes' duration. Such a contract may be terminated by either party upon giving notice in writing a specified number of days in advance.

cancellation date The last date on which an order for space may be canceled.

CATV Community Antenna Television. CATV provides network and local TV programming in "difficult reception areas" where normal TV reception is either very poor or nonexistent. The CATV system has three principal components to perform this function: a sensitive antenna that picks up the signals; a coaxial cable that transmits them to subscribers; and amplifiers to insure delivery of signals of acceptable strength.

CC Conclusion of a program—for example, 11:30 P.M. CC.

checkerboard programming Running completely different programs each day in each time period.

chromalin A four-color process proof made on a sensitized paper using powdered dyes.

circulation In radio and TV, the number of households or individuals that are tuned in to a station once or more often in a week. The total is the station's weekly circulation. In newspapers and magazines, the average number of copies per issue sold on newsstands or through subscriptions (paid circulation), or distributed free to a selected audience (controlled circulation).

closed circuit A telecast transmitted from camera to monitor, but not broadcast publicly.

close-up A tightly framed or cropped picture of a person or object, or a portion of such.

closing date The last date for submitting artwork or negatives to a publication.

clutter Frequent interruptions of program material with commercials, promotions, and public service announcements.

coarse-screen halftone A screened photograph with vertical and horizontal lines spaced far apart—65–85 lines to the inch. Generally used for newspaper reproduction of photographs and illustrations.

cold type Direct-impression type composition as set by phototype compositors.

collate To assemble or gather printed sheets or signatures of sheets for binding or collecting into a whole group.

color correction Dot etching, re-etching, or masking to improve color in process color printing.

color filter An optical glass sandwich with color gelatin or plastic cemented inside, used in photography for special effects.

color keys Sometimes called "3M proof" or "Geva proof." The least expensive method of making a four-color proof. Made with four different color overlays (yellow, magenta, cyan, and black) on clear vinyl.

color proof A small-run four-color proof, printed in advance to show what the finished piece will look like before it goes on a larger press for the final printing.

color separation A photographic separation of art or photos by filters to isolate four-process colors for printing.

color separation negatives The negatives used in making plates for color printing. Each negative possesses a color characteristic of the original artwork. In four-color printing, there would be one negative for each of the primary colors and one for black.

column inch A unit of measurement for printed matter, one column wide, one inch deep (14 agate lines).

combination negative A negative combining both line art (unscreened) and halftone (screened), the material being adjacent or overlapping.

commercial impressions The total audience, including duplication, for all commercial announcements in an advertiser's schedule.

composition The organization or arrangement of all the components of a design or layout.

comprehensive A layout done in detail sufficient enough to make it look like a finished advertisement.

condensed type Narrow, slender type.

confirmation A verbal or written acceptance of a space or time contract by station or publication.

contact print A photoprint made by exposure of a film negative or positive directly against print paper.

contrast The difference between color-tone qualities, or black–grays–white, needed for good separation of elements.

copy All material to be broadcast (radio) or put on TV (audio) signal; the written portion of an advertiser's message.

copy fitting Specifying manuscript copy to type size, line width, and depth to fit a given area.

cost per point (CPP) Used as a budgeting method by most agencies to obtain an advertising level at a predetermined cost; for example, 100 rating points per week at $50 CPP = $5,000 budget per week.

cost per thousand (CPM) The advertising cost of reaching 1,000 units, messages, households, viewers, etc., with a particular media vehicle or media schedule. It is computed by dividing the advertising cost by the number of households or viewers and multiplying by 1,000.

coverage (area) The number of sets or homes in a geographic area, usually designated by counties, in which a radio or television station signal can be received.

cropping The cutting or deleting of any unwanted portions of a picture or illustration to make the image fit a given space.

crossmarks Register marks. Used to align one printing element or plate with others.

cue A signal for action to begin. Dots on a film to indicate the end.

cumulative audience (cume) The total, unduplicated audience reached by a station during two or more time periods or by successive issues of a publication. May also be used with an advertiser's schedule to show how many different households or people a schedule reaches. (Also called "net audience" or "unduplicated audience.")

demographics The statistics of an audience broken down by age, sex, income, marital status, education, etc.

direct-response advertising Any direct advertising to recipients through the mails or through print or broadcast media that is designed to pull an order or inquiry.

dissolve A fade-out of one picture and the overlapping fade-in of another in television.

dress Stage clothing. Final rehearsal. Set properties and dressings.

drop A large, painted background for staging a show.

dropout (halftone) A screened photograph with no dot pattern in certain areas to give highlights or greater contrast. See *halftone*.

dry run   A rehearsal.

dubbing   Transcribing a sound track from one source to another, or one or more sound tracks onto a single film.

duotone   Separation of a black-and-white illustration or photo into two separate halftones for two-color printing.

early fringe   The time period preceding prime time TV (usually from 4:30 to 7:30 P.M., except in the Central Time Zone, where it extends from 3:30 to 6:30 P.M.).

editing   Putting significant story parts in proper sequence and eliminating unimportant matter.

end rate   The lowest rate an advertiser pays after all discounts have been applied.

fade   To decrease sound. To increase black (fade to black), or decrease black (fade in).

film positive print   A film print made by exposing a negative to negative film. A reverse film print of a negative.

flat   Art or photo lacking in contrast.

flight   An advertising campaign that runs for a specified number of weeks, followed by a period of inactivity.

flip cards   Lettered or printed cards flipped off an easel in sequence as they are read or televised.

flop   To reverse direction; to turn a negative over before printing so the image faces the direction opposite that in the original copy.

flush right (left)   Type set to align on the right (or left). The other side may be flush or irregular (ragged).

folder   A direct-mail advertising piece folded one or more times.

folio   Page number (left-hand pages have even numbers; right-hand pages have odd numbers).

font   A complete assortment of type in one size and style of letters, figures, and symbols.

format   The makeup of a publication, including size and shape. The style, content, and design of any printed piece. Also, a plan or agenda outlining all show elements, in sequence, including all programming and script from opening to closing.

four-color printing   Printing that employs the three primary colors plus black to give a full-color reproduction.

fourth cover   The back or outside portion of the cover of a magazine.

frequency   The average number of times an audience is exposed to a given TV or radio schedule (either programs or announcements or both) within a stated period of time. See *reach* and *cumulative audience*.

fringe time   The time periods preceding or following prime time. See *early fringe* and *late fringe*.

full position   Advertising space at the top or bottom of a page, flanked by reading matter other than advertising.

galley proof   A proof of type, for verification before it is printed.

grid card   A rate card that allows a station to price its spots individually on the basis of audience delivery and so have a variety of rates within each time period.

gross audience   The total number of households or people delivered by a particular television schedule without regard to any duplication that may occur. This is distinguished from a net, unduplicated audience, which gives the number of different households or individuals reached. Also called "total audience."

gross impressions   The sum of the audiences of every vehicle used in a media schedule. Since people exposed to the same vehicle more than once, or people exposed to more than one vehicle, are counted in the total, gross impressions includes duplication. It is an expression of the gross audience of a schedule of announcements or insertions.

gross rating points (GRPs)   The total estimated size of the television or radio audience for a given program (or advertisement), expressed as a percentage of the total audience, in terms of either households or individuals. It may be defined for a specific period. Like gross impressions, it includes duplication. (Reach × frequency = GRP.) See *reach* and *frequency*.

gutter   The margin or blank space between the printed area and the binding edge.

halftone   An illustration or photograph that has been screened to re-create the tonal values of the original.

high key   Brightly illuminated; all tonal values light and bright.

highlight   The lightest, whitest, brightest spots in art, in a photo, or on a TV screen. On a halftone, dots will be very tiny or completely absent.

horizontal publication   A publication having an editorial content of interest to only one group of professionals—for example, lawyers.

house organ   A company magazine or newspaper. It may be edited for internal, external, or a combination of internal and external distribution.

imposition   The arrangement of printed pages on a flat sheet that will be in correct numerical order when folded for gathering and binding.

impressions   The total number of commercials or advertisements scheduled, multiplied by the total target audience exposed on each occasion.

independent stations   Stations that have no network affiliation and are programmed independently of the three major networks.

insert   In magazines or newspapers, a page or booklet printed by the advertiser and inserted in the publication by the publisher. It is often printed on different stock from that used for the publication. In television, the term refers to a picture inserted in another picture to emphasize detail or to dramatize an idea.

insertion order   An order to an advertising medium to publish an advertisement according to agreed-upon specifications.

island position   The placing of a commercial announcement away from any other commercial announcement—that is, with program content on both sides.

isolated 30   A 30-second commercial announcement that runs by itself, not in combination with any other commercial announcement. Usually found on network television.

laminate   A printed sheet, photo, or illustration covered by a clear plastic sheet attached by pressure and heat.

late fringe   The time period following prime time TV (usually after 11 P.M., except in the Central Time Zone, where it starts at 10 P.M.).

layout   The drawing of an advertisement by an artist. Also used in agency planning for obtaining a client's approval.

line art   Artwork with black lines and no tonal values, as in a pen-and-ink drawing.

list house   A business organization (list broker) that sells or rents names and addresses for use in direct-mail advertising and mail-order selling.

lithography   The process of printing from a flat surface, based on the principle that grease and water will not mix.

logo   An abbreviation of "logotype." The nameplate, usually distinctive in appearance, of an advertiser. A trademark of a company.

lower case   The noncapital letters of any typeface or alphabet.

makegood (MG)   A rerun by the medium at no cost to the advertiser because of an error during the first run.

marketing   An analysis of the marketplace, including the problems and opportunities, and the use of the results of such an analysis to deliver a particular service at a profit.

mechanical   A pasteup with all elements in place and ready for camera.

media buyer   A person responsible for purchasing advertising in any medium.

media planner   A person responsible for determining the proper use of an advertising medium or combination of media to fulfill the marketing objectives for a specific product or advertiser.

medium   A vehicle that carries advertising, such as a newspaper, a magazine, radio, and television.

metro rating   The percentage of television households within the Standard Metropolitan Statistical Area (as defined by the U.S. Bureau of the Budget) that views a station during a specific time period. The metro area normally extends beyond the city limits.

moiré   Halftones with an undesirable, distracting pattern caused by incorrect rotation of screen.

negative   A reverse film picture of the actual photographed object. On a negative, all values are opposite from actual values: black is transparent on the film and white is opaque.

newsprint   A printing paper made of chemicals and ground wood pulp, used mostly by newspapers.

offset   A term for lithographic printing. A reverse imprint of an image from a roller onto paper. Also called "set-off."

one-time rate   A rate charged when the advertiser has not placed sufficient advertising to get a frequency discount.

OTO   One time only. A commercial announcement that runs only once.

overrun   The number of pieces of printed matter produced in excess of the specified quantity.

package A combination of announcements, not sold separately, offered by a station or its representative. Packages are developed to fulfill client objectives in the most efficient manner with the best available inventory.

participation An announcement within a program, as contrasted with one scheduled between programs.

pass-along circulation The number of readers for each copy of a newspaper or magazine. Some magazines will have three or four readers per copy.

pasteup Type, photos, line art, etc., pasted on art board, and ready for camera.

penetration The extent to which a certain medium, or an individual newspaper, magazine, or radio or TV program, reaches a market—for example, 25 percent of metro.

perfecting press A press that prints both sides of paper in one pass-through.

photocomposition Any type reproduction proofs prepared directly from typesetting machines using film negative masters.

pica A unit of linear measurement used by printers and typographers equaling ⅙ of an inch (6 picas per inch).

piggyback A commercial announcement from an advertiser, part of which promotes one product or service and part another product, with each part able to stand alone.

point A standard of measurement of type used by printers and typesetters equaling ¹⁄₇₂ of an inch (72 points per inch).

position requested A request for preferred position in newspapers or magazines, not an order for it. No special or extra charge is made if the paper allows the service.

positive A reverse negative. A faithful reproduction of the original copy.

posting The act of putting up a transit or outdoor sign.

preempt To have a special program supersede or take over the time for a regularly scheduled program.

preemptible rate A discounted rate that subjects the advertiser to cancellation by another advertiser paying a higher rate. The preemption protection varies by station.

preferred position Especially desirable space in a newspaper or magazine, either in terms of location within the publication or location on any given page. Such a position sells for a higher price than nonpreferred, or *ROP*, space.

press proofs Final proofs pulled on the engraver's printing press before the quantity run begins.

pressure-sensitive paper A paper with an adhesive backing protected by a peel-off sheet.

primary or target audience The specific audience sought for a particular service or product.

primary colors In pigmented colors, red, yellow, and blue. In printing inks, yellow, magenta (process red), and cyan (process blue). In light, red, green, and blue.

primary reader A person who qualifies as a reader, living in the household in which the publication is initially received.

progressive proofs   Full-color, four-ink process proofs pulled to inspect color quality. Pulled in same sequence of yellow, magenta, cyan, and black as they will be printed to show the result after each additional color has been applied.

pub-set   All type set by the publication.

quintile   Viewers or households divided into five equal groups, ranging from the heaviest to the lightest viewers. Based on amount of TV viewing, radio listening, and newspaper or magazine reading, as well as on demographics.

raised printing   See *thermography*.

rate base   The specific quantity of circulation guaranteed by a magazine on which rates are based.

rate card   A station's printed card or folder giving rates, mechanical requirements, and closing dates.

rate protection   The length of time an advertiser is guaranteed a specific rate.

rating   A percentage of a target group population, within a defined area, tuned to a particular radio or TV station at a specific time period. The rating may be expressed in terms of households or individuals. A 25 rating in metro Los Angeles means 25 percent of all households in the metropolitan Los Angeles area tuned in at a particular time period.

rating service   A research organization that offers a syndicated service of periodic measurements of the television audience.

reach   The number of different households or people exposed to a program, a group of programs, or an advertiser's schedule. Reach is usually expressed as a percentage of the total population in a defined area.

readers per copy   The estimate of the average number of people who read an issue of a publication. (Readers per copy × circulation = total audience.)

ream   500 sheets of paper.

reflective art   Any opaque copy, lit from the front by lights near the camera, that reflects its image into the camera.

register   In printing, the correct positioning of two or more colors so that the images are in perfect alignment. "In register" means that the printing is in perfect position on the sheet. "Out of register" means that the colors are not in position; this may cause the printing to look blurred.

register marks   Positioning guides or marks on artwork and negatives used to insure perfect alignment of multi-image printing.

remote   Any telecast or broadcast originating away from the home studio.

rep   Station representative. A company or salesperson who serves as a national sales arm for a station or publication.

replacement   The substitute for a commercial announcement that did not clear on the original order.

reproduction proof (repro)   Any press proof or photoprint sharp enough for final reproduction.

resolution   Definition; degree of detail in any photograph or television picture.

retouching   A method of improving the appearance of photographic artwork, usually by use of an airbrush.

reverse   To change to tonal images opposite those of original copy; usually refers to light copy or art on dark background.

right-angle fold Two or more folds at right angles (90°) to each other.

road block Horizontal saturation. An advertising technique designed to deliver the greatest unduplicated audience (reach) through the purchase of the exact time on all stations on the same day.

ROP Run of paper. The placement of an advertisement anywhere within the publication that the publisher elects. Normally nonpreferred position.

ROP color Color advertisements placed anywhere in regular sections of a newspaper, using the normal printing method, regularly available inks, and standard newsprint.

ROS Run of schedule. Commercial announcements that can be scheduled at any time. Each announcement is moved progressively through either the time periods of the day (vertical) or the days of the week (horizontal).

rotation The sequential movement of an announcement from one commercial availability to the next within a specific time block or program to insure even distribution of the audience for each advertiser.

rough A rough or crude sketch of a planned advertisement, to give some indication of the appearance or layout of the finished advertisement.

sans serif Any typeface without serifs (short lines stemming from the upper and lower strokes of a letter).

saturation The use of many announcements within a short space of time to give maximum impact to an advertiser's message.

scaling Proportioning artwork or photos by specifying reduction or enlargement of any copy for camera lens.

scanner An electronic device used in preparation of full color separations for process printing.

schedule Times of day and dates an advertiser's commercials run in a specific or continuing campaign.

score To make an indentation in heavy printing paper for easier folding by hand or machine.

screen Contact or crossline screens used in halftone production for printing. In television, the face of a TV tube in a receiver or monitor.

screen ruling The number of lines per inch on a halftone screen. Coarse screens: 50, 65, 85 lines per inch. Fine screens: 100, 110, 133, 150, 300 lines per inch.

screened print A photoprint made from a halftone negative.

secondary (pass-along) reader A reader who lives in a household that receives the publication secondhand.

second cover The inside front cover of a magazine.

second-generation tape A videotape recording that is copied from an original or master recording.

self-mailer Any direct-mail advertising piece that requires no envelope for mailing.

share of audience The percentage of the total television (or radio) audience in a specific time period that is tuned to a particular station or program.

short rate The difference between the contract rate and the earned rate when the latter is higher. An advertiser not using enough space to earn the quantity discount specified in his contract is charged the short rate.

silhouette halftone   A halftone in which the shading effect of the halftone screen has been removed from the background, leaving the illustration standing against the background color of the paper.

sixty   A one-minute announcement.

slide   A transparent picture mounted in glass or on cardboard for projection (2" × 2", 3" × 4", or 4" × 5").

small caps   The small capital letters, usually available in any type font, that are as high as the main body of the lower-case letters.

snow   Electronic interference showing as white flecks on the TV screen.

SNR   Subject to nonrenewal. Commercial announcement time that is available if the current advertiser does not renew.

spectacular   An outdoor sign with many lights, motion, or 3D elements.

split run   A means of testing advertisements by placing one advertisement in half of the copies of a given issue of a magazine and another advertisement in the other half of the copies of the same issue. Both advertisements occupy identical locations and are exposed to the same editorial and advertising competition for readers' attention.

sponsor   An advertiser who buys the exclusive right to the time available for commercial announcements in a given program segment.

spot   Commercial announcement time available for sale or purchased from local radio or TV stations by advertisers to air their commercials. Commercial announcements are frequently called spots (e.g., 60-second, 30-second, and 10-second spots).

spot broadcast   The use of individual radio or television stations as opposed to the networks, for either a sponsored program or spot announcements.

standing type   Set type being held by the typographer for corrections or reuse.

stet   Leave as is. Proofreader's mark indicating that copy is OK as originally written and no corrections should be made.

stock   Any paper or other material to be printed.

stock photos and artwork   Any photograph or art available for use in publishing or advertising. Libraries of stock photos and artwork are available from various private firms.

storyboard   A series of sketches with dialogue that roughs out highlights of a story, TV commercial, or motion picture.

stretch   To slow down the pace of a show.

strike-through   The penetration of ink through a printed sheet.

substance   The weight in pounds of a ream (500 sheets) of business paper cut to standard size (17" × 22"). Similar to basis weight of other printing papers.

super   A slide or picture superimposed over another on the TV screen, providing additional information.

surprint   To expose two separate negatives in the same area.

sync   Synchronization. The simultaneous projecting or telecasting of picture and sound.

tabloid   A newspaper usually comprising 1,000–1,200 lines per page.

tag   Information usually added to the end of a commercial announcement to advise viewers where the product or service being advertised can be purchased in that market.

take   Director's cue for a cut from one TV camera to another. An exposed section of film or tape. An "outtake" is discarded film. A "good take" is a good shot. A "bad take" has to be done again.

talent   Actors, performers.

target audience   The prime prospects toward which an advertising message is directed. This information is obtained from the demographics and buying patterns of the audience.

TBA   To be announced.

tear sheet   A sheet of newspaper containing an advertisement of a specific advertiser. Serves as proof of publication.

television set saturation   The percentage of total homes having at least one television set.

ten   A 10-second announcement.

text   The reading matter of body copy, as distinguished from the headlines.

TFN (UFN)   Till further notice, or until further notice. Pertains to a schedule placed on a station.

thermography   A printing process using heat and powder on wet ink to get a raised engraved-like effect.

third cover   The inside back cover of a magazine. Cf. *fourth cover*.

thirty   A 30-second announcement. Also a sign-off signal. The number 30 or the symbol # is usually used at the end of news stories.

time buyer   A person responsible for purchasing advertising on radio and television stations.

time sheet   A sheet used by a buyer to keep track of the data on a buy. Also called "buy sheet."

tint   The light degree of a color.

tissue overlay   A tracing paper overlay for indicating printing specifications and for protecting art.

titles   Studio title cards or slides, or any graphic material shown on camera.

total audience   The total number of people who read an average issue of a magazine, newspaper, or Sunday supplement. Total audience is composed of primary readers and secondary, or pass-along, readers.

total audience rating   A type of rating computed for some specified interval of time, such as the length of a television or radio program or 15 or 30 minutes.

trademark   A name, picture, or symbol used to identify a product (registered with the U.S. Copyright Office).

transcription   A record made for broadcast. Any recording.

transparency   Any color art or color photo on a clear or translucent film base for viewing with back lighting.

transparent inks   Inks that allow the paper color or other inks beneath them to show through.

transpose   To switch the places of two elements, such as two words in a sentence or two photographs.

trim size   The size of a magazine after pages and cover have been trimmed on the three outer edges. The size of the magazine as it is purchased on the newsstand or received by subscribers.

twenty   A 20-second announcement.

upper case   The capital letters in any typeface or alphabet.

video   The visual portion of a television broadcast.

videotape   Tape on which both sound and picture are recorded simultaneously, as contrasted with audiotape, which records only sound.

voice-over   The voice of the announcer, usually off camera, in a TV commercial.

work and turn   To print one side, then turn the sheet over from left to right and print the other side.

APPENDIX 1

Federal Information Centers

Alabama

Birmingham
322-8591
Toll-free tieline to Atlanta, Ga.

Mobile
438-1421
Toll-free tieline to New Orleans, La.

Arizona

Phoenix
(602) 261-3313
Federal Building
230 North First Ave.
85025

Tucson
622-1511
Toll-free tieline to Phoenix

Arkansas

Little Rock
378-6177
Toll-free tieline to Memphis, Tenn.

California

Los Angeles
(213) 688-3800
Federal Building
300 North Los Angeles St.
90012

Sacramento
(916) 440-3344
Federal Building and U.S. Courthouse
650 Capitol Mall
95814

San Diego
(714) 293-6030
Federal Building
880 Front St.
Room 1S11
92188

San Francisco
(415) 556-6600
Federal Building and U.S. Courthouse
450 Golden Gate Ave.
P.O. Box 36082
94102

San Jose
275-7422
Toll-free tieline to San Francisco

Santa Ana
836-2386
Toll-free tieline to Los Angeles

Colorado

Colorado Springs
471-9491
Toll-free tieline to Denver

Denver
(303) 837-3602
Federal Building
1961 Stout St.
80294

Pueblo
544-9523
Toll-free tieline to Denver

Connecticut

Hartford
527-2617
Toll-free tieline to New York, N.Y.

New Haven
624-4720
Toll-free tieline to New York, N.Y.

District of Columbia

Washington
(202) 755-8660
Seventh and D Sts., S.W.
Room 5716
20407

Florida

Fort Lauderdale
522-8531
Toll-free tieline to Miami

Jacksonville
354-4756
Toll-free tieline to St. Petersburg

Miami
(305) 350-4155
Federal Building
51 Southwest First Ave.
33130

Orlando
422-1800
Toll-free tieline to St. Petersburg

St. Petersburg
(813) 893-3495
William C. Cramer Federal Building
144 First Ave., South
33701

Tampa
229-7911
Toll-free tieline to St. Petersburg

West Palm Beach
833-7566
Toll-free tieline to Miami

Georgia

Atlanta
(404) 221-6891
Federal Building and U.S. Courthouse
76 Spring St.
30303

Hawaii

Honolulu
(808) 546-3620
Federal Building
300 Ala Moana Blvd.
P.O. Box 50091
96850

Illinois

Chicago
(312) 353-4242
Everett McKinley Dirksen Building
219 South Dearborn St.
Room 250
60604

Indiana

Gary/Hammond
883-4110
Toll-free tieline to Indianapolis

Indianapolis
(317) 269-7373
Federal Building
575 North Pennsylvania
46204

Iowa

Des Moines
284-4448
Toll-free tieline to Omaha, Nebr.

Kansas

Topeka
295-2866
Toll-free tieline to Kansas City, Mo.

Wichita
263-6931
Toll-free tieline to Kansas City, Mo.

Kentucky

Louisville
(502) 582-6261
Federal Building
600 Federal Place
40202

Louisiana

New Orleans
(504) 589-6696
U.S. Postal Service Building
701 Loyola Ave.
Room 1210
70113

Maryland

Baltimore
(301) 962-4980
Federal Building
31 Hopkins Plaza
21201

Massachusetts

Boston
(617) 223-7121
J.F.K. Federal Building
Cambridge St.
Room E-130
02203

Michigan

Detroit
(313) 226-7016
McNamara Federal Building
477 Michigan Ave.
Room 103
48226

Grand Rapids
451-2628
Toll-free tieline to Detroit

Minnesota

Minneapolis
(612) 725-2073
Federal Building and U.S. Courthouse
110 South Fourth St.
55401

Missouri

Kansas City
(816) 374-2466
Federal Building
601 East Twelfth St.
64106

St. Joseph
233-8206
Toll-free tieline to Kansas City

St. Louis
(314) 425-4106
Federal Building
1520 Market St.
63103

Nebraska

Omaha
(402) 221-3353
U.S. Post Office and Courthouse
215 North 17th St.
68102

New Jersey

Newark
(201) 645-3600
Federal Building
970 Broad St.
07102

Patterson/Passaic
523-0717
Toll-free tieline to Newark

Trenton
396-4400
Toll-free tieline to Newark

New Mexico

Albuquerque
(505) 766-3091
Federal Building and U.S. Courthouse
500 Gold Ave., S.W.
87102

Santa Fe
983-7743
Toll-free tieline to Albuquerque

New York

Albany
463-4421
Toll-free tieline to New York

Buffalo
(716) 846-4010
Federal building
111 West Huron St.
14202

New York
(212) 264-4464
Federal Building
26 Federal Plaza
Room 1-114
10007

Rochester
546-5075
Toll-free tieline to Buffalo

Syracuse
476-8545
Toll-free tieline to Buffalo

North Carolina

Charlotte
376-3600
Toll-free tieline to Atlanta, Ga.

Ohio

Akron
375-5638
Toll-free tieline to Cleveland

Cincinnati
(513) 684-2801
Federal Building
550 Main St.
45202

Cleveland
(216) 522-4040
Federal Building
1240 East Ninth St.
44199

Columbus
221-1014
Toll-free tieline to Cincinnati

Dayton
223-7377
Toll-free tieline to Cincinnati

Toledo
241-3223
Toll-free tieline to Cleveland

Oklahoma

Oklahoma City
(405) 231-4868
U.S. Post Office and Courthouse
201 Northwest 3rd St.
73102

Tulsa
584-4193
Toll-free tieline to Oklahoma City

Oregon

Portland
(503) 221-2222
Federal Building
1220 Southwest Third Ave.
Room 109
97204

Pennsylvania

Allentown/Bethlehem
821-7785
Toll-free tieline to Philadelphia

Philadelphia
(215) 597-7042
Federal Building
600 Arch St.
19106

Pittsburgh
(412) 644-3456
Federal Building
1000 Liberty Ave.
15222

Scranton
346-7081
Toll-free tieline to Philadelphia

Rhode Island

Providence
331-5565
Toll-free tieline to Boston, Mass.

Tennessee

Chattanooga
265-8231
Toll-free tieline to Memphis

Memphis
(901) 521-3285
Clifford Davis Federal Building
167 North Main St.
38103

Nashville
242-5056
Toll-free tieline to Memphis

Texas

Austin
472-5494
Toll-free tieline to Houston

Dallas
749-2131
Toll-free tieline to Fort Worth

Fort Worth
(817) 334-3624
Fritz Garland Lanham Federal Building
819 Taylor St.
76102

Houston
(713) 226-5711
Federal Building and U.S. Courthouse
515 Rusk Ave.
77208

San Antonio
224-4471
Toll-free tieline to Houston

Utah

Ogden
399-1347
Toll-free tieline to Salt Lake City

Salt Lake City
(801) 524-5353
Federal Building
125 South State St.
Room 1205
84138

Virginia

Newport News
244-0480
Toll-free tieline to Norfolk

Norfolk
(804) 441-3101
200 Granby Mall
Room 120
23510

Richmond
643-4928
Toll-free tieline to Norfolk

Roanoke
982-8591
Toll-free tieline to Norfolk

Washington

Seattle
(206) 442-0570
Federal Building
915 Second Ave.
98174

Tacoma
383-5230
Toll-free tieline to Seattle

Wisconsin

Milwaukee
271-2273
Toll-free tieline to Chicago, Ill.

APPENDIX 2

Federal Agencies

National Institute of Education (NIE)
1200 19th St., N.W.
Washington, D.C. 20208

Public Health Services (Offices)
5600 Fishers Lane
Rockville, Md. 20852

Health Care Financing Administration
330 C Street, S.W.
Washington, D.C. 20201

Department of Housing & Urban Development (HUD)
451 7th St., S.W.
Washington, D.C. 20401

Federal Bureau of Investigation (FBI)
J. Edgar Hoover Bldg.
935 Pennsylvania Ave., N.W.
Washington, D.C. 20535

Drug Enforcement Administration
1405 1st St., N.W.
Washington, D.C. 20537

Department of Labor (DOL)
200 Constitution Ave., N.W.
Washington, D.C. 20210

Department of State
2201 C Street, N.W.
Washington, D.C. 20520

Department of Transportation
400 7th St., N.W.
Washington, D.C. 20590

Advisory Commission on Intergovernmental Relations (ACIR)
726 Jackson Place, N.W.
Washington, D.C. 20575

Office of Human Development
330 Independence Ave., S.W.
Washington, D.C. 20201

Public Health Service
Office of the Assistant Secretary
200 Independence Ave., S.W.
Washington, D.C. 20201

National Institutes of Health (NIH)
9000 Rockville Pike
Bethesda, Md. 20015

Child Support Enforcement
330 C Street, S.W.
Washington, D.C. 20201

Department of Justice
Constitution Ave., Btwn 9th & 10th Sts., N.W.
Washington, D.C. 20530

Law Enforcement Assistance Administration (LEAA)
633 Indiana Ave., N.W.
Washington, D.C. 20531

Immigration & Naturalization Service
425 I St., N.W.
Washington, D.C. 20536

Bureau of Labor Statistics
441 G Street, N.W.
Washington, D.C. 20212

Agency for International Development (AID)
21st and Virginia Ave., N.W.
Washington, D.C. 20523

Department of the Treasury
15th & Pennsylvania Ave., N.W.
Washington, D.C. 20220

Chamber of Commerce
1615 H St., N.W.
Washington, D.C. 20006

Energy Research & Development Administration (ERDA)
20 Massachusetts Ave., N.W.
Washington, D.C. 20545

General Services Administration (GSA)
18th and F Sts., N.W.
Washington, D.C. 20405

Institute of Medicine
Constitution & 21st St., N.W.
Washington, D.C. 20418

National Labor Relations Board (NLRB)
1717 Pennsylvania Ave., N.W.
Washington, D.C. 20570

National Science Foundation
1800 G St., N.W.
Washington, D.C. 20550

Small Business Administration (SBA)
141 L St., N.W.
Washington, D.C. 20416

U.S. Information Agency (USIA)
1750 Pennsylvania Ave., N.W.
Washington, D.C. 20547

Federal Labor Relations Council (FLRC)
1900 E St., N.W.
Washington, D.C. 20415

National Academy of Sciences
Constitution & 21st St., N.W.
Washington, D.C. 20418

National Research Council
Constitution & 21st St., N.W.
Washington, D.C. 20418

National Mediation Board (NMB)
1425 K St., N.W.
Washington, D.C. 20572

Occupational Safety & Health Review Commission (OSHRC)
1825 K St., N.W.
Washington, D.C. 20006

U.S. Commission on Civil Rights (USCCR)
1121 Vermont Ave., N.W.
Washington, D.C. 20425

Veterans Administration (VA)
Vermont at H St., N.W.
Washington, D.C. 20420

REGULATORY AGENCIES

Federal Aviation Administration (FAA)
800 Independence Ave., S.W.
Washington, D.C. 20591

Federal Trade Commission (FTC)
Pennsylvania Ave. at 6th St., N.W.
Washington, D.C. 20580

Interstate Commerce Commission (ICC)
12th & Constitution Ave., N.W.
Washington, D.C. 20423

Federal Communications Commission (FCC)
1919 M St., N.W.
Washington, D.C. 20554

Food & Drug Administration (FDA)
5600 Fishers Lane
Rockville, Md. 20852

APPENDIX 3

Key Professional and Advertising Associations

American Bar Association
1155 E. 60 St.
Chicago, Ill. 60637
(312) 947–4000

American Institute of Certified
Public Accountants
1211 Ave. of the Americas
New York, N.Y. 10036
(212) 575–6200

American Medical Association
535 N. Dearborn St.
Chicago, Ill. 60610
(312) 751–6000

American Dental Association
211 E. Chicago Ave.
Chicago, Ill. 60611
(312) 440–2500

American Association of Advertising
  Agencies
666 Third Avenue
New York, New York 10017
(212) 682-2500

American Osteopathic Association
212 E. Ohio St.
Chicago, Ill. 60611
(312) 944–2713

American Chiropractic Association
200 Grand St.
De Moines, Iowa 50312
(515) 243–1121

Newspaper Advertising Bureau
485 Lexington Ave.
New York, N.Y. 10017
(212) 557–1800

Institute of Outdoor Advertising
485 Lexington Ave.
New York, N.Y. 10017
(212) 986–5920

Radio Advertising Bureau
485 Lexington Ave.
New York, N.Y. 10017
(212) 599–6666

TV Bureau of Advertising
485 Lexington Ave.
New York, N.Y. 10017
(212) 661–8440

Direct Mail Marketing Association
6 E. 43 St.
New York, N.Y. 10017
(212) 689–4977

National Yellow Pages Association
999 W. Big Beaver Rd.
Troy, Mich. 48084
(313) 362–3300

Eight Sheet Outdoor Advertising
  Association, Inc.
P.O. Box 2584
Springfield, Mass. 01101
(413) 736–7259

Standard Rate and Data Service
5201 Old Orchard Road
Skokie, Ill. 60077
(312) 583–1333 (Chicago)
(312) 470–3100 (Skokie)

Association of National Advertisers
155 E. 44 St.
New York, N.Y. 10017
(212) 697–5950

Transit Advertising Association
60 E. 42 St.
New York, N.Y. 10017
(212) 599–2352

American Marketing Association
222 S. Riverside Plaza
Chicago, Il 60606
(312) 648–0536

Marketing Research Association, Inc.
221 N. LaSalle St.
Chicago, Il 60601
(312) 346–1600

Media Networks Inc.
600 Third Ave.
New York, N.Y. 10016
(212) 661–4800

Index